SO-BEP-894

the Unofficial Guide™ to Climbing the Corporate Ladder

Jack Griffin

IDG Books Worldwide, Inc.
An International Data Group Company
Foster City, CA • Chicago, IL • Indianapolis, IN
• New York, NY

IDG Books Worldwide, Inc.
An International Data Group Company
919 E. Hillsdale Boulevard
Suite 400
Foster City, CA 94404

For general information on IDG Books Worldwide's books in the U.S., please call our Consumer Customer Service department at 800-762-2974. For reseller information, including discounts and previous sales, please call our Reseller Customer Service department at 800-434-3422.

ISBN: 0-02-863493-4

Manufactured in the United States of America

10 9 8 7 6 5 4 3 2 1

First edition

Dedication

For Monique

Contents

The *Unofficial Guide* Reader's Bill of Rights xvii

The *Unofficial Guide* Panel of Experts xxiii

Introduction xxvii

I Strictly Personal 1

**1 Cube Roots: The Basics of Today's
   Corporate Climb 3**

"I'm Not Political"..4
   A Quiz on Political Savvy 4
   Evaluating the Results..........................9
   Where's Grandpa's Gold Watch? 9
   Eat or Be Eaten.................................10
   Be Eaten or Go Stale 10

The *Real* Rules of the Game 11
   How "Executive Decisions" Are Made 11
   *Your Own Horn: If You Don't Toot It,
      Who Will?* 12
   No One Is Indispensable 13

It *Is* Who You Know...............................13

Just the Facts.......................................14

2 Fitting In and Standing Out.....................15

Before You Say a Word 16
   Walking Tall 16
   Let Your Smile Do the Talking..................17
   Eye to Eye.......................................18
   Eye to Eyebrow..................................19

Hail to the Handshake 20

All about Breathing 21

A Body-Language Phrase Book 22
   Conveying Relaxed Energy......................22
   A Show of Hands 23
   Body-Language Blunders 24

Making an Entrance 25
  Greetings! 26
  Unmusical Chairs 26
  Putting Names to Faces 27
Dress Codes: Send the Right Message 27
  I Gotta Be Me 27
  A Question of Focus 28
  Being Comfortable 29

Come Clean 29

Getting in Gear 29
  Suit Yourself 29
  Shirts, Blouses, Tees, and Ties 30
  Aim for the Middle; Dress a
      Notch Above 31
  Why Less Is More 31

Just the Facts 32

3 Uncommon Courtesy 33
"Nice Guys" Don't Always Finish Last 33
  An Exercise in Empathy 34
  Increasing Rapport 35
  Helping Words 36

Rapport Wreckers 37
  A Language of Exclusion 37
  Selfish, Nasty Habits 37

Relieving Peer Pressure 38
  Starting on a Good Note 39
  Cubicle Questions 39
  The Territorial Imperative 40
  Make It Yours 41

Help! 42
  Offering It 42
  Asking for It 43
  Accepting It 43

Praise and Constructive Criticism 44

Bones to Pick—Anger 47
  Off Your Chest 48
  All About Apologies 48

Making Time Special 50
  Birthdays and Babies 50
  Anniversaries and Achievements 51
  Sharing the Sadness 52

Just the Facts 53

II Beyond Yadda Yadda—Effective Communication.....................55

4 Getting Your Message Across 57

First, Try Talking to Yourself....................58
 What Do You Want to Say? 59
 Create a "Script" 61

Power Dictionary 64

Openers and Closers.............................67
 Your First Words...............................68
 Follow-throughs 68

Just the Facts....................................70

5 Big Results from Small Talk....................71

Make the Time 72

Conversation Killers 73
 Not Listening 73
 Interrupting....................................74
 Negativity......................................75
 Patronizing....................................75

Recipe for Great Conversation 76
 Prepare to Be Spontaneous.....................76
 Seize the Opportunity 77
 Come Out with a Good Opening 78
 Lighten Up 79

The SOFTEN Solution...........................82
 Smile...83
 Open Up..83
 Forward, Lean 83
 Tone It Down 84
 Eye Contact Now...............................84
 Nod—and Nod Some More......................84

Talking with Your Ears..........................84
 Conversation Killers 85
 Conversation Builders 86

Taking Talk to the Next Level 87

Just the Facts....................................88

6 Meaningful Meetings—Not an Oxymoron 89

Why Good Meetings Go Bad 90
 Individual Problems 90
 Organizational Problems........................91

What's the Use? 92
   The Importance of the Agenda *93*
   Roll Call *95*
   Size Counts *95*

Invitation Etiquette...............................96

Making Space for Flexibility 97
   Problem Polling *97*
   Brainstorming *98*
   Break It Up! *99*

Stoking the Furnace...............................99
   Be Clear *99*
   Manage Time *99*
   Reflect and Facilitate........................*100*

On Power...101
   Power Seats *101*
   Power Plays...................................*102*
   Power Ploys...................................*103*

Meeting Manners 104
   For the Leader................................*105*
   For the Others *105*
   Conflict—It's Not All Bad *106*

The Call to Action................................106

Just the Facts 108

7 Busy Signals.....................................109

Before You Pick Up That Phone... 110
   PTA: What It Is and Why You Want It......*111*
   Famous First Words...........................*111*
   Ugh! That Voice *113*
   Stand Up and Smile (No One
     Can See You)...............................*114*

You Own the Call 115
   Taking Possession............................*116*
   Selling the Call *117*

Rules for Putting the Caller on Hold 118

Singed Wires: Coping with the
Irate Caller 120

A Way out of Voice Mail Hell 123
   Dodging Telephone Tag.......................*123*
   Call Screening Etiquette *123*
   The Effective Phone Message.................*124*

How to Get Your Call Through....................126
  Name Names...126
  On Hold? Don't Agree to It 127
  Use the Call Ownership Principle 128
Just the Facts 128

8 Letters Perfect 131

The Memorable Memo 132
  Official Junk Mail.................................132
  Good Form 133

A Menu of Memorable Memos....................134
  Light Their Fire 136
  Keeping Everyone on the Same Page........137
  What to Say When Things Get Ugly..........137
  Invitation to a Solution 139
  Might I Suggest... 140

Looking Good on Paper............................142
  The Elements of Style 142
  Who Writes Letters Anymore? 144
  Forms and Formats................................145
  Envelope Rules.....................................146
  Hello and Goodbye 147

Some Major Themes 148
  So Sorry 148
  We've Got a Problem with That 150
  Please Help..151
  The Magic of Thanks 153

Just the Facts 154

9 Putting Yourself Across Online...............155

The E-mail Challenge...............................155

E-mail Etiquette 157
  This Is Just to Say—We're Drowning!.......159
  Who's in This Loop?..............................160
  More E-mail Abuses 160
  Oops! Can I Take That Back?...................161
  Greetings and Felicitations.....................162
  Telegraphic or Conversational?...............163
  Room for Style? 164
  Meet the Emoticons...............................165
  Bells and Whistles 166

Safe and Secure...Right?............................166
  Big Brother Lives...............................169
  Keeping Copies 170
  Deleted—or Not? 170
Just the Fax 171
  Getting It There...............................171
  Cover Page Basics.............................172
  Between You and Me 173
Just the Facts 174

III Dealing with (and Being)
the Boss..175

10 Who's the Boss? 177
Setting the Tone....................................178
R-E-S-P-E-C-T.......................................178
Pressing the Right Buttons.......................182
A Guide to Bosses..................................183
  Tyrannical Types...............................184
  Dealers in Guilt.................................187
  Dealers in Blame...............................189
  The Impractical Leader........................190
  The Incompetent Leader......................192
  The Emotional Volcano........................193
How to Bond with Your Boss 194
  Accepting a Compliment......................195
  Apologizing......................................196
Typical Scenarios 197
  Salary Review 197
  Promoting Yourself............................198
  Promoting an Idea 199
  Extending a Deadline.........................200
Just the Facts 201

11 On Loyalty and Leadership 203
Listen to Some Leaders on Leadership 204
The Credibility Blueprint..........................204
  Lay It Out..205
  Choose Carefully...............................208
  Empowerment...................................208
  Giving the Right Feelings 209

Motivating ASAP....................................211
   Critical Feedback..............................*212*
   Meaningful Praise.............................*215*
Team Talk 215
   Fifty Team-Building Words and
      Phrases *216*
   Twenty-Five Words and Phrases to
      Avoid....................................*217*
Just the Facts 218

12 Using the Carrots and the Sticks............219
Motivational Speech................................220
   Information, Please.............................*222*
   Positive Praise.................................*223*
   Progress Report................................*225*
   Criticism Without the Crush....................*225*
Ethics of Progressive Discipline.................227
When You Have to Say "No" 229
   "I Want a Raise" *230*
   "It's My Turn" *231*
You as Role Model 232
Just the Facts 233

IV Let the Games Begin 235

13 The Good, the Bad, the Ugly..................237
You Can Run, but You Can't Hide...............237
Ethical Manipulation 238
   Become Influential.............................*239*
   As Usual, Follow the Power....................*240*
   Selling Benefits................................*240*
   The Undercut: a Master Stroke................*241*
   Bonding *241*
   If You Can't Beat 'Em, Make 'Em
      Join You.................................*242*
   Great Idea! *242*
The Rumor Mill: Don't Be Grist.................243
What's That Sticking Out of Your Back?.......246
   Dodging the Schemers.........................*246*
   Credit Where Credit Is Due *247*
   The Smiling Killers.............................*248*

Emotional Manipulation *249*
Removing the Shiv *250*

Network News 251
Making Connections...........................*251*
Keeping Doors Ajar............................*252*

Just the Facts 253

14 Office Diplomacy **255**

Conflict Is like Death and Taxes 256

Causes of Conflict 257

The Conflict Management Concept.............258

Baby Steps 261
Label It..*261*
Pick Your Fights *262*
A Time and a Place *262*
One at a Time *263*
Speak Specifically................................*263*
Address Issues, Not People....................*263*
Listen and Hear *264*

Everybody's a Winner............................264
A Mutual Solution Is the Holy Grail........*265*
Speak Again Specifically *265*
Agree on an Action Plan......................*266*
Then Execute the Plan.........................*266*

Thorns among the Roses 266
Dealing with Office Bullies.....................*266*
*Coping with Passive-Aggressive
    Personalities* *268*
Handling the Complainer *269*
Verbal Abuse *271*
Workplace Violence: It's Real.................*273*

Just the Facts 274

15 Old Boys and Glass Ceilings................**277**

The Power of Diversity............................278
Your Multicultural Assets *278*
Know Thyself......................................*280*
Sensitivity Training..............................*282*

The Etiquette of Inclusion 283
Male/Female Issues.............................*284*
Enabling the Disabled *287*
Squash Stereotyping *290*

Good Manners or Good
Risk Management? 290
   A Shade of Blue.................................*291*
   If It Gets Ugly..................................*291*
Just the Facts 293

**16 Office Romance: The Most
Dangerous Game?** **295**
Is It Love? Passion? Sexual Harassment? 296
   Nature Meets the Corporation................*297*
   The H Word....................................*300*
   If You Are a Victim...........................*302*
   A Question of Rank..........................*303*
Consenting Adults...................................305
   Better Than a Singles Bar....................*305*
   Is It Romantic? *306*
Staying Professional................................306
   Company Policy...............................*307*
   Oh, Behave! *307*
   Kiss and Tell? *308*
Just the Facts 308

V The Savvy Schmoozer....................**311**

17 An Out-of-Office Experience **313**
Be There or Be Square 314
   Open to All Possibilities........................*314*
   Me? Keep a Social Calendar?.................*316*
   RSVP..*317*
   Show Up (On Time)...........................*317*
Networking Lite.....................................318
   The Schmoozer's Art *318*
   Meeting and Greeting.........................*320*
   Play the Name Game *320*
   Practice the SOFTEN Touch....................*321*
   The Business Card Ceremony.................*322*
Social Savvy..322
   Social Dressing *322*
   Accentuate the Positive, Eliminate the
      Negative....................................*323*
   The Cocktail Party *323*
   The Office Party................................*324*

The Company Picnic...............................325
The Boss's House..................................325

It's Your Call 327
Invitation to Your Boss 327
Having the Gang Over 328
Your Family's Role 329

Just the Facts 330

18 Please Don't Drink the Finger Bowl........331

The Many Meals of Business 332
Power Breakfast....................................332
Power Lunch...333
A Civilized Dinner.................................334

Table Manners Refresher Course 336
Napkin First 336
Ordering Wisely.....................................338
The Golden Mean 341
Settling Up 341

Table Talk...342
Steering the Conversation 343
You Said a Mouthful 343
Keep It Light...343

Surviving Embarrassing Moments...............343
Self-Inflicted Spills 344
Spills by Others....................................344
Spills on Others 344

Just the Facts 345

VI Promoting Yourself........................347

19 Movin' On Up..349

Your Best Prospects 349
Finger on the Pulse 350
Ear to the Ground 351
Eye on the Stars 351

Niche Versus Pigeonhole 352

A Word from Our Sponsor........................353
Find the Power, Follow the Power............353
Should You Use HR? 354

When You Want to Make Your Move 355
Focus on the Firm, the Department,
and the Boss.................................355

Build Your Case..................................356
Glad You Thought of It! 356

Do-it-yourself Kit................................356
Why You Should Build a New Position......357
What You Need 357
Selling It..358

Lateral Moves and Strategic Steps Down......358

Just the Facts 360

20 **Movin' On Out** **361**

What You Owe Yourself 362

What You Owe Your Employer 362
The Unwritten Contract 362
Time Thief 363
Don't Stab Yourself in the Back 364
Keeping It Positive 365
Weaving Your Net................................366
Casting Your Net 367
Telephone Manners 367
Correspondence Course 367

Acing the Interview 368
A Matter of Time.................................368
Pressing the Flesh 369
Taking Names.....................................369
Helping Out......................................370

Aim for Closure 370
And I Thank You 371
Easy on the Spurs 371

Don't Slam That Door 372

Just the Facts 373

A **Glossary**....................................**375**

B **Resource Guide**..............................**383**

C **Recommended Reading** **391**

D **Important Documents** **395**

E **Important Statistics**.........................**423**

Index..**427**

The *Unofficial Guide* Reader's Bill of Rights

We Give You More Than the Official Line

Welcome to the *Unofficial Guide* series of Lifestyles titles—books that deliver critical, unbiased information that other books can't or won't reveal—*the inside scoop*. Our goal is to provide you with the *most accessible, useful* information and advice possible. The recommendations we offer in these pages are not influenced by the corporate line of any organization or industry; we give you the hard facts, whether those institutions like them or not. If something is ill-advised or will cause a loss of time and/or money, we'll give you ample warning. And if it is a worthwhile option, we'll let you know that, too.

Armed and Ready

Our hand-picked authors confidently and critically report on a wide range of topics that matter to smart readers like you. Our authors are passionate about their subjects, but have distanced themselves enough from them to help you be armed and protected, and help you make educated decisions as you go through your process. It is our intent that, from having read this book, you will avoid the pitfalls everyone else falls into and get it right the first time.

Don't be fooled by cheap imitations; this is the *genuine article Unofficial Guide* series from IDG Books. You may be familiar with our proven track record of the travel *Unofficial Guides*, which have more than two million copies in print. Each year thousands of travelers—new and old—are armed with a brand new, fully updated edition of the flagship *Unofficial Guide to Walt Disney World*, by Bob Sehlinger. It is our intention here to provide you with the same level of objective authority that Mr. Sehlinger does in his brainchild.

The Unofficial Panel of Experts

Every work in the Lifestyle *Unofficial Guides* is intensively inspected by a team of three top professionals in their fields. These experts review the manuscript for factual accuracy, comprehensiveness, and an insider's determination as to whether the manuscript fulfills the credo in this Reader's Bill of Rights. In other words, our Panel ensures that you are, in fact, getting "the inside scoop."

Our Pledge

The authors, the editorial staff, and the Unofficial Panel of Experts assembled for *Unofficial Guides* are determined to lay out the most valuable alternatives available for our readers. This dictum means that our writers must be explicit, prescriptive, and above all, direct. We strive to be thorough and complete, but our goal is not necessarily to have the "most" or "all" of the information on a topic; this is not, after all, an encyclopedia. Our objective is to help you narrow down your options to the best of what is available, unbiased by affiliation with any industry or organization.

In each *Unofficial Guide* we give you:

- Comprehensive coverage of necessary and vital information

- Authoritative, rigidly fact-checked data

- The most up-to-date insights into trends

- Savvy, sophisticated writing that's also readable

- Sensible, applicable facts and secrets that only an insider knows

Special Features

Every book in our series offers the following six special sidebars in the margins that were devised to help you get things done cheaply, efficiently, and smartly.

1. "Timesaver"—tips and shortcuts that save you time.

2. "Moneysaver"—tips and shortcuts that save you money.

3. "Watch Out!"—more serious cautions and warnings.

4. "Bright Idea"—general tips and shortcuts to help you find an easier or smarter way to do something.

5. "Quote"—statements from real people that are intended to be prescriptive and valuable to you.

6. "Unofficially..."—an insider's fact or anecdote.

We also recognize your need to have quick information at your fingertips, and have thus provided the following comprehensive sections at the back of the book:

1. **Glossary**—Definitions of complicated terminology and jargon.

2. **Resource Guide**—Lists of relevant agencies, associations, institutions, Web sites, etc.

3. **Recommended Reading List**—Suggested titles that can help you get more in-depth information on related topics.

4. **Important Documents**—"Official" pieces of information you need to refer to, such as government forms.

5. **Important Statistics**—Facts and numbers presented at-a-glance for easy reference.

6. **Index**

Letters, Comments, and Questions from Readers

We strive to continually improve the *Unofficial* series, and input from our readers is a valuable way for us to do that. Many of those who have used the *Unofficial Guide* travel books write to the authors to ask questions, make comments, or share their own discoveries and lessons. For lifestyle *Unofficial Guides*, we would also appreciate all such correspondence, both positive and critical, and we will make best efforts to incorporate appropriate readers' feedback and comments in revised editions of this work.

How to write to us:

Unofficial Guides
Lifestyle Guides
IDG Books
1633 Broadway
New York, NY 10019

Attention: Reader's Comments

About the Author

Author Bio

Jack Griffin is an Atlanta-based writer specializing in business communication, marketing topics, and corporate history. A former university professor and publishing executive, Mr. Griffin has served as an adviser to top federal officials, presented speeches to a variety of corporate and service organizations, and worked as a communications consultant and speechwriter to customer service organizations, sales forces of major corporations, and motivational speakers. He is president of a consulting firm serving cultural institutions and publishers.

Mr. Griffin is the author of *The Complete Handbook of Model Business Letters, How to Say It Best; The Business Speaker's Almanac; The Do-It-Yourself Business Promotions Kit; The Lifetime Guide to Business Speaking and Writing; How to Say It at Work: Putting Yourself Across with Power Words; Phrases, Body Language, and Communication Secrets; How to Say It from the Heart: Putting Yourself Across with Power Words; Phrases, Body Language, and Communication Secrets;* and other books.

The *Unofficial Guide* Panel of Experts

The *Unofficial* editorial team recognizes that you've purchased this book with the expectation of getting the most authoritative, carefully inspected information currently available. Toward that end, on each and every title in this series, we have selected a minimum of three "official" experts comprising the "Unofficial Panel" who painstakingly review the manuscripts to ensure: factual accuracy of all data; inclusion of the most up-to-date and relevant information; and that, from an insider's perspective, the authors have armed you with all the necessary facts you need—but the institutions don't want you to know.

For *The Unofficial Guide to Climbing the Corporate Ladder,* we are proud to introduce the following panel of experts:

Susan M. Osborn, Ph.D. Dr. Osborn is the author of *The System Made Me Do It! A Life Changing Approach to Office Politics* (www. netcom.com/~sosborn/) and writes a monthly column on office politics for *High Technology*

Magazine. She is also a consultant, seminar facilitator, and adjunct professor in northern California. Her courses on systems thinking, organizational change, leadership, and global issues are offered at Chapman University, National University, and the University of Phoenix.

In addition to 25 years as an adult educator and management consultant, Dr. Osborn has held positions of leadership in the computer industry, aerospace, and the criminal justice system. She earned her doctorate in Human and Organizational Systems from the Fielding Institute and holds an M.S.W. from U.C. Berkeley. She is also the senior author of *Assertive Training for Women.*

Jill Frank Jill Frank works for Atlanta-based MindSpring Enterprises in business development, and is a partner of Sterling Communications, Inc. Frank has a successful track record of guiding executives through tough political situations at work through her column and her weekly radio guest segment on the nationally syndicated show Business First (on the Business News Network). She is also the author of *9 Steps to Surviving in the Jungle of Office Politics.* Her Website is http://jillfrank.home.mindspring.com/.

Sara Unrue Koulen Sara Unrue Koulen (SUnrue@willowsolutions.com) is a consultant and software developer, creating custom applications for companies of all sizes. As a consultant in a variety of office situations, she has gained unique insight into how different companies work. A cum laude graduate of Yale

University with expertise in interpersonal relations, she specializes in integrating technology
and office politics, helping managers and other
corporate professionals identify the best allies,
avoid or work constructively with potential enemies, and navigate inefficient or hostile office
settings to complete the tasks at hand.

Introduction

There's one in every office. A person not necessarily handsome or pretty, but nevertheless irresistibly attractive—magnetic, even. A person no more or less competent than any number of the other high achievers in the office, yet someone who consistently *seems* more competent and who certainly *is* just a little more self-confident than anyone else. Recalling Muhammad Ali in his youthful prime, this person floats like a butterfly and stings like a bee. Only nobody really seems to mind getting stung, and the floating is a wonder to watch.

This person is a savvy office politician, the person who seems to know intuitively how to get ahead in the workplace, how to climb the corporate ladder. And if you envy him or her, this book is for you.

But if you cringe at the very sound of phrases like *office politics* and *climbing the corporate ladder*, this book is also for you. In fact, maybe you need it even more urgently. For perhaps no aspect of career building is more misunderstood or more casually maligned than office politics. For some people, *corporate ladder* evokes a picture of savage competition, as the unscrupulous schemer climbs over the bodies of those he's defeated, clawing and fighting his way to higher and higher rungs. Likewise, most people think that *office politics* is:

- Inherently dirty, sleazy, sneaky, and underhanded.

- A synonym for "ruthlessness."

- Something someone else is good at.

- A shabby substitute for good, sound, solid work.

- Incompatible with ethics and values.

- Incompatible with their personality or character: "I could never do that!"

But consider this:

- Even in times of high employment and the availability of significant opportunity, "most people" still don't make it to the top. And they never will.

- Much of the time, "most people" are or have been wrong. Some of us are old enough to have spent a good deal of our working lives in the dark days before the personal computer, and what Digital Equipment president Ken Olsen said in 1977 seemed right as rain to most people at the time: "There is no reason for any individual to have a computer in the home."

The fact is that by picking up this book, you have already demonstrated that you are not like "most people." Maybe you don't like office politics, but you accept it as an inescapable feature of work-a-day reality. Maybe you've seen it work, and you want it to work for you.

But just what is "office politics"? The short answer is found in Appendix A, the glossary at the back of this book:

Office politics The ways in which people interact with one another in the workplace; also, the strategies savvy employees use to achieve and maintain a competitive advantage in the workplace.

The longer answer is the entire contents of this book. Office politics includes:

- How to fit in at work while simultaneously standing out (Chapter 2)

- How to create rapport with colleagues, subordinates, and bosses (Chapter 3)

- How to speak effectively and persuasively (Chapters 4 and 5)

- How to transform routine business meetings into occasions of genuine creativity (Chapter 6)

- How to transform the telephone, written correspondence, e-mail, and the fax into communication power tools (Chapters 7, 8, and 9)

- How to work effectively with any kind of boss (Chapter 10)

- How to become and be an effective leader (Chapters 11 and 12)

- How to practice ethical manipulation without becoming the victim of unethical manipulation (Chapter 13)

- How to resolve conflict productively (Chapter 14)

- How to make the most of workplace diversity (Chapter 15)

- How to survive an office romance and navigate the shoals of sexual harassment (Chapter 16)

- How to schmooze your way to the top (Chapter 17)

- How to mind your manners when business moves outside of the office (Chapter 18)

- How to use political savvy to build your career (Chapters 19 and 20)

There's more to office politics than sweet talk and back-stabbing. It is nothing less than the human side of business. And, ultimately, what other side matters?

Strictly Personal

PART I

Cube Roots: The Basics of Today's Corporate Climb

There are phrases in business that are guaranteed to bring a smile to the face—phrases like "signing bonus," "merit promotion," "company car," and "corner office." Then there are phrases like "office politics" and "climbing the corporate ladder." From some people they elicit pursed lips and a knowing nod of the head, from others a grimace.

Few people like to admit to dedicating a good part of their lives to what sounds like a dirty business. For some, "politics" sounds sleazy or manipulative, and "climbing the corporate ladder" connotes grubbing and groveling. But this is to deny three truths. First, everyone who works with more than two other people is involved in office politics and is currently stationed somewhere on the corporate ladder. Second, while there is no substitute for talent, training, and just plain knowing your job, these factors

3

alone are rarely enough to boost you to the top. Climbing the corporate ladder requires the savvy practice of office politics. But—and here's the third truth—office politics doesn't have to be dirty. It can be a highly effective, humane, and profitable way to do business and build a career. And "climbing" can be far more invigorating, satisfying, and enriching than "groveling."

This chapter will help you decide how you stand on office politics and where you stand on the corporate ladder.

"I'm not political"

Even the most blissfully naive among us admit to the existence of something called office politics. "It's the underhanded way people manipulate other people to climb the corporate ladder," they'll say. "I don't believe in office politics. It's all about back-stabbing," others remark. Or, "I guess that's how a lot of people get ahead. Me, I just try to do the best job I can and leave everyone else alone. I just stay in my cube. I'm not political."

So at least these people know that office politics is real. That's a step in the right direction. But here are three more essential truths about office politics that every working person should know:

1. Everyone is political, but not everyone realizes it or is good at being so.

2. You either use or are used by office politics.

3. Office politics doesn't have to be underhanded, dirty, or cruel. In fact, it is most effective when it is above-board, positive, and nurturing.

A quiz on political savvy

Whether you become an effective practitioner of office politics or its helpless victim depends on the degree of your political savvy. Here is a little self-test to help you measure where you are at right now. Answer "true" or "false" to each of the following questions:

Bright Idea
Answer the quiz questions as honestly as possible. If you're tempted to cheat and just answer everything "true," you'll make the highest possible score, but you won't learn anything.

True False

T F 1. I know the first and last names of everyone I see and work with on a regular basis.

T F 2. I've socialized with at least three peer-level coworkers in the last six months.

T F 3. I've socialized with my boss at least once in the past 12 months.

T F 4. I say "good morning" to everyone I see when I come into work.

T F 5. I have at least four "small-talk" conversations with coworkers each day.

T F 6. I answer my own phone.

T F 7. I avoid screening calls.

T F 8. I enjoy collaborative approaches to problems.

T F 9. I think of myself as part of a team.

T F 10. I am eager to help coworkers.

T F 11. I do not hesitate to ask for help and advice.

T F 12. I accept compliments easily and with pleasure.

T	F	13.	I deserve praise.
T	F	14.	I find frequent occasion to praise coworkers and subordinates.
T	F	15.	People find me persuasive.
T	F	16.	I find meetings productive.
T	F	17.	I am willing and able to deal with difficult people.
T	F	18.	More often than not, I can get people to do what I want them to do.
T	F	19.	I avoid victimization.
T	F	20.	I regard workplace diversity (the presence of men, women, people of different racial, cultural, and ethnic backgrounds, gays and lesbians, and people with disabilities) as an asset in today's business environment.
T	F	21.	Every once in a while, I bring food (like doughnuts and coffee) to work for everyone to share.
T	F	22.	I keep personal business to myself.
T	F	23.	I have a talent for acting calm when others are hysterical.
T	F	24.	I participate in corporate social events (like joining the office bowling team).
T	F	25.	I would be willing to take charge of a corporate social event.

> **"**
> You lose a lot of time hating people.
> —Marian Anderson, African-American singer who broke down color barriers, 1965
> **"**

T	F	26.	To enhance our corporate image, I do charitable work in the community.
T	F	27.	Even though it seems silly, I knock on the partition before entering anyone's cubicle.
T	F	28.	I believe that many "business" decisions are made for personal reasons.
T	F	29.	I believe you must promote yourself, because you can't depend solely on high performance to earn a reward.
T	F	30.	I must prove my value to my colleagues, subordinates, and bosses every day.
T	F	31.	I am both valuable and replaceable.
T	F	32.	In the working world, what goes around comes around.
T	F	33.	I set realistic objectives.
T	F	34.	I set realistic goals.
T	F	35.	I know the difference between objectives and goals.
T	F	36.	I communicate goals and objectives clearly.
T	F	37.	I give full and clear instructions to others.
T	F	38.	People find me very approachable.
T	F	39.	I am often asked for advice.
T	F	40.	I am "in the loop."

T   F   41. I am on the "A list" for memos and meetings.

T   F   42. I am invited to important company social events.

T   F   43. I communicate effectively.

T   F   44. People believe what I say.

T   F   45. I feel good when I speak.

T   F   46. I admit it: I like the sound of my own voice.

T   F   47. I have no trouble saying what I mean.

T   F   48. I have a good vocabulary.

T   F   49. I look a person in the eye when I speak.

T   F   50. I'm good at remembering names.

T   F   51. I have a warm handshake.

T   F   52. I enjoy listening to others.

T   F   53. I enjoy making small talk.

T   F   54. I look and feel relaxed when I speak.

T   F   55. I negotiate effectively.

T   F   56. The measure of successful negotiation is the degree to which everyone wins.

T   F   57. I like talking about money.

T   F   58. I am prepared to move on to a better job—a job with greater rewards and more opportunity.

T   F   59. I honestly look forward to the workday.

Evaluating the results

Go back and count the number of "true" responses. Give yourself one point for each "true." If you score under 44, you are probably not practicing office politics effectively.

If your score disappoints you, take another good look at the questions. There is one thing they all have in common. Not one of them concerns a trait, habit, style, or attitude that's genetically based. All the traits, habits, styles, and attitudes touched on in the questions can be learned, practiced, and honed. This book will help you do just that.

- If you scored below 45 points, this book will help you inventory what you need to learn and practice, and it will guide you in the first steps toward learning and practicing.

- If you scored 45 points or better, this book will help you practice and hone the skills you already have, and it will suggest a few more to add to your toolbox.

No business organization today functions without office politics, and there was never a "golden age of business" in which politics played no part. Whenever more than two human beings embark on a common enterprise, politics plays a role.

Where's Grandpa's gold watch?

In your grandpa's day, there was office politics. But your grandpa worked for the same company for 40 years and retired with a shiny gold watch. Was he a better office politician than you? Possibly. Who knows? What we do know is that 20, 30, or 40 years ago, employees changed employers—and employers changed employees—far fewer times than they do now. Today, according to the U.S. Department of

Watch Out!
Does a low score on this quiz mean you are doomed to failure and a dead-end job? Not at all. It does mean, however, that you aren't doing everything possible to maximize your opportunities for advancement. This book will address the issues mentioned in the quiz and help you make the most of your chances.

Labor, the average worker changes employers seven times during his or her career. In fact, that same worker can expect to change *careers* at least three times during his or her working life.

Eat or be eaten

Employers and employees both demand more of each other than at any other time in history. Employers expect a higher level of performance and a greater range of skills from each employee, while employees make unprecedented demands in salary, perks, opportunity, and equality of access to these items. Yet the "social contract" between employer and employee has never been looser or less secure.

Employers view employees as "human resources"; this sounds noble and generous until you stop to consider that resources can be swapped and upgraded and, on an individual basis, are generally expendable. Most employees have caught on to this, realizing that, in today's working world, it's either eat or be eaten. The prevailing attitude is driven by desperation and resentment—the feeling that the ax may fall at any time, and understandable resentment of the powers that wield the ax.

Under these circumstances, employees may become sharks, ready to devour bosses, subordinates, and colleagues—whoever gets between them and their next meal. The flaws with this philosophy are many, but they boil down to one: Who really wants to live this way?

Be eaten or go stale

Then there are the employees who don't want to be sharks, but who don't want to get eaten alive either. They avoid risk. This sounds like a good strategy until you stop to realize that all rewards entail risk. Risk is the inevitable by-product of all movement, all progress. Everyone knows that walking on two legs involves continually losing and regaining your balance. Each step risks a potentially fatal fall.

Many employees hunker down and hole up, accepting the same old responsibilities and the same old paycheck in return for the favor of not being consumed.

What's wrong with this approach? Well, not only is it life-denying and deadly dull, it provides nothing more than the *illusion* of safety. You don't have to be a sharpshooter to know that it's easier to hit a stationary target than a moving one. The corporate slugs are by no means immune to the ax of downsizing. And when you are chopped, where do you go from there?

The *real* rules of the game

The truth is that you needn't approach your career from either extreme—shark or slug. Start with three rules:

1. Know your job now.

2. Keep learning.

3. Behave well to everyone. That means adhering to the Golden Rule: Do unto others as you would have them do unto you. Treat those you work with as you would like them to treat you.

Beyond this, be willing to grow up to the basic realities of office politics.

How "executive decisions" are made

People in upper management never purposely make a bad decision. Often, a great show—and even a sincere effort—is made to objectively weigh all the

Watch Out!
Don't glamorize the idea of sticking with the same job for years. If you don't ever take on new skills and challenges, are you really able to make the transition to a new job? Can you even come up with a resume solid enough to get a new job?

pros and cons, the benefits and the liabilities. "Numbers" are looked at. "Products" are evaluated.

Everyone assumes that business is about creating *products* in order to make *numbers*. "I'm in the *shoe* business, and I spent *X dollars* this year and took in *Y dollars*, resulting in a profit of *Z dollars*."

But before you're in the shoe business or the pickle business or the banking business or the computer business, you are in the *people business*.

- Executive decisions are made by people who work with people, and are based on information supplied and presented by people.

- Decisions involving people are never objective and are always political.

- Executive decisions are, by definition, political.

The preceding three statements are *true*. Accept them, and you are in the game. Act effectively according to everything they imply, and you are in position to win the game. Ignore or deny them, and you may still play the part of predator or prey—but either way, you are out.

Your own horn: if you don't toot it, who will?

A politician running for government office talks about running on his record, but never does so. A successful politician continually creates and recreates that "record" through tireless self-promotion. The successful office politician must do the same. After all, the only person who is intimately familiar with "your record" is you. You can't count on the boss's keeping score in your favor.

Look for opportunities to toot your own horn:

- When you promote a project
- When you bid for a key assignment

Bright Idea
Resolve to do at least three *intensely human* things each workday: Say good morning to people in the office. Ask about a subordinate's family or outside interests. By being people-oriented yourself, you remind everyone at the office that they, too, are in the people business.

- When you ask for a raise or promotion
- When you attend a salary or performance review session

Shape your achievements to make them most appealing:

- Say what you did.
- Explain the positive impact of what you did.
- Use numbers—expressions involving dollars, days, hours—to quantify your achievements.

No one is indispensable

History presents not a single example of a human being who lived forever and kept his job forever. We understand this. Yet, at some level of our being, we decline to accept it.

So Joe Shmoe in accounting is fired. Who knows the reasons the company has for letting him go? He didn't do such-and-such, or he wasn't very good at that, or this project failed. Or maybe it's just that the boss doesn't like people named "Joe." Whatever the reasons, he got the ax, and you didn't.

Most of us *understand*, as an abstract idea, that the company doesn't regard us as indispensable. Yet few of us *accept* this truth, and even fewer act on it.

The more politically effective you are, the less dispensable you will *seem*. (And therefore, the less dispensable you will *be*.)

It *is* who you know

As old as the Dead Sea Scrolls is the lament of the cynical middle manager passed over for promotion yet again: "It's not *what* you know, it's *who* you know."

That cynic is right. And that is precisely the point.

Watch Out!
Don't let errors stand in the way of your ability to promote yourself—transform errors into achievements. If, for example, a project fails, emphasize what you did to avert outright disaster and what valuable data or lessons the company acquired as a result of the experience.

If we accept the fact that all business is ultimately *people* business, then we must understand that *what* you know is *who* you know. The route to mastery of your trade is traversed through people. Opportunity is built not on abstract knowledge, but on relationships with a series of human beings.

So, read on. None of what you'll encounter will seem strange to you. Office politics? You've been in it all your working life.

Just the facts

- The concepts "office politics" and "climbing the corporate ladder" have negative connotations, but they are as positive or as negative as we choose to make them.

- We are all deeply involved in office politics; through awareness and practice, we can master the political situation rather than become victims of it.

- Office politics is about dealing effectively with people.

- No matter what business you are in, you are in a *people business*.

GET THE SCOOP ON...
The importance of nonverbal communication ▪
Asserting authority nonverbally ▪ The power of
eye contact ▪ Cultivating a memorable hand-
shake ▪ Working a room without saying a word ▪
What your appearance says about you

Fitting In and Standing Out

Chapter 2

The title of this chapter expresses the goal I wake up with at the start of each business day. Because the phrase pulls in two directions, however, it's not easy to reach; in fact, it might sound like a contradiction in terms. A research and development expert once explained to me that developing new products is easy: All you have to do is create something entirely new that's worked well before. Trying to fit in *and* stand out at the same time is like this. But doing something well is never easy, and in fact, people who master the art of office politics are quite adept at walking the high wire, balancing conformity and individuality.

This high-wire act begins even before a single word is spoken. The master office politician makes many nonverbal statements using the language of the body. Body language helps you put yourself across, laying the foundation and providing the context for whatever verbal messages you want to deliver. This chapter shows you how to tell the world

Unofficially...
In 1971, psychologist Albert Mehrabian found that 55 percent of a speaker's persuasion is the product of her facial expressions and body movement. Vocal qualities (voice tone, pitch, and the pace of delivery) accounted for another 38 percent. The actual *words* the speaker used contributed a mere 7 percent to the persuasiveness of the speech!

of the office something about who you are without saying a thing.

Before you say a word

Human beings are visual animals. More of the "higher part" of the brain—the cerebral cortex—is devoted to processing visual information than to any other single function. This means that even before you've said a word, before you can make your case, before you can tell people verbally who you are and what you are about, the judging and evaluation have already begun.

Walking tall

Napoleon was a short guy who made it big. Well, he bucked the odds. The fact is that tall people have a built-in advantage with respect to how others perceive their credibility and authority. It's no accident of language that the word *stature* refers to physical height as well as achievement and reputation. Traditionally, Hollywood heroes have been tall. At five-foot-seven, 1950s leading man Alan Ladd had to stand on a box for those medium close-ups opposite Lana Turner. And what's true for men holds for women as well: Tall women (5'7" and up), like tall men (6' or more), command greater authority.

Is this shallow? Yes. Is this fair? No. But it is a fact of life, so you'll have to keep it in mind as you become more aware of the importance of nonverbal cues in interpersonal relations.

If you happen to be relatively short, you're not out of luck. You merely need to do what you can to give yourself as much height as possible. For example:

- Avoid boxy-looking suits.
- Avoid clothing with horizontally striped patterns, especially if the stripes are wide.

- Shorter men should shun baggy, loosely cut pants, while shorter women should favor longer hemlines.

Do you need to invest in "elevator shoes"? Probably not. But, in a business context, short men (5'7" and shorter) should consider shoes with a slightly built-up heel and moderately thick soles, while short women (5'4" and shorter) should consider wearing heels rather than flats. Be reasonable, though. If you try too hard to look taller, you'll only underscore the absence of height.

More important than what you wear, however, is how you walk. What your mother told you about posture is still good advice: Stand up straight, don't slouch, and don't stoop. Concentrate on maintaining an erect posture as you move forthrightly and without hesitation. And walk with a purpose. Think about what you need to accomplish as you approach Mr. Smith or Ms. Jones. The message is delivered nonverbally, but it can be put into words: "I know how to carry myself."

Let your smile do the talking

Walking straight and tall and with a purpose will help you command attention and respect, but it doesn't require stalking the office halls with a look of grim determination. In fact, it's always a good strategy to smile. This doesn't mean keeping a mindlessly plastic grin across your face, but rather developing a look that broadcasts a pleasant and approachable attitude.

As trite and simple-minded as it may sound, a smile wins acceptance. A smile is an invitation. In contrast, a sour look or outright scowl sets up resistance that is difficult to overcome. If you come on like a "tough nut to crack," many people will

Bright Idea
Try bringing a natural smile to your face by thinking of something that pleases you. Visualize a favorite person or place, or run through your mind a favorite piece of music.

immediately dismiss you as someone not worth dealing with.

Eye to eye

Just about everyone knows this cardinal rule of effective body language: Make eye contact. If you want to convey openness and honesty, look a person straight in the eye.

It sounds simple, right? But putting it into practice can be difficult. As an experiment, start taking note of how many people you meet and talk to who consistently fail to make eye contact. Many of us, perhaps most of us, instinctively avert our gaze from the person we're talking with. Some people actually look away or stare at the floor; most of us glance aside more subtly, just far enough to avoid catching and holding the other person's gaze.

Why is it so difficult to make and maintain eye contact? Probably hundreds of unconscious motives, pieces of unconsciously learned behavior, and unspoken social taboos are at work in each of us, driving us to divert our gaze. Nevertheless, most of us fully realize how important it is to make and maintain eye contact.

The eye-contact stakes are indeed high. After all, a synonym for a sleazy, suspect, or downright dishonest human being is "shifty-eyed." Unless a person is a very accomplished liar, someone who is telling something less (or something more) than the truth has trouble saying it "to your face" and cannot look you "straight in the eye." If, however, you make eye contact while delivering your message, chances are you'll be taken at your word. You will *sound* persuasive because you *appear* sincere.

But the power of eye contact is even greater than this. Not only does it convey honesty, sincerity, and trustworthiness, it also transmits energy. We've all

> **"**
> Eyes can speak and eyes can understand.
> —George Chapman (1559?–1634), English poet and translator of Homer
> **"**

heard people speak of the "sparkle" in someone's eye, as if that were a most remarkable phenomenon, a rare thing. Actually, if you stop to think about it, you'll realize that we all have a sparkle in our eyes—eyes are naturally shiny. This sparkle is rarely noticed, however, because so few people make full eye contact.

Use the sparkle you surely have. Its effect can be electric.

The crucial element of office politics—indeed, the objective of most business encounters—is to get others to "see eye to eye" with you. You may think of this as merely a shopworn figure of speech, but figures of speech are often rooted in physical reality. To persuade someone to see eye to eye with you is much easier if you begin the process of persuasion by ensuring that, in physical fact, you *do* see eye to eye with the other person.

Just remember the unfortunate fact that, for most of us, the pleasure of seeing eye to eye does not come naturally. It's a skill that must be practiced, and you may well find that you are resistant to it at first. Don't let this discourage you, however. Keep making a conscious effort to meet the eyes of the person you're speaking with. Transmit your sincerity. Convey your energy. You'll find that with practice it comes more naturally to you, and the results are worth the effort.

Eye to eyebrow

Most of the time, eye-to-eye contact works all the magic you need. But in certain situations and with some folks, the issue is not seeing eye to eye, but avoiding a steamroller.

Let's face it: Power struggles happen. And for some people, "office politics" consists of coercion, domination, and just plain bullying. We'll have

Bright Idea
Remember, your object is to make pleasing eye contact, not to drill your gaze into the very soul of your partner in conversation. While it's always a bad idea to speak to another person with your eyes averted, don't go overboard in the other direction and stare at the person.

Watch Out!
Avoid the temp-
tation to use the
eye-to-eyebrow
technique indis-
criminately on
everyone you
encounter. You
don't want to
appear hostile
or, even worse,
as a bully
yourself.

much more to say about coping with and defending against intimidation in Chapters 6, 9, 11, and 12, but here's a quick body-language antidote to the machinations of an office bully. Instead of making eye contact, set your gaze a notch higher. Don't look at the other person's eyes, but just above them, at the level of the eyebrows. This can send a subtle but unmistakable signal of dominance, and it telegraphs the message that *you* are not easily cowed.

Hail to the handshake

Although it may seem somewhat quaint nowadays, like something out of a Horatio Alger novel or an Andy Hardy movie, people used to take handshakes very seriously. Dutiful fathers would take their sons aside (remember, in those days it was exclusively the little boys, not the little girls, who were expected to grow up into the world of business) and explain to them in solemn fatherly tones the importance of a "good, solid handshake." That gesture was passed down from man to boy as if it were the skeleton key to commercial success, an all-purpose, 100-percent-guaranteed open-sesame. "Son, this is *important*."

Cute, huh? Most of us probably think that business people today are too sophisticated for such mystical notions about a handshake. After all, isn't a handshake just a preliminary to getting down to *real* business?

But think about this for a minute. Can you recall a particularly memorable handshake in your life? You probably can. We remember touch even more vividly than we remember words. Think about that memorable handshake. Was it memorable because it was especially warm and powerful? Or because it was a "limp, dead-fish" handshake?

Whether positive or negative, a handshake makes an impression. At the very least, that impression lingers longer than whatever else occurs during a particular encounter. Sometimes, however, the impression created by a handshake lasts a lifetime.

Is a handshake really mystical? No, its power can be explained—it's the power of touch between two people. Fortunately, it's not hard to deliver a handshake memorable for warmth, sincerity, openness, and a willingness to communicate:

1. Keep it dry. Nobody likes a clammy handshake. If necessary, carry a handkerchief with you and use it to wipe your hands before you go into a meeting or conference that is likely to involve handshakes.

2. Grasp the other person's hand fully. Take hold of the palm, not just the fingers.

3. Deliver a grip that is *moderately* firm. No one appreciates a bone-crunching handshake. It's both painful and childish. On the other hand, avoid the limp, dead-fish grip. As with eye contact, the transaction taking place is an exchange of energy—positive, warm, controlled energy.

4. Hold on to the other person's hand a few fractions of a second longer than you might be inclined to do naturally. This quite literally *holds* the other person's attention as you exchange greetings.

5. Start talking *before* you let go. Say (for example) "How are you, Fred?" Then release your grip.

6. During the handshake, establish and maintain eye contact. And be sure to smile!

All about breathing

"Wait a minute. I *know* how to breathe."

Obviously. But breathing is not always easy—for example, when we are excited or scared. The way we

Bright Idea
Gentlemen, women appreciate a firm handshake as much as men do—maybe even more. Gripping the hand of a woman associate firmly immediately disposes of certain gender issues by not suggesting that you treat female business associates any differently from male associates.

Watch Out!
Remember, anxious breathing aggravates anxiety. But relaxed breathing makes you feel less anxious. Focusing on your breathing will not only make you sound more confident, it will actually increase your confidence.

breathe is an accurate barometer of emotion, a barometer others can read as easily as you can.

Anxiety disrupts normal breathing patterns. Typically, we say it makes us "short of breath"; more accurately, anxiety causes us to take short, shallow, and rapid breaths. This has two results:

- We look and sound nervous.

- We feel nervous; the rapid breathing resulting from anxiety actually increases anxiety.

Fortunately, to a significant degree you *can* override anxious breathing patterns. This will help you relax, and when others see you relaxed, they'll take you more seriously. To overcome anxious breathing:

- Don't rush into any important communication.

- Out of sight of others, take a few deep breaths before speaking.

Musicians, especially singers, may spend years learning how to regulate their breathing. All you have to do is focus on slowing down your breaths and making them deeper.

A body-language phrase book

Psychologists have made extensive studies of body language. The most popular book on the subject is Julius Fast's classic *Body Language,* first published in 1970. In the workplace, the following body-language strategies are most useful.

Conveying relaxed energy

The most valuable, positive quality anyone brings to an enterprise is energy—not frenetic, aimless nervousness, but energy in repose. It is what our parents (or grandparents) called *poise.*

In addition to keeping your breathing regular and deep, you can convey relaxed energy by doing the following things:

- Making eye contact. Remember, a meeting of the eyes telegraphs not only honesty and frankness, but also a sense of energy.

- Opening your eyes wide. This expresses engagement with others and generally heightened interest.

- Sitting (relatively) still. Avoid a rigid posture, but do sit upright, without fidgeting.

- Smiling.

- Nodding to communicate understanding and assent. Avoid nodding too vigorously, however. Easy does it.

- Leaning forward in your seat from time to time to express intensity of interest. Actively engage others.

If you consciously bear in mind that your objective is to convey energy—not nervous energy, but relaxed energy—you will find it easier to express these values with your body.

A show of hands

Many people are self-conscious about hand gestures. They don't know "what to do with" their hands. What *should* you do with your hands? The short answer is—*use* them.

Hand gesturing is normal, natural, and human. While you should avoid making a lot of distracting gestures, especially those near your face and head, using your hands to help you make your point is yet another aspect of relaxed energy. Try these gestures:

- **Open-handedness.** Gestures with open hands, held palm up, suggest honesty and general receptiveness to the needs and ideas of others.

Bright Idea
Rub your hands together to indicate that you are looking forward to what the other person is about to say. But don't confuse this with wringing your hands. The latter is one of the more destructive "phrases" of body language, conveying extreme anxiety and unhappiness.

- **Steepling.** Putting the fingertips of both hands together, steeple-fashion, conveys confidence.

- **Rubbing hands together.** Used sparingly, this gesture powerfully conveys positive expectancy.

Body-language blunders

As powerful as positive body language is, the negative nonverbal messages we sometimes send are even more compelling, taking us in directions we don't want to go. Avoid the following:

- **The tentative entrance.** Don't shuffle or sneak into a room. Move forthrightly, as if you have a purpose.

- **The downcast look.** Make and hold eye contact.

- **The lowered chin.** Not only does this tend to make eye contact impossible, it is a defensive posture.

- **The dead-fish handshake.** This conveys a lack of interest in the other person and is perceived as creepy—there is no other word for it.

- **The death-grip handshake.** There is never any business benefit in making another person feel uncomfortable.

- **Fidgeting.** Like yawning, fidgeting is contagious. Fidget, and everyone around you will begin to feel nervous, frustrated, and eager to leave.

- **Sighing.** This sets off alarm bells, suggesting that the situation calls for despair.

- **Yawning.** Convey intense interest, not utter boredom.

- **Head scratching.** This suggests confusion.

- **Lip biting.** This is a strong signal of anxiety.

- **Rubbing the back of the head or neck.** Such a gesture conveys frustration and impatience.

- **Narrowing of the eyes.** This is a particularly strong negative gesture, which suggests disagreement and even resentment or anger. Outright squinting communicates clueless bewilderment.

- **Raised eyebrows.** Be careful with this. It conveys disbelief, as if you don't trust what the other person is saying.

- **Peering over the top of your eyeglasses.** This too conveys disbelief.

- **Crossing arms in front of your chest.** This common stance is a strong message of defiance and a closed mind. The tighter and higher the arms are crossed, the greater the degree of aggression conveyed.

- **Rubbing eyes, ears, or the side of the nose.** All these gestures telegraph doubt and self-doubt. They sabotage any message.

Making an entrance

Parents and teachers have always liked to lecture about the importance of first impressions. They are indeed important, because they create the context in which subsequent communication is interpreted and accepted or rejected. And "first" doesn't just apply to the first time someone meets you; other firsts are equally important. For example, consider how the first encounter you have with a coworker each morning affects your expectation of how productive and helpful the person will be that day. Each time we enter a room, we create a new first impression. Be sure to use good, positive body language when you perform this important action.

Greetings!

Walk tall and smile. Treat everyone in the room to a pleasant greeting, such as "good morning" or "good afternoon." As I'll discuss elsewhere, it's also good to personalize your greeting as appropriate: "Joe, how's that golf game of yours?" Greet people by name, and, if there's time, bring up a subject you know is of interest to whomever you greet.

Unmusical chairs

Good entrances are often compromised by awkward moments involving what should be the simple act of taking a seat.

Don't rush to a seat. Doing so will make you seem overanxious or even selfish. More important, by standing in a room in which others are already seated, you will enjoy a few moments in which everyone will look up to you—both literally and figuratively. The standing figure has an aura of authority, however temporary. Take advantage of it.

Also think about where you will sit. Given a choice, take a firm chair rather than a soft chair or sofa. You are seen to your best advantage sitting upright, not swallowed up and small-looking in a piece of overstuffed furniture. If you're seated at a table, be aware that a kind of geopolitical power map comes into play. The position of greatest authority is always at the head of the table. The number-two position is at the foot of the table. Some authorities regard the *weakest* positions as those on either side of the head of the table, while others see the second most powerful position as to the leader's left, and the least powerful to his or her right. Also note that it takes a certain amount of self-confidence to take a seat at the foot of the table. If this makes you uncomfortable, don't do it.

Putting names to faces

Make free and frequent use of people's names. If you're walking into a meeting with new people, make a determined effort to learn their names and to associate a face with each name. A good way to do this is to look the person in the eye as you shake his or her hand and repeat the person's name: "John, it's good to meet you."

Dress codes: send the right message

Most of us feel we shouldn't "judge a book by its cover" or be overly concerned with clothes. Henry David Thoreau stated this view well: "Beware of all enterprises that require new clothes, and not rather a new wearer of clothes."

Of course, Thoreau didn't work for a living, and he lived part of his life in a shack built on borrowed land on Walden Pond. For those of us who work around others, let's face it—clothes are important. They send strong nonverbal messages. At the very least, your working wardrobe should be:

- Impeccably clean
- Well-maintained
- Appropriate to what you do

Office success won't require you to become a fashion plate, but by keeping these simple points in mind, your clothing will send the message that you are organized, someone to be taken seriously.

I gotta be me

Of the three clothing suggestions just mentioned, it's the last that gives some people trouble. Just what is "appropriate"? And how does "appropriate" fit with making an individual statement? The fact is that dressing for work—dressing in a politically

> 66
> A monkey in silk is still a monkey.
>   —Spanish proverb
> 99

Bright Idea
Some organiza-
tions have
explicitly stated
dress codes. If
this is the case
where you work,
follow the code
to the letter. In
most business
situations, how-
ever, the dress
code is not
handed down
from on high and
stated in so
many words.
You'll have to
discover it
through
observation.

savvy way—may involve modifying your self-image. "I
gotta be me"? Well, not necessarily.

Styles change, of course, and no single prescrip-
tion for dressing works best in all situations at all
times. But keep your eyes open, and you will soon
decipher the dress code operating in your particular
place of business.

Identify the people with clout in your organization and observe how they dress. Take this as a statement of the company's dress code. Don't imitate
your model slavishly, but do take inspiration from
her.

Keep your ears and eyes open. Don't solicit comments on your outfit. To the question, "Do you like
my suit?" few people will respond with anything
other than a compliment, regardless of their true
feelings. But do listen for *unsolicited* compliments. If
you regularly get positive comments on what you
wear, you can be sure that you've tuned into the
code. Keep it up.

A question of focus

Practicing effective office politics is in large part a
matter of drawing attention to yourself for the right
reasons: your ability to do the job, your sage and
savvy approach to business, your good sense, your
imagination, and so on. Don't let your wardrobe
obscure the focus that should be on you rather than
on your clothes. Follow these two rules:

1. In general, dress a bit more conservatively than
   your heart or taste tells you to do.

2. Keep your outfits simple. Use vivid accents—a
   sharp tie or a beautiful scarf, for example—to
   make an otherwise simple, conservative, under-
   stated ensemble distinctive.

Being comfortable

Question: When is a suit and tie more comfortable than sweat pants and a T-shirt? Answer: When you're on the 23rd floor sitting around a conference table with a lot of other people in suits and ties.

Dressing for comfort does not automatically mean soft, loose, and sloppy, because comfort has to do with context and purpose as well as feel and fit. To make a consistently effective statement with your wardrobe, you need to become comfortable with the code, dressing in a way that feels right *in context*. Your clothes should express something of who you are, as well as mark you as a team player.

Come clean

No matter how carefully you select your wardrobe, the effect is spoiled if what you wear is anything less than fresh, clean, and in impeccable repair. Office politics shouldn't be a dirty business!

Your personal grooming is also key. Come to work freshly showered, with your hair well attended to.

Getting in gear

Although styles change, and what's right in some contexts may be inappropriate in others, here are some tried-and-true principles of politically effective dressing.

Suit yourself

Men as well as women may benefit from dark colors, at least as seasonally appropriate, because these convey authority. Dark blue, for example, is strongly associated with power and authority. Most women find that a small pinstripe looks better than a solid dark suit.

Watch Out!
Don't douse yourself in perfume, cologne, or aftershave. No human sense is more sensitive than the sense of smell. Strong scent may be perceived as intrusive and annoying. Worse, many people are allergic to perfumes. You don't need to avoid using scents completely, but use them *very* sparingly.

Bright Idea
If you like black,
go ahead and
wear it.
Conventional
wisdom says to
stay away from
black suits
because the
color is more
appropriate for a
funeral than for
business. But a
smartly tailored
black suit, for
men and women
alike, accented
with a bit of
color—a tie or a
scarf—suggests
quiet authority.

Pay close attention to suit fabric, because others will. Men should choose natural fabrics only, with 100 percent wool as the number-one choice. Even in warm weather, summer-weight wool fabrics look great and hold their shape well.

Because of the way they are tailored and the usually lighter weight of body fabric and linings, women's suits are more prone to wrinkling than men's. For this reason, women might consider high-quality blends of natural and synthetic fabrics.

Unless your understanding of the prevailing dress code convinces you otherwise, favor conservative cuts. A man with a slender build might look great in a European-cut suit, but most men do better in more generous American cuts.

Shirts, blouses, tees, and ties

For men, long-sleeve shirts are usually a must. If you are following a rather conservative course, white or pale-blue solids are best. If you like a stripe or other pattern, choose something muted.

Choose cotton for the shirt material. While polyester is less likely to wrinkle, natural fabric looks much better. Have your shirts professionally laundered with light starch.

For women, long-sleeved blouses are most desirable, although short-sleeve blouses are also acceptable in most workplaces. It is probably safest to avoid sleeveless blouses altogether, although in some warm climates, the sleeveless look is popular and acceptable. Note, however, that climate alone is not an infallible guide. In Miami and Atlanta, for example, going sleeveless will raise no eyebrows, whereas it will look out of place in many New Orleans or Charleston offices. Look around, and see what others do.

Worn with a smart suit jacket, well-made T-shirts are increasingly popular even in fairly conservative business environments. For blouses as well as tees, natural fabrics are best, especially cotton or silk.

Clothes-conscious folk disagree whether shoes or necktie commands the most immediate attention in a man's outfit. But all agree that a necktie can make or break a look.

Avoid ties that scream. Favor traditional patterns, including foulards, stripes, and muted paisleys. Hunting dogs, duck heads, and other assorted flora and fauna should be shunned. Buy 100 percent pure silk only.

Women can create wonderful effects with the right scarf. Avoid the matching scarf-and-blouse look, and instead choose a pure silk scarf in a color and pattern that complement your suit.

Aim for the middle; dress a notch above

Sales professionals in many fields have long advised dressing "a notch above" their customer. For example, instead of cotton, try silk. Rather than jeans, how about khakis? This is a reasonable rule of thumb to follow when choosing a politically effective wardrobe for yourself. Gauge the level of the office "look" and aim just a little bit higher. This way, you accomplish the feat of standing out *and* fitting in.

Why less is more

The politically savvy workplace dresser will not take any of this advice as absolute. By all means, exercise personal taste and judgment. But I can't resist issuing *one* hard-and-fast rule. Beyond providing warmth, protection, and a means of avoiding arrest for indecent exposure, clothes, in a business context, are a form of self-expression. This means that

Watch Out!
Some people are turned off by monograms, considering them egotistical and even vulgar. If you like monogrammed shirts, place the initials discreetly on your left sleeve at the top of the cuff rather than over the breast pocket.

Bright Idea
Women can choose from a spectrum of colors for blouses and T-shirts; however, bear in mind that in more conservative business environments, especially in financial firms, white, pale blue, and pearl gray are the most universally accepted colors for women's tops.

your outfits should not express *themselves,* but should ultimately draw the focus to *you.* For this reason, keep in mind what the great modern architect Mies van der Rohe said about building design: *Less is more.*

Keep your look simple, but pay close attention to the details and the quality. In this way, your clothes will always express business values universally regarded as desirable, and you will never be written off as just another suit.

Just the facts

- Psychological studies have shown that the most persuasive elements of communication are non-verbal, principally the body language of the communicator.

- Body language and general appearance make positive office politicking easier.

- Although many aspects of body language are habitual and unconscious, we can learn to become aware of how we express ourselves non-verbally, so that we can consciously improve these vital communication skills.

- Effective workplace dressing is mainly a matter of reading the dress code where you work.

- A great career look focuses attention on you, not your clothing.

GET THE SCOOP ON...
Building workplace community and rapport ▪
How to praise and criticize ▪ Handling anger ▪
Apologizing effectively ▪ Celebrating special
occasions ▪ Acknowledging grief and loss

Uncommon Courtesy

Chapter 3

The office: You spend about a third of your working life in it. It is a place populated by individuals whose common interests and goals almost certainly outweigh their differences and conflicting goals. These days, it probably houses people of diverse cultural and ethnic backgrounds. It is, in short, a community, and thinking of it as such is the first big step toward winning at office politics, because building a community in the workplace is a foundation for an entirely new view of political power. Truly effective, career-building politics is not about the dog-eat-dog survival of the fittest, but about creating an environment in which the whole is greater than the sum of the parts. That is an environment in which you can excel.

"Nice guys" don't always finish last

We have all heard clichés about the workplace, and we sometimes believe them. The trouble with running our lives and careers according to clichés is that one cliché often cancels out another. Just consider the following two:

- "What goes around comes around."
- "Nice guys finish last."

If one is true, the other must be false. The second advises you to be lean and mean. The first tells you that if you act lean and mean, you'll get lean and mean treatment in return—hardly a formula for success.

My vote is for the first. Remember, the workplace is a *community*. You are a member of that community, and like all communities, you get from it what you put into it.

An exercise in empathy

Being a "nice guy" is not about passivity, letting things slide, or taking it on the chin. It's about developing an ability to see beyond your own ego.

"
Do as you would be done by.
—Lord Chesterfield, to his son (1748)
"

Think about the last time you purchased something from a really good salesperson. There may be a hundred little details that made the encounter successful, but almost certainly the salesperson you judged to be effective did two things: She took the focus off herself, and she put it on you.

In contrast, an ineffective salesperson focuses not on the customer but on the sale. And a truly disastrous salesperson focuses on neither the sale nor the customer, but on herself: "Please, buy this car. I have to pay the mortgage this week."

An effective salesperson works to see the world from the customer's perspective, discovering the customer's wants and needs, as well as doubts and fears, and then addressing those. This is *empathy:* an identification with another person.

The savvy office politician is an effective salesperson, always endeavoring to empathize—not out of a sense of altruism or self-sacrifice, but because she knows that to get you've got to give. A good salesperson makes sales. A great one makes customers. In the workplace, think beyond the specific occasion, and always try to make each interaction with subordinates, colleagues, and bosses satisfying to them.

Increasing rapport

What, exactly, is an "interaction"? Well, exactly, an interaction can be momentous—asking a boss for a promotion, perhaps, or persuading a colleague to support a major project of yours. Or it can be as apparently inconsequential as a glance, a smile, or a kind word.

Linger on that word "apparently," because the little things you do every day in the workplace are only *apparently* inconsequential. Their cumulative effect is, in fact, of great consequence. It is the little things that do most to either build or tear down rapport.

"Rapport" is another key word for the skilled practitioner of office politics. It's a relationship of mutual trust and emotional affinity. But just how is rapport established?

- Rapport may build slowly, over a period of years, between good friends, between teachers and students, between spouses, and between long-time business partners and associates.

- Rapport may be established instantly and spontaneously. Some people just "hit it off" with one another.

But you can't afford to wait years or to trust to chance that rapport will develop. You need to take proactive steps to accelerate the process. Don't leave your future to chance; build relationships with your

Bright Idea
Think of the people you work with—subordinates, colleagues, and bosses—not as your coworkers, but as your customers, people to whom you give value in exchange for value. An important part of your job is to satisfy them.

subordinates, colleagues, and bosses. Remember: 70 percent of the reason people get fired has nothing to do with poor job performance, but is the result of unresolved personality conflicts.

Helping words

One way to build rapport quickly is to use helping words. The most basic helping words are forms of the first-person plural pronoun:

> we
>
> us
>
> our

Timesaver
Think about your language. Look for places to use *we* instead of *I* or *you*. This is a quick, efficient way to create rapport.

As quickly as possible, try to move each conversation from the monologues of *I* and *you* to a dialogue of *we, us,* and *our.* For example, suppose a colleague complains, "I just can't get Shipping to fulfill all these orders on time." There are two ways to respond. If you reply "You have a real problem there," you show that you've been listening. But the pronoun *you* will not build rapport. If, however, you say "We have a real problem here," you will be more successful. The pronoun *we* is a rapport builder. It forges a bond between you and your colleague.

Just as important, this second response invites constructive continuation of the conversation: "What can *we* do about it?" In contrast, the first response invites only an off-putting challenge: "What are *you* going to do about it?"

Here are some other helping words, all of which can help build rapport by promoting a bond between you and another, typically by suggesting a cooperative activity or process:

> analyze   brainstorm
>
> collaborate   confer

cooperate   huddle

learn   listen

solve   team up

work together

Rapport wreckers

While rapport can be quickly built, it can, unfortunately, be quickly destroyed as well.

A language of exclusion

One way to wreck rapport is to use the language of exclusion instead of the language of inclusion. Using words like *I* and *mine* or *you* and *yours* builds barriers; instead use the inclusive plural pronouns—*we, us, ours.*

Negative words, such as words that deny, contradict, or refuse, also build barriers. Here are a few examples of negative words—all sure-fire rapport killers:

afraid	fail	impossible
bad luck	fault	lose
cannot	fear	non-negotiable
crisis	final	stupid
delay	forgot	tired

Selfish, nasty habits

Another way to wreck rapport is through plain bad behavior. Typical breeches of office etiquette include:

- Using inappropriate language. This includes making vulgar comments and telling tasteless jokes or using inappropriate or demeaning nicknames.

- Arriving late to appointments or meetings.

Bright Idea
Why not make your own list of helping words? The more sensitive you are to the language you use, the more effectively you will build rapport.

- Sloppy or inappropriate dress or grooming.

- Poor telephone manners. This includes a multitude of sins, such as keeping callers on hold, failing to take or relay messages, slamming down the phone, starting to talk before the receiver is in position, and eating while talking.

- Knee-jerk sour attitude. No one likes to hang out with a negative person who doesn't want others to succeed.

- Failure to honor your word or to muster the courage to support it.

- Habitual jealousy. Jealousy is a virus. It arises from fear and then spreads to anger and hatred. Don't be jealous of others for their success; it is only your fear of success that is stopping you from being successful.

- Failure to greet or to greet appropriately. Avoid the limp handshake as well as the bone-crushing handshake. Don't fail to make eye contact. (See Chapter 2 for pointers on both these topics.)

- Refusing to listen. Do you habitually cut people off or interrupt them?

- Failure to respect the privacy and space of others. This is a major problem in the age of the doorless office and the cubicle.

- Failure to share appropriately. Do you put more paper in the copier when needed, or do you use the machine, then walk away, leaving it empty?

- Being a gossip or breaking confidentiality.

Relieving peer pressure

Let's face it: Success in business is largely a matter of numbers. Your sales figures are up, or they're not. You're within budget, or you're not. You meet projections, or you don't. But success is also built on things that cannot be readily measured. It's built, in part, on giving people the right feelings.

Starting on a good note

Start each day off on a positive note by saying "good morning" to your coworkers. Use the person's name: "Good morning, Ben." When time and circumstances permit, extend the morning greeting: "Good morning, Ben. How was your weekend?" If possible, make the greeting even more personal: "Good morning, Ben. How'd your son do in the game Saturday?"

Cubicle questions

These days, if you have a "real" office—one with windows and a door, plus walls that don't move—you're either very lucky or you rank fairly high on the office totem pole. There was a time when only entry-level personnel were herded into cubicles. These days, however, even higher-level employees are penned into spaces without doors, windows, or solid walls.

Managers and owners love cubes because they are cheap and efficient ways of handling space. Most other employees, however, hate and resent them as an affront to their dignity. The best—that is, the most productive—course is to accept cubicles as the grim reality of today's workplace. Here are three suggestions.

1. Don't complain about your work space.

2. Treat your cubicle as your office.

3. Treat the cubicles of others as their offices. This means that you should always respect the privacy of your colleagues, as if they occupied an office with a door. Don't barge in. Ask permission to enter.

Bright Idea
Make your greetings personal by learning something about the people you work with. How do you do that? Try engaging in some productive small talk. (See Chapter 5.)

Unofficially...
Anthropologists call the study of how we use space *proxemics*. But you don't have to be a professor to study it. For example, the next time you're in a meeting with more than a few people, notice how many people choose, time after time, the same place at the conference table.

The territorial imperative

Why do folks find cubicles so depressing? The most likely reason is that they rob us of privacy; more essentially, they rob us of our territory. Human beings are territorial animals. It's built into our genes. We can't help it, and we resent, from deep in the gut, any attack on our turf.

It's bad enough that management has done so much to undermine people's sense of territory. Don't add insult to injury by failing to respect whatever precious territory your colleagues have left. Follow these rules of "cube etiquette":

- As just mentioned, ask permission before entering a cubicle.

- Do not enter another's cubicle if that person is not present—except, for example, to deliver something or leave a note.

- If you are supposed to meet someone in an office or in a cubicle, wait outside until the person shows up.

- In a meeting, ask permission before rearranging any furniture: "Do you mind if I move this chair?"

- Take your trash with you when you leave.

- Don't put your coffee cup or anything else on a person's desk without asking permission. The desk is the "inner circle" of one's territory. Respect this.

- Don't borrow equipment without permission, and always return whatever you borrow.

- Don't snoop or appear to be snooping. Never rifle through papers on somebody else's desk.

Make it yours

Territoriality is not just something for you to respect. It is something for you to establish for yourself as well. If you have a choice, choose your office carefully:

- A "real" office is always preferable to a cube.

- A corner office is preferable to any other. Why? A corner office is usually bigger and has more windows. Also, corner offices are by necessity more rare and, therefore, more exclusive.

If you have a choice of office furniture, pay most attention to your seat. There is a good reason why kings and queens have elaborate thrones: What you sit on conveys a message about the power you wield. Generally, the more expensive a chair is, the more it puts others in mind of a throne, and, therefore, the more power you are perceived to have. Even if you can't afford something bigger, you should at least have a chair with armrests.

By all means, personalize your space with artwork you like and pictures of the family. Observe some cautions, however:

- Make yourself aware of any company rules concerning the decoration of offices. Respect them.

- Awards and certificates are almost always appropriate.

- If you decorate with personal photos, make certain that the subjects in them are properly attired.

- Avoid decorating with religious items.

- Avoid decorating with "clever" sayings, especially if they are of questionable taste.

- Avoid stuffed animals.

Bright Idea
How you arrange the furniture in your work space influences your perception of the adequacy of the space. If possible, position your chair so that you can lean back without touching a wall or bookcase. Even a fairly large office will seem cramped if you can't lean back freely.

Watch Out!
Putting an inap-
propriate or
potentially offen-
sive photograph,
joke, or motto
on your office or
cubicle wall can
be a career killer.
Offensive mater-
ial in the work-
place can lead to
legal action,
including law-
suits by employ-
ees who claim
that such mater-
ial creates a
"hostile work
environment."

- Avoid anything with a sexual connotation or a message of hostility (such as military memorabilia).

- Remember that everything you put in your office says something about who you are and, even more important, who you *think* you are.

Keep your office or your cubicle neat and clean. Unless security and confidentiality are at stake, it is not necessary for you to clear your desk every evening. But do keep it looking organized.

You should also feel free to enforce your personal territory—without being nasty about it. If, for example, someone borrows your stapler and neglects to return it, ask for it back: "I need my stapler back, please." If you don't want people waiting in your office when you're not there, mention it—gently but firmly: "Bob, next time you get here before I do, please wait outside."

Help!

If you want to create instant rapport, offer help when help is needed. And here's a surprise: If you want to create rapport even faster, *ask for help*. Few things make people feel better about themselves than being asked for advice or help. By asking for help, you give the other person good feelings about himself. Your appeal for help ends up helping the other person as well. So don't be shy.

Offering it

If you are asked for help, give it. If you cannot give the help asked for, help the person find someone who *can* help: "Dana, I don't know a thing about installing modems, but Sarah Smith does. Let's give her a call."

If you are not directly asked for help, but you see a colleague in difficulty, take a sensitive but straightforward approach: "Bill, can I help you with that?"

Asking for it

Before you ask for help—or information—from colleagues, try to take the time necessary to identify the best sources of aid. Ask yourself:

- Who does what job?
- Who seems to command influence and enjoy respect?
- Who is "in the loop"?
- Who is clearly climbing the corporate ladder?
- Who is frequently asked? Frequently quoted?
- Who makes the important decisions?
- Who is a natural leader?

These are the people to identify as sources of information and aid. Get to know them.

Never apologize when you ask for help. Don't think of your request as *taking* something, but as *giving* something. You are giving somebody the opportunity to be helpful, which is an opportunity to feel good.

If you need help right away, just ask: "Sally, I need your help." If the situation isn't urgent, temper your request: "Sally, I need your help with something. When's a good time to talk?" If the help or information you seek is even less pressing, approach the issue casually: "Sally, mind if I pick your brain about something?"

Accepting it

In accepting help, once again, do not apologize: "I'm really sorry I bothered you." By apologizing in this way, you are sending the signal that the person

Bright Idea
When you make an offer of help, phrase the offer in the form of a question: "Can I help?" Never say "You look like you're in trouble!" Or "You look like you can use some help!" These suggest that the person *looks* stupid or incompetent.

Timesaver
Asking for help
is a positive
move—as long
as you don't sim-
ply dump a prob-
lem in someone
else's lap.
Respect the
other person's
time by being as
specific as possi-
ble about the
help you need.
Provide as much
information as
you can. If you
do this, you'll
discover that
others begin to
respect your
time, as well.

should feel annoyed with you. Why even imply such a thing?

Nor should you cast yourself in the role of a clue-less dunce: "I'm just a helpless moron when it comes to computers." This invites the other person to agree with you. Chances are she won't come out and say, "Yes, you really *are* a helpless moron," but that thought will cross her mind. Also, by presenting yourself as stupid, you make the other person feel bad about having helped you: "Why did I waste my time with this dope?" Remember, just as you want to associate yourself with the company's movers and shakers, so do other people. Don't give them the message that you're a dolt.

Praise and constructive criticism

It's common courtesy to acknowledge the achieve-ments of colleagues, as well as subordinates and bosses. But it is *uncommon* courtesy to acknowledge their screwups—by way of offering genuinely con-structive and creative criticism.

Certainly, it is easier to offer praise than to criti-cize, but even praise has potential problems. Keep the following tips in mind:

- In praising a colleague or subordinate, make sure that your words are conveyed sincerely. There should be no trace of sarcasm. "Damning with faint praise" will only insult the recipient.

- Be careful not to patronize or talk down to a col-league or subordinate. Don't express astonish-ment: "*You* did *this!* I can't believe it!"

- Be specific in your praise. Don't say: "You're doing a great job!" Instead, say: "Increasing the profit margin by 2 percent! Well, that's just out-standing!" Sincere praise is not conveyed by adjectives, no matter how well chosen. It is conveyed by precise nouns, which show that you fully understand and appreciate the accomplishment you are praising.

- Being specific will also help you avoid a major pitfall when you praise a boss—the sucking-up syndrome. When congratulating a boss on an achievement, focus on the facts of the achievement rather than on the personality of the boss. This will save you from looking like a sycophant.

A little praise / Goes a great ways.
—Ralph Waldo Emerson
99

Offering criticism is, of course, a more delicate matter than offering praise, but it doesn't have to be any less positive an act. Before making any critical remarks to colleagues, subordinates, or bosses, do a quick reality check:

- First and most important: Do not criticize any *person*. Focus your remarks on an issue, a project, an action, or an outcome—not on a person, trait, or personality.

- Before you say a word, be sure that the situation really does call for criticism. Really stop and consider: Is the issue really worth criticizing?

- Ask yourself if the situation you are criticizing can be improved or corrected. If a problem is not fixable, don't just dump it in another person's lap.

- Don't bludgeon your listener. Ask permission to offer criticism. That is, ask the person if he would "like to hear" how you feel about what he is doing. Asking for permission in this way will help the other person to receive what you say as "feedback" rather than "criticism."

- Choose an appropriate place and time. Don't embarrass the person by criticizing her in front of others. Establish a time: "Mary, there's some-thing I want to discuss with you. What would be a good time for you when we might have a few uninterrupted moments?"

- Always support criticism with substance. Don't be vague. Cite specific problems, incidents, or actions.

- Be prepared to offer helpful alternatives. You don't want to tear down without helping to build up. However, don't present your sugges-tions in a way that belittles the other person.

- Present your criticism in an informal manner and with a friendly tone of voice. Avoid the lan-guage of command: "you must," "you have to," and so on.

- Combine praise with criticism, if at all possible. You don't want your listener to think that he is a total failure.

- Avoid overwhelming your listener with multiple criticisms. Try to identify and tackle one issue at a time.

- Don't leave the other person hanging out to dry. Follow up with positive feedback, including praise, congratulations, and thanks.

Don't use threats, predicting punitive or other dire personal consequences if a problem goes uncorrected. The inadvisability of threatening your boss is obvious. But threats also poison relationships with colleagues and subordinates. It may be neces-sary to discuss consequences, but make certain that what you discuss are objective, factual conse-quences, not criticisms of personality or compe-tence. Focus on issues, not egos.

What about when you're on the receiving end of criticism? How you respond to criticism profoundly influences how coworkers, bosses, and subordinates think about you. Here's some advice:

■ Think of criticism as an opportunity to learn and improve. Accept it as something useful.

■ Fight the very understandable and normal impulse to respond defensively. Listen.

■ Use body language and make remarks that show that you are listening to—and hearing—the criticism.

■ Don't take a critical remark as gospel. It is a perception. Get beyond the critical remarks. Explore the substance on which they are based.

■ If the criticism is clearly unjust, don't respond in anger, but don't roll over and take it, either. Learn from it. Even if the criticism has little or no merit, you need to find ways to create more positive perceptions.

■ Even if you strongly feel the criticism is unjust, you should avoid responding defensively. Ask for an example. Say your boss criticizes you for making hasty decisions. Politely and sincerely ask for an example. If the criticism has no merit, your boss won't have any examples to cite. With luck, this lack will be as apparent to your boss as it is to you and will, therefore, be an effective argument against the criticism.

Watch Out!
When listening to criticism, try to suppress such body-language signals of resistance as a hand placed over the mouth or on the forehead (as if to shade the eyes). Don't fold your arms across your chest. Maintain eye contact with your critic. Your objective is to appear open and willing to listen.

Bones to pick—anger

Sometimes workplace situations escalate beyond the reach of constructive criticism. In a utopia, there would be no anger or conflict. But even the most congenial of workplaces is no utopia.

What's the best way to handle annoyance and anger? If possible, follow the FIDO formula: Forget It; Drive On. Anger usually passes and annoyances fade. Why give such emotions and incidents potentially destructive permanence?

Off your chest

You can't always ignore anger and annoyance, however. If a situation is making your work life miserable or interfering with your productivity or that of the organization, it's time to act. But remember:

- Keep it low-key. As with constructive criticism, focus on the issues, the actions, and the behavior, rather than on personalities.

- Keep it at a low volume. Speak in a normal conversational tone.

- Express your feelings.

Watch Out!
Workplace anger will usually not escalate into full rage; however, if you ever feel that emotions are getting out of hand—if, for example, a coworker becomes abusive—remove yourself from the situation *immediately*. And if you feel that your safety is physically threatened, get out and talk to a supervisor or, if necessary, security.

This last point merits further discussion. Just telling a person that she is making you angry is not helpful. Don't tell the person how she is making you feel. Instead, focus on the issue for which the person is responsible and *explain* how that issue makes you feel: "Bob, when you took credit for the widget idea I worked so hard to come up with, I really felt hurt."

The object is to create empathy, to make the other person see reality from your perspective. Most of the time, this will elicit an apology, which you should accept gracefully.

It may also be helpful to look toward the future. For example: "I appreciate your apology, Bob, and I understand that you didn't mean to cut me out of the loop. But I don't mind admitting that recognition for what I do is important to me, and I hope that, in the future, you'll be more careful when we work on something together."

All about apologies

Most of us find apologies difficult. Certainly, we don't look forward to having to make them. But let's think about this. It's not so much the apology we dread, but the pain of having made a mistake. Once the mistake has been made, the constructive approach is neither to dwell on it nor to think about the apology for it as a grim necessity. Instead, accept the mistake as a fact—the egg is broken—and embrace the apology as an opportunity. Apologies can go a long way toward building and strengthening workplace relationships.

We have often been told that to err is human; to forgive, divine. When you err, you present others with an opportunity to forgive—in short, to become divine! It's your job to apologize in such a way that others are made aware of this wonderful opportunity.

Effective apologies rest on two ground rules:

1. **They are timely.** Be proactive and take the initiative. When something goes wrong, don't wait to be asked for an explanation. Offer one, together with an apology.

2. **They are helpful.** Don't stop with saying that you're sorry. Offer solutions, remedies, and help.

The ideal apology consists of three parts:

1. **The apology proper**—saying that you are sorry.

2. **Empathy**—an expression of understanding of the other person's feelings.

3. **Remedy**—trying to move the conversation from the *I* and *you* to the *we*.

Here's an example of a productive apology between you and a colleague:

> **You:** I'm very sorry that I was late with the report you needed. I know what an uncomfortable spot that put you in.

Bright Idea
Begin your apology by showing that you clearly understand how you hurt the other person. By doing so, you reduce his need to make you hear his perspective. This will make him more receptive to your apology and the remedy you suggest.

Colleague: I have to tell you, I was pretty ticked off.

You: I bet you were. Let me go to the boss and explain what happened. We just didn't get back the results of the first two tests in time. I should have given you a heads-up. I'll explain.

Colleague: Well, that would be great. Thanks.

You: I'm just sorry I put you on the receiving end of any heat.

Note that the tone of the apology is straightforward and sincere, empathy is introduced immediately, and a remedy is offered. Also note the absence of groveling. Don't tell the other person how to feel, and certainly don't suggest that she should hate you: "What a jerk I am. You must really hate me!"

Making time special

Make it your business to learn something about the special days in the lives of your colleagues, subordinates, and bosses. Consider being the person who keeps track of everyone's birthday and anniversary with the company. At the appropriate time, send an e-mail inviting all to acknowledge Joe Smith's fifth anniversary with the firm, or Jane's birthday.

Birthdays and babies

Many colleagues will bashfully protest a fuss being made over their birthdays, but, make no mistake, they really appreciate it. Just how much of a fuss you make depends on the prevailing atmosphere and culture of your firm, as well the company's size. Disrupting the workday several times a week to celebrate this or that birthday among a large group of employees is neither productive nor practical. But everyone has to eat lunch. Why not arrange a gathering among the birthday person's friends? At the very least, you may want to circulate a card to be signed by everyone in the office.

Just don't be *too* pushy. Always take the person's feelings into account. Not everyone is comfortable being the center of attention on their birthday. If you have a colleague like this, opt for the low-key approach. A group card, for example, may be better than a birthday lunch.

Births among employees' families are much rarer than birthdays, and they are strong reasons to celebrate. Everyone feels good about a new life coming into the world. Consider organizing a collection for the purchase of a modest gift. Just realize that passing the envelope can become annoying and even burdensome if it becomes an office routine. If this becomes a real threat, consider setting up a petty cash "kitty," to which people make a monthly voluntary and anonymous contribution of, say, $5. Use this to pay for cards, gifts, and so on.

Anniversaries and achievements

Celebrating personal milestones humanizes a workplace, and if you are the one who initiates such acknowledgments, your prestige among your coworkers will be enhanced. As important as marking birthdays and births is, it is even more important to come together as a business community to acknowledge employment anniversaries and firm-related achievements. Marking these milestones goes a long way toward building a team feeling in an organization.

The key to making the commemoration of anniversaries and achievements effective is to make them relevant. This is achieved through explanation and specificity. Take time to compose an e-mail congratulating Sarah Jones not for having worked

Watch Out!
Some companies have strict rules restricting or prohibiting solicitation of money among employees for *any* reason. Always respect such rules. Even if your organization doesn't regulate collecting money, go about it sensitively. Present it to fellow employees as an opportunity, not an obligation. Never pressure anyone into giving money.

10 years with the company, but "for having helped us become the number one supplier of widgets in this region over the course of 10 years."

If you feel that you are not in a position to circulate a memo or e-mail acknowledging a company-related achievement, you can still honor the person face to face:

> John, I hear that we're coming up on your 10th anniversary. Congratulations! You know, I've really benefited from your knowledge.

Or:

> Hey, I just heard about your getting the Customer Service Award. Way to go! When you made all those calls to get Mr. Jones's widget repair expedited . . . well, I learned what it means to go the extra mile for a customer. Thanks for the lesson!

Sharing the sadness

Communities have to deal with losses as well as achievements. Many of us just don't know what to say when a coworker experiences a loss such as the death of loved one. We are afraid of intruding on another's grief. It is, however, important to overcome our natural reticence and acknowledge the loss.

If it falls to you to inform others of the loss, a tasteful e-mail or a memo circulated through the office is called for. Include in your message only those details concerning the loss that have been made public or that the family of the deceased has authorized. If you are announcing the death of a colleague, it is appropriate to include a memory or two from life: "We will miss Harry's wise counsel and those truly terrible jokes he was so famous for."

When a bereaved colleague returns to work, it's important to empathize with her loss without smothering her in melancholy sentiment. If possible, add a personal detail that focuses on the life lived rather than on the life lost: "I'm so very sorry about your loss. I met your mother only the one time, but she really struck me as a wonderful person."

Uncommon courtesy, a hallmark of the savvy office politician, is first and last about injecting *your* humanity into the workplace. You can do this in times of happiness and achievement and on occasions of congratulation—and also when criticism and correction or understanding and condolence are called for. Embrace all these occasions as opportunities for developing a workplace community in which you will excel.

Moneysaver
When it comes to gestures of support and condolence, bigger is not better. Rather than expressing your sympathy with an expensive but impersonal gift, choose something creative that fits the recipient's personality. This really is a case in which the *thought* counts.

Just the facts

- Think of the workplace as a community of which you are a member and on which your success depends.

- Build rapport with your colleagues, subordinates, and bosses by using a vocabulary of inclusion and by developing empathy—imaginative sensitivity to the feelings and needs of others.

- How you offer, ask for, and accept help, praise, and criticism communicates how you feel about yourself, your coworkers, and your job.

- Learn all you can about the people with whom you work; use this information to personalize everyday greetings and other casual interactions.

Beyond Yadda Yadda— Effective Communication

PART II

GET THE SCOOP ON...
The spontaneity problem ▪ Strategies for
reducing workday randomness ▪ Determining
your objectives for the workday ▪ Scripting
your workday

Getting Your Message Across

Chapter 4

When Henry Ford, inventor of the Model T, introduced the modern assembly line in 1908, he forever changed the lives of a large segment of American labor. If the assembly line made it possible to turn out one identical flivver after another, it also meant that one day in a worker's life would be pretty much the same as the next.

The assembly line made it possible to turn out mass quantities without having to put much thought into it. The unpredictable nature of the task—people's spontaneity and improvisation—was taken out of the equation. It reduced the risks of mistakes while also reducing the cost of labor, justifying the reduction of Ford's salary levels.

Sounds pretty dreadful. No wonder few of us want to work on an assembly line. In fact, the most sought-after jobs are the *least* routine—the jobs that offer the most variety and require the most spontaneity. These also tend to be the highest-paying jobs.

But if variety and spontaneity are sought after, why do employers feel the need to compensate such jobs at higher levels? The answer is that it isn't easy to handle variety and spontaneity productively. It requires education, training, experience, and skills that are unnecessary in the cut-and-dried world of the assembly line.

Ford's assembly line was designed to reduce the costs and risks of spontaneity. Maybe it wasn't fun, but it did provide security and ensured a certain level of productivity. This chapter suggests ways in which you can inject just a touch of assembly-line routine into your workday, without compromising the creativity you and your employer prize. By making effective communication a habit instead of an accident, you build, each and every work day, the muscles you need for the corporate climb.

First, try talking to yourself

You wake up in the morning, about to face the work-day. Just what is it that you face?

Almost certainly, it's not "The Unknown." You have ongoing projects, certain clients to contact, other clients you expect will contact you, matters to discuss with a colleague or your boss, and so on. At the very least, you have a pretty good idea of the *kinds* of issues, problems, and activities with which you'll be involved that day. Of course, there may be surprises, both welcome and unwelcome, but for the most part your job offers a substantial degree of continuity from one day to the next. You don't have to reinvent yourself every morning.

Once you become aware of the continuity that links one workday to another, you can:

- Plan each day more effectively

Unofficially...
A trained pianist doesn't have to read and decipher each note on the sheet music. She comes to the keyboard with a mind stocked with "recognizable clusters"—a set of allowable and familiar chords and sequences. There is a high degree of continuity from one to the next. In this chapter, we'll be looking at the "identifiable clusters" that will help you communicate in your daily work life.

- Reduce the number of unpleasant surprises in each workday
- Communicate more effectively with your colleagues, subordinates, bosses, and clients
- Appear more creative

This last point presents a bit of a paradox. We tend to associate creativity with spontaneity, an ability to think on our feet. But some kinds of spontaneity can actually be a waste of time, effort, and emotional and mental energy. The more efficiently we can come up with a workable solution to a problem, the more creative we appear. And, almost always, we can more readily come up with solutions to familiar problems—to known problems, ones for which we are prepared—than we can to problems that blindside us.

So here's a theorem that runs counter to the received wisdom of the working world:

In many cases, creativity is inversely proportional to spontaneity and proportional to preparation.

What do you want to say?

Here's another way of looking at your workday: Think of it as a series of equations. Equations consist of known and unknown variables. The fewer unknowns, the easier it is to solve the equation. So it should be your goal to reduce the number of unknown variables in your day.

As you do this, remember that *you* are always one of the variables. You have a choice: You can enter the equation as a known or an unknown. It's much easier if you write yourself in as a known. Make the effort to take frequent stock of yourself, your needs, your goals, your strengths, your weaknesses. Learn what *you* are about.

Bright Idea
The title of a best-selling book by the great trial attorney Louis Nizer, *Thinking on Your Feet*, expressed a prospect that intimidates most people. But in fact, Nizer did everything he could to *avoid* having to think on his feet. By carefully preparing before stepping into the courtroom, he eliminated as many surprises as possible. Follow the lawyer's lead in your work life.

Of course, some people spend their entire lives on an analyst's couch trying to discover "who they are." Fortunately, successfully negotiating your workday does not require so substantial an investment of time and money. It calls for a simple, two-stage preparation.

Before you begin the day, jot down a short list of objectives and issues for that day: things you want to accomplish and issues or problems that you believe you will confront.

Once you've made this list, you're halfway ready to go to work. Your next step is to look at the list, item by item, and ask yourself what your position is relative to each item—how you feel about the item, what kind of outcome you want in dealing with the item, what it means to you, what you need to do in order to deal with it, and what you need from others in order to deal with it.

Here's a sample list of items to address on a certain day:

1. Estimate costs for ABC project.

2. Speak to boss about XYZ idea.

3. Talk to Sam about expediting shipments to customer DEF.

Next, take these one by one and jot down what they mean to you:

1. **Estimate costs for ABC project.** I'll need to talk to Phyllis to get figures. I need for her to make this a priority. If I can get these costs estimated today, I can get to my customer before the competition does. It's important to me to make this sale.

2. **Speak to boss about XYZ idea.** She's resistant. I think this is a good idea, and it would do my career good to take charge of a project like

this—if it works. I *think* this is a good idea, but I'm not sure. I need more information on the demographics of the proposed territory.

3. **Talk to Sam about expediting shipments to customer DEF.** DEF is giving me a hard time about shipping delays. It makes me look bad—makes the company look bad, too. It's important that this issue get resolved. How can I motivate Sam?

Now you have a good idea not only of your objectives for the day, but of what they mean to you and (in a general way) what you have to do to achieve them.

The second objective, talking to your boss about the XYZ idea, looks like it needs to be put on hold, pending your getting more information. So that bumps up in priority the first and third. Although objective number 3 is pressing, number 1 probably needs to get underway first. So, now you have your day's priorities mapped out:

1. Estimate costs for ABC project.

2. Talk to Sam about expediting shipments to customer DEF.

3. Get more information on the demographics of the proposed territory for the XYZ idea before talking to the boss about it.

Create a "script"

In jotting down objectives for the day and establishing how you feel about these objectives and what you have to do to accomplish them, you take a big step toward increasing the day's potential for productivity by reducing its randomness and thereby reducing the amount of spontaneity that may be required from you.

Timesaver
Keep your priority list flexible. As you start to think in more detail about each item you want to achieve in the day, you might become more aware of what things really are the most important. Revise your list as needed to keep your tasks moving ahead as efficiently as possible.

You can now take planning a step further. Think of the advantages you would enjoy if you could walk through your workday the way a Hollywood star walks through a film role. You'd always know just what to do and say. All you would have to do is follow the script.

The problem with real life, of course, is that it doesn't come with a script. But that doesn't mean you can't create one. Focus on the most important and difficult of your day's objectives, and plot out your approach. This might take the form of a few quick notes, or it might be a genuine script, with your lines written out.

To do this, look at what is now your number-one objective for the day. Recall our earlier example: "Estimate costs for ABC project. I'll need to talk to Phyllis to get figures. I need for her to make this a priority. If I can get these costs estimated today, I can get to my customer before the competition does. It's important to me to make this sale."

How will you go about motivating Phyllis? Give some thought to this now, before you approach her. This will help you identify important facts. For example, you might note:

- The most powerful motive is self-interest.

- Phyllis takes pride in doing a good job.

The first is a safe assumption about most people. The second relates directly to Phyllis. Now, write a script that exploits both of these facts about what motivates Phyllis.

> **You:** Phyllis, we have an opportunity to hook up with a major customer. We need to give him the most competitive bid possible, and you're the only one who can get us the

Bright Idea
If you know that you are about to face a particularly demanding or critical encounter—for example, a job interview or a request for a promotion—why not try a little role playing? Ask a friend to play the part of the interviewer or your boss. Then rehearse your approach. Encourage the other person to be difficult, challenging, and resistant.

figures we need to present a lean but realistic bid.

Here, you've written an opening that plays on Phyllis's self-interest (she'll be part of a big deal) and her pride in her job (she's the only one who can furnish what's needed). Notice also the consistent use of the language of inclusion (see Chapter 3): The emphasis is on the pronoun "we." It's "we need," not "I need," and certainly not "you must."

Now that you have a good approach scripted, don't stop preparing. A really effective script anticipates possible resistance. Suppose, for example, that you hear the following response:

> **Phyllis:** I'll get to it just as soon as I can, but I'm pretty busy now.

How do you keep your project on the front burner, in the face of such an obstacle? Try something like the following:

> **You:** Don't I know it! But this is such a high-profile, high-visibility deal that I'm sure you'll want to be part of it. We need to be aggressive. We don't want to let it slip.

Don't *tell* the other person what to do. Instead, arrange reality so that she'll decide for herself to do what you want her to do. Be the great salesperson, the one who keeps the focus on the customer's needs, not his own.

Now you have a script for your day's top-priority objective. Because you have decided to defer your conversation with your boss about the XYZ idea until you get some additional information, you may proceed to the next step down on your day's list of priorities: motivating Sam in Shipping to expedite shipments to customer DEF.

Unofficially...
The People's Almanac Book of Lists tells us that speaking spontaneously before a group is the worst fear of American citizens. Ease your anxiety by preparing as thoroughly as possible.

What makes Sam tick? It's safe to begin with the same assumption as we noted earlier: The most powerful motive is self-interest. What else do you know about Sam? Not much—except that he's touchy and defensive about his turf. He certainly won't respond well if you imply that his department is not doing its best; therefore, don't imply anything. Show him what's been happening. For example:

> **You:** Sam, I've been getting some grumbling from one of our major customers, DEF. You know them, right?
>
> **Sam:** Yes, sure.

Put the burden on DEF, not on yourself. Start to define the problem not as yours, but *ours.* The phrase "one of *our* major customers" and the question "You know them, right?" bring Sam into the picture.

> **You:** Jane Smith at DEF is concerned about shipping time. Now, my first reaction to this is, well, *everybody's* worried about shipping time. But take a look at this. Maybe you can help me figure it out...

You decide that you'll *show* Sam log entries that demonstrate the sizable gap between request date and ship date. Let him draw his own conclusions. Let the decision to improve be *his* decision, *his* idea, not yours.

Power dictionary

Scripting is a powerful tool. Of course, you can't try to script every business conversation you have, and you don't need to; days may go by without the need for a script. But it is important to identify the big moments, the major exchanges, and to prepare for them by:

- Knowing what you feel, want, and need
- Defining a set of objectives
- Sketching a verbal plan by which you can work with others to attain your objectives

Scripting is a very specific tool, a way of preparing to address specific problems or to achieve specific objectives. Your verbal preparedness kit should include some general-purpose equipment as well. Consider the 50 power words listed in Appendix A. These are words that motivate positive action and recruit people to your cause. Study the words and how they invite cooperation and positive responses.

There are also powerless words and phrases, as listed below. Most of the following words need no explanation beyond the fact that they set up one or more of the following adverse conditions:

- They divide instead of unite.
- They set an *I* against a *you*.
- They define a winner and a loser.
- They emphasize limits rather than potential.

Weed these words out of your conversation whenever possible.

Afraid

Bad luck

Blame

Cannot

Cheated

Circumstances

Company policy: This one is surprisingly destructive, because it is frequently used as an excuse for rejecting an idea or proposal out of hand: "We can't do that: Company policy won't allow it." Have a good, independent

Timesaver
By using a vocabulary of proven effectiveness and avoiding powerless words, you can make your case more quickly and efficiently.

reason for what you do. If your reason does involve company policy, explain and justify that policy—don't just invoke it.

Cornered

Crisis

Delay

Delinquent

Demand

Disaster

Don't worry about it: This phrase is usually taken to mean just the opposite of what it says: Start worrying.

Excuse

Fail

Fault

Fear

Final

Forgot

Frustrating: It is often a good thing to share feelings; however, it is usually destructive to confess frustration. This word is often read as a synonym for giving up.

Guess

Hopeless

Impossible

Impractical

Inadequate

Insist

Loser

Loss

Lost

Watch Out!
Be careful of overusing the word "experiment." Used carelessly, this word suggests a lack of control and planning. You may intend it to express an exercise of imagination and innovation; others, however, may see it as an admission that you're simply winging it.

Make do

Must

Nervous

No

Non-negotiable: Avoid coercive language. It does not invite compliance or agreement, but defiance and rejection.

One-time offer: Same comment as for the previous phrase.

Overloaded

Panic

Relax

Rules

Slipped

Sorry

Stupid

Tired

Unaware

Unfair

Unreasonable

Wasted: Words like this imply that the actions of the past are absolute and without remedy—hopeless.

Worry

Openers and closers

You and your coworkers swim in an ocean of words. How can you make what you say stand out and get noticed? Sell the people around you on the notion that what you have to say is valuable—valuable *to them*. Since this is first and foremost a sales job, why not take a leaf from the salesperson's book? Just

We are all sales-men every day of our lives. We are selling our ideas, our plans, our enthusiasms to those with whom we come in con-tact.
—Charles M. Schwab

Bright Idea
Even if you simply want to strike up a conversation with a stranger, you can still address self-interest. Just start off with a leading question aimed at getting the person to talk about herself: "I was intrigued by what you said in the meeting about cost tracking. Can you tell me more about your approach to it?"

about any book on the art of selling offers this acronym, which sounds like the title of a Verdi opera: *AIDA*.

*A*ttention

*I*nterest

*D*esire

*A*ction

AIDA describes the four essential steps in moving a prospect toward a sale. You begin by getting the person's attention, move on to developing his interest, then building desire, and, finally, moving that person to action. This formula applies whether you are selling widgets or mere words.

Your first words

As you've probably guessed by now, the most effective way to command attention is to address the other person's self-interest. There is nothing wrong with saying to someone, "I want to talk to you." But if you really want to command instant attention, say instead, "This will interest you," or "I've got something important for you to know," or "I've got big news for you."

Remember, your first words should serve to begin a transaction, not to conclude one. Don't *deliver* information (for example, don't start talking about yourself). Instead, *solicit* information—get the other person to talk about himself.

Follow-throughs

After you've commanded attention, what do you do next? Follow through by developing the other person's interest. Ask questions and listen. As long as possible, avoid making statements. Statements tend to end an exchange, whereas questions perpetuate conversation. Remember: When you are "selling" an idea to a colleague, subordinate, or boss, ask questions about the other person's needs.

The object of asking questions is to learn how you can shape your proposal or idea to the needs of the other person. Once you begin to connect what you want to do with the other person's needs, ratchet up the conversation to create in the other person a *desire* for what you offer. Finally, propose an action. Tell the person what she needs to do to help you realize your idea or project.

How does all this work? Let's go back to the example objective mentioned earlier in the chapter, about estimating costs for the ABC project. You approach Phyllis:

> **You:** Hey, Phyllis, I've got some important news for you!
>
> **Phyllis:** Really? What is it?
>
> **You:** We have an opportunity to sell a *huge* customer on the ABC project. You'll be playing a big part in this.
>
> **Phyllis:** What do I need to do?
>
> **You:** This is an opportunity for you and your department to shine. We need to move on this project super-fast. The customer has other vendors on the line, but we can bag him if we get a very aggressive bid out to him very quickly. That's where your creativity comes in. We need accurate and thorough cost estimates, and we need them by Wednesday.
>
> **Phyllis:** That's not going to be easy.
>
> **You:** Everyone is well aware of that—which is why we need your magic on this. We all know this bid won't get out without you. You're our

> 66
> Selling is essentially a transference of feeling.
> —Zig Ziglar
> 99

secret weapon. I've got all the specs ready. I'll
e-mail them to you so that you can get into
action on this immediately.

When the pressure is on, we tend to focus on
ourselves—on our own predicaments, problems,
and needs. It is precisely when the pressure is at its
greatest, however, that we need to enlist the attention and collaboration of others; that means shifting
the focus to their self-interest and their needs. This
is the heart and soul of putting yourself across, even
under the most difficult circumstances—which, of
course, is when putting yourself across is most vitally
important.

Just the facts

- The typical workday is not as random and
  unpredictable as you may think; you can plan
  for it and even rehearse for it.

- Get into the habit of beginning each day by
  determining your objectives for the day and
  what you must do to attain them.

- Script and rehearse—in advance—such important conversations as those that promote your
  ideas, your projects, or your career.

- All important business conversations are about
  selling your point of view; learn the vocabulary
  of effective salesmanship.

GET THE SCOOP ON...
Career and business benefits of small talk ▪
Finding out what others need, want, and feel ▪
Avoiding conversation killers ▪ Small-talk
subjects ▪ Conversational body language ▪
Effective listening

Big Results from Small Talk

Chapter 5

"He's all business." How many times have you heard this comment made about a colleague, client, or boss? It's probably meant as a compliment, but it never quite comes across as one. After all, who wants to spend more time than is absolutely necessary with someone who's "all business"? Moreover, such a person sounds unapproachable: He probably wouldn't want to spend any time with you, either.

The fact is, business isn't "all business." Business is also about building the relationships and creating the trust that are the foundation of career-building office politics. That means it's about getting to know people not just as they are described by a job title, but as fully dimensional human beings.

How do you reach this deeper level in the workplace?

When an astronomer wants to see a very faint star, he never looks directly at it. The experienced stargazer knows that the most sensitive area of the human retina is not in the center of the field of vision, but off to the side. To detect a faint light, it's best to look slightly away rather than to focus on the object directly.

The same is true of conversation. Want to learn more about the people you work with? Don't always jump directly into the business at hand. Look to the side. Be indirect. Make small talk.

Make the time

Old-school managers think of small talk as an activity for "clock watchers" and "goldbricks" (old-school terms). Shooting the breeze, they say, is the enemy of productivity—a waste of time.

Of course, small talk sometimes *is* a waste of time. But this can also be true of most business activities. You might, for example, put in hours of research on a project that never gets off the ground. Or you might pursue a sales lead that doesn't result in a sale. In the same way, some small talk is productive and some is not.

This doesn't mean it isn't worth trying, however. Consider some of the possible results of *effective* small talk:

- Team building

- Heightened visibility for you

- Increased workplace leverage, which will enable you to secure support or compliance when you need it

- A generally more harmonious, enjoyable work environment

- Awareness of the needs and attitudes of others

The benefits of the first four items are self-evident. But why should you want to become more aware of the needs and attitudes of others? First, the

Bright Idea
Some salespeople claim that there are two reasons people decline to buy a product: the reason the customer gives for not buying, and the *real* reason, which he does not express. How do you get at these deeper, more compelling reasons? Just ask: "Is there any other reason?" Or: "Is there something else?" Use small talk to gently probe. It is worth investing time and effort to gain knowledge about the needs and wants of those you work with.

more you know about your colleagues, subordinates, and bosses, the more effectively you can communicate with them. Even more important, the people you work with are all your "customers." That is, you are continually selling yourself, your ideas, your projects, your point of view, and your value to those around you. A big part of selling is knowing your customer, identifying his or her needs, desires, and concerns, and then addressing your sales appeal to these issues. How does a sales professional find out about his or her customers? By getting them to talk about themselves. The more you know about the people you work with—your customers— the better your chances for creating "customer satisfaction."

So, instead of regarding small talk as a waste of time and feeling guilty whenever you indulge in it, start looking for more ways to *make time* for it.

Conversation killers

Small talk is conversation. These days, you often hear people complain that the art of conversation is dead. "People used to be able to *talk* to one another," folks lament. "Not anymore!" Probably every generation has lamented the death of the art of conversation. This suggests that the failure of conversation is less a product of the times than an indicator that people throughout the ages have lacked certain skills. Since the lament for lost conversation is so common, let's begin with the negatives, the verbal moves that squash small talk before it begins.

Not listening

The number-one conversation killer is the failure to listen. Typically, this is the result of being preoccupied: Something else is on your mind. It's also

Watch Out!
Don't let your
eyes wander
during a conver-
sation. This
undermines your
ability to focus
on what the
other person is
saying, and it
sends the mes-
sage that
you aren't
interested.

possible that what the other person is saying doesn't interest you. Or you may be self-conscious, so focused on yourself that you just can't concentrate on what someone else is saying.

How can you be sure to listen?

- Choose the right time for small talk. If you are preoccupied—engaged in something really important—don't interrupt yourself to start a conversation; if someone wants to talk to you, reply gently that you'd love to talk, but you're up against a deadline or you're in the middle of a demanding problem. If possible, offer a raincheck for the conversation: "Can I drop by your cube for a chat after lunch?"

- Look at the other person.

- Read "The SOFTEN solution" later in this chapter. It will tell you how to send the right signals of attention. If you send these signals to your partner in conversation, you'll find that your own level of attention increases accordingly.

- Ask questions. You don't have to bombard your partner with queries, but do insert a question if the conversation suddenly flags and you're stuck in an awkward silence. When the other person trails off, just try, "And then what happened?" Or: "What did you do next?" Or: "How did you feel about that?"

Interrupting

Another sure-fire conversation killer is interrupting the speaker. This brings a conversation to an abrupt end, and it generates a good deal of anger and resentment. Interrupting is insulting and hurtful. Conversation is a game of give and take. That is the pleasure of it. Be patient and wait your turn.

Negativity

Negativity of any kind almost always kills conversation, especially casual small talk, which, by its nature, should be light and breezy. Follow these tips to keep your conversation upbeat:

- Don't use small talk as an occasion for criticism. Criticism is something best done in private, never in the guise of friendly conversation. The other person will feel ambushed, angry, and defensive.

- Avoid sarcasm and ridicule. Praise and expressions of admiration are always welcome surprises in casual conversation. Sarcasm and ridicule are not only impolite, they are destructive.

- Avoid gossip. Gossip and rumor mongering are the most common and pernicious forms of negative small talk. For many people, they are also difficult to resist. Unfortunately, the price of gossip is often far greater than killing a conversation. Gossip makes enemies and generally undermines the trust that is so essential to a working community. See Chapter 12 for more on this important subject.

Patronizing

Yet another way to make yourself an unattractive conversation partner is to patronize or talk down to people. Resist the need to demonstrate that you're smarter than the other person. The objective of casual business conversation is not to show off, but to acquire information. You already know what you know. Give the other person a chance to tell you what *she* knows.

Bright Idea
When you start a conversation, stretch your imagination. Imagine yourself talking *with* your conversation partner, not *to* her.

Recipe for great conversation

Now that we've removed the biggest roadblocks to small talk, we can proceed to the positive ingredients of effective conversation.

Prepare to be spontaneous

Small talk is typically spontaneous, on the spur of the moment. In a workplace context, however, small talk is potentially so important that it is best not to leave it entirely to chance. Just as you can rehearse parts of your workday (see Chapter 4), you can prepare for small talk. Doing so isn't difficult. In fact, you probably already do many if not all of the following:

- Keep well-informed of current events. You should try to read the newspaper daily. Read at least one good news magazine each month. Listen to Public Broadcasting Service television and radio, or other media that cover news stories in depth. And when you travel on business, pick up the *local* paper, skimming it for local small-talk material.

- Keep your eyes open. Watch people. Watch what's going on in the community.

- Stay well-informed about developments in your business or profession. This is valuable for your career in a general way, and it will provide you with plenty of interesting material for conversation.

- Keep a journal, diary, or informal scrapbook. Jot down or cut out interesting news, commentary, statistics, and other items you find from time to time.

Remember that the object of this preparation is *not* to enable you to deliver an impromptu·

Watch Out!
Sports is *not* a safe topic for small talk, unless you are certain that your conversation partner is as interested in the subject as you are. Few things kill a conversation more quickly than talking sports to someone who has no interest in the topic.

monologue. Rather, it is to provide material that will spark small talk. Your principal role is to listen and respond, not to make a speech.

Seize the opportunity

Your preparation for it notwithstanding, small talk should have the feel of spontaneity. It fills the odd places and moments in the day. There are many opportunities for small talk. Look for some of the following:

- Encounters in passing: hallways, elevators, commuter trains

- Natural pauses in the day: arrival at the office, departure from the office, the lull before a meeting

- Break periods in conferences

- Office social occasions

- Unofficial social occasions: Create your own events by inviting someone to join you for lunch, fishing, golfing, or playing tennis. Find out what you have in common, then jump on it.

You should also be aware of *non-opportunities:*

- If a colleague seems lost in thought, it's probably best not to bother her.

- Know when to take a hint. If your prospective conversation partner doesn't follow through with a conversation when you open with him, stop. Just say "See you later, Fred," and move on.

- Be sparing with small talk in a busy office. Speak softly. Be considerate of others who are trying to concentrate.

- Know when to end the conversation. And it's best for *you* to end the conversation, rather than wait for the other person or people to do so.

Unofficially...
Architects, office designers, and management gurus tout the open-design, cubicle-divided office space as conducive to informal, creative conversation. True enough, the modern office invites small talk, but it also requires that we modulate it so we don't lose our own privacy or intrude on what little privacy is left to others.

When you're ready, just say "Well, I'd better get back to work," or "Time for me to prepare for my meeting," or "I've got some financial statements that aren't going to do themselves."

Small talk humanizes business, helps you learn about and address the needs and wants of those you work with, and presents you as a caring, decent, likable person. Like all good things, however, small talk can be abused and overused. It should lubricate the business day, not drown it.

Come out with a good opening

Breaking the ice is a lot easier than you may think. Don't try to be clever. Instead, come out with an opening line that clearly signals your desire to talk. If you've done your homework, it might be a remark about a news story or industry-related news. If you are approaching a stranger, it's best to draw on non-controversial material.

The most effective openers incorporate material of likely interest in open-ended questions:

- "Have you tried the new accounting software MIS has distributed?"

- "What do you think of the new accounting software MIS has distributed?"

- "Pete, I've been meaning to ask you: Where are you from?"

- "What's your commute like from that part of Long Island?"

Questions are not the only openers that work well, however. Sometimes self-revelation will start the ball rolling:

- "This is my first annual conference."

- "I just flew in from the Chicago conference. I'm really excited about it."

Bright Idea
A joke can be a very effective ice-breaker—provided that the joke is funny and that you are good at telling jokes. Be sure you have good comedic timing and know the punch line before you start telling the joke. Avoid off-color humor or jokes at the expense of another. Sexual, religious, political, and ethnic humor are all taboo in a business situation.

- "I just started using that new accounting software."

If one opener doesn't break the ice, try another. But be sensitive to signals indicating the person just doesn't want to talk. Informal conversation should never be forced.

Lighten up

Don't confuse small talk with conversation about specific business issues or problems. When you see an opportunity for impromptu conversation with a subordinate, colleague, or boss, decide whether you want to bring up a major business issue or whether you want to exchange a moment or two of small talk. Do *not* try to combine the two.

If you begin with, "So I hear your kid was really something on the soccer field Saturday," then shift gears to the crisis in accounting ("Heads will roll!"), you'll destroy the rapport created by the small talk, and make it difficult to talk about the crisis.

The cardinal rule of small talk is to keep it light. Of course, if your conversation partner uses the occasion to shift to issues of greater weight, whether related to business topics or personal problems, don't bail out of the conversation or try to shift gears. Help out. Go with the flow. If the topic that comes up requires privacy, suggest that you move out of the hall and into your office or his: "John, I want to hear more. Let's step into my office." But you should not be the one who initiates the shift to the heavy stuff.

Some topics are generally "safe" for small talk, and some are not. Safe topics include:

- **The weather.** Safe, but dull—unless the weather is truly remarkable, exceptionally pretty, or exceptionally bad.

Watch Out!
Nobody likes to feel ambushed. If you begin a serious, issue- or crisis-focused conversation with light, small-talk banter, your conversation partner will feel blind-sided, even betrayed, and certainly resentful. Separate small talk from serious talk.

- **Commuting traffic.** Most "gripe" subjects are poor small-talk choices, but *everyone* likes to share commuting war stories. Besides, you or someone else may have helpful advice to share.

- **Current events.** But avoid the controversial ones, such as issues involving political affiliation, liberal versus conservative positions, and so on.

- **Travel.** The danger here is not knowing when to stop. Be careful.

- **The other person's interests or hobbies.** Most people enjoy talking about themselves, especially their special interests.

- **Positive comments** Talk about a place or an event, such as a recent business meeting.

- **Books.** Again, avoid controversy.

- **Arts and entertainment.** This can include (non-controversial) television programming.

Sports can be a good, safe small-talk topic *if and only if* you are interested in a particular sport and you know that the other person is also. Sports topics should not be used as ice-breakers with persons you know little about. Trying to start a sports-related conversation with someone who has no interest in sports can lead to a minor disaster. It makes the other person feel bad, and it may reflect poorly on you, as your would-be conversation partner may think to herself: "Another jock jerk!"

Some topics are too weighty or risky for small talk and should be avoided, such as:

- **Health.** Avoid the innocent-sounding "Hey, how are you?" This could get into topics that are unpleasant or overly personal. In general, avoid talking about your health or the health of others.

Of course, if your conversation partner brings up a personal health issue that concerns him, respond appropriately.

■ **Cost of personal items.** It is gauche and insensitive to ask a person how much he has paid for a piece of jewelry or article of clothing. And it is usually ill-mannered to discuss the cost of items you own, unless you want to steer an associate to an exceptional bargain. If you admire something a colleague has—a watch, perhaps—and you would like to buy one for yourself, just say something like: "That is one great-looking watch. Do you mind if I ask where you bought it?" Then you can go to the store to find out the price for yourself.

■ **Income.** Many firms actually prohibit employees from discussing salaries, under penalty of dismissal. Even if your company has no explicit policy on the subject, salary is never an appropriate topic for casual conversation.

■ **Misfortune or personal problems.** If your purpose is to make small talk, don't bring up your personal problems or invite discussion of those of others. Of course, you should be a sensitive listener if someone comes to you with a problem of a personal nature. And you should certainly express condolences and sympathy for a coworker who has experienced a loss (see Chapter 3). Do avoid water-cooler psychoanalysis, however. Remember, you should not give "professional" advice outside of your area of competence. If you feel that a coworker is in serious trouble, suggest professional counseling or, perhaps, a conversation with a priest or rabbi.

Watch Out!
Don't give health-related or financial advice to coworkers. This includes tax and investment tips. Giving advice beyond your area of expertise is dangerous—to the other person and to you (you might get sued)—and is especially risky if you are giving advice to a subordinate, who might be inclined to take your word as gospel.

Bright Idea
Should you
restrict all work-
place conversa-
tion either to
small talk or to
specific business
topics? Not nec-
essarily.
However, it's
best to limit dis-
cussion of
weightier topics
to your good
friends, and if
the conver-
sation is likely
to become
involved or time-
consuming, you
should wait until
lunch or after
work.

- **Off-color stories.** Locker-room humor, sexual jokes, ethnically-based humor, and the like has no place in the office. It may or may not directly offend the person with whom you are speaking at the moment, but it will certainly get around. At the very least, it will embarrass you and others. It may even cause others emotional pain. At worst, it may result in your losing your job or in legal action against you or your company.

- **Religion.** Religion is a strictly personal matter for you and your coworkers. It should not be discussed in the workplace. Your firm may even have an explicit policy against doing so.

- **Politics.** Political discussions, especially in support of or opposition to particular candidates, have no place in the office. Your company may even prohibit such discussion. And under no circumstances do you want to appear to be soliciting support for a candidate.

- **Highly charged issues.** Steer clear of issues people feel very strongly about, pro or con. Abortion is a prime example.

- **Intimate revelations.** It's good to reveal your human side to your business associates, but don't go too far. Avoid intimate details about your personal life or that of your family. Don't solicit such details from others.

The SOFTEN solution

Even if you prepare for them, small-talk encounters are essentially spur-of-the-moment situations. It's difficult to remember just what you should and should not do. Most people find that acronyms are a handy aid to memory. In their *Complete Business*

Etiquette Handbook (Prentice-Hall, 1995), Barbara Pachter and Marjorie Brody suggest a formula they call SOFTEN. I've borrowed from it and adapted it to the small-talk situation.

Smile

The smile is the single strongest signal you can send to the world that you are open for conversation. The smile is the first facial expression infants learn, and it is probably the first expression they learn to respond to. From very early in our lives, we look for smiling faces. Unfortunately, as we grow into adulthood, smiling often comes to us less naturally. We may even have to work at generating a smile. But it's worth the effort. No business succeeds by closing its doors; no businessperson succeeds by appearing unwelcoming and unreceptive.

Open up

In addition to smiling when you converse, use open body language. Face the other person. Avoid folding your arms across your chest (this indicates resistance). Also avoid putting your hands on your hips, a gesture that tends to convey defiance. Don't be afraid to gesture with your hands, but try to favor open gestures, palms upward.

Forward, lean

In American business and professional culture, maintaining personal space is a major body-language issue. Most people are comfortable with face-to-face distances of about three feet. However, feel free to lean forward from time to time to make a point or to listen more attentively. Don't touch the other person. Don't point. But occasionally leaning forward underscores your interest in what the other person is saying.

Watch Out!
It is not always appropriate to smile. If you are delivering or receiving bad news, a smile is inappropriate. Smile as much as possible, by all means, but be sensitive to what is fitting for different situations.

Unofficially...
Many studies
have shown that
people listen
more intently to
lower-pitched
voices than to
higher-pitched
ones. Further-
more, listeners
tend to attribute
greater authority
to lower-pitched
voices. This is
true whether the
voice is male or
female. So it
pays to exercise
the lower regis-
ter of your voice.
Practice your
deeper tones.

Tone it down

Speak distinctly. Don't mumble. Don't trail off. Don't speak while looking downward or looking away. However, keep the tone and volume of the conversation conversational. Don't shout. Avoid speaking in a high pitch; indeed, you might practice consciously lowering your voice.

Eye contact now

Always make eye contact with your conversation partner. This not only communicates your interest, it powerfully conveys your trust and your trustworthiness. On the other hand, if you fail to make eye contact, if you deliberately look away, or if your eyes habitually wander, you suggest two things:

- You are bored with the other person.

- You are hiding something. You are dishonest— "shifty-eyed."

While eye contact is vitally important, don't try to stare down your conversation partner. Don't do anything to intimidate the other person or make him or her feel uncomfortable.

Nod—and nod some more

You don't have to inject frequent comments into a conversation just to prove that you're listening. The first five elements of the SOFTEN formula will go far to communicate your interest and attention. In addition, nod periodically. This is a powerful body-language signal that communicates understanding and acceptance of what is being said. Furthermore, it tells the other person that he should continue talking.

Talking with your ears

The most important organs of speech you possess are your ears. If you listen to what others are telling you, you will know what to say to them. You will be able to shape your messages to their needs. You will satisfy all of your "customers"—whether internal (colleagues, subordinates, and bosses) or external (actual clients).

The problem is that we hear far more than we take in or "attend to." Our bodies and minds are wonderfully equipped to aid our survival. Our senses are bombarded by stimuli, always receiving the sights, sounds, and smells around us. If we stopped to "attend to" each of these bits of information, our conscious minds would be quickly overloaded, and, at the very least, we would be unable to concentrate on useful work. Fortunately, our subconscious mind reviews and rejects most of the stimuli without bringing it to our attention. Only when something seems important—your baby cries, or someone calls your name—is the signal sent into consciousness so that we can act on it.

Selective attention is a valuable gift of biological evolution, but it also means that, day to day, a great deal tends to get past us. How many times have you been in a meeting and suddenly realized that you've "zoned out"—haven't really heard a thing that's been said for the past 5, 10, 15 minutes?

In conversation, it's important to recognize the roadblocks to effective listening and overcome them. The most common listening problem is a wandering mind. For this, there is only one remedy—forcing yourself to concentrate. Doing so takes self-discipline.

Conversation killers

Here are some roadblocks to good concentration. You will have to work on overcoming them if you want to become an effective listener.

Bright Idea
Conversation is give and take, so even if you're anxious to add your own thoughts to the discussion, be patient: You'll get your turn.

- **Allowing yourself to be distracted by eavesdropping on neighboring conversations.** It's just not possible to follow two conversations at once. Stick to your own.

- **Allowing your eyes to wander.** This not only distracts you, it is very impolite. Maintain eye contact with your conversation partner.

- **Interrupting.** This is a sure conversation killer, and it generates a lot of resentment in the other person.

- **Overly critical listening.** Some people listen to others chiefly to find fault with what they say. Such people soon find themselves without anyone to talk to. Instead of waiting to pounce on errors, practice *admirative listening*. Speak to others with the intention of admiring what they tell you. It will make you more receptive.

Conversation builders

As you learn to overcome the worst conversation killers, you can also begin to practice conversation builders. Here are four important ways to enhance conversation:

1. Use the SOFTEN approach just discussed.

2. Reflect what the speaker says. Paraphrase the speaker's statements to let her know that you are listening. This not only reassures the speaker, it helps keep you truly focused. Consider the following example:

   Speaker: I told him that the best computer for him was a desktop, not a laptop, because he never traveled and really did a lot of typing. He needed a full-size keyboard and a decent-sized monitor.

Listener: The desktop was the way to go for him, then?

Speaker: Exactly. Now, if he were more mobile...

3. Ask questions. As long as you keep them relevant, questions will help propel a conversation.

4. Respond in ways that stick to the subject. Don't take the conversation in odd tangents. Your remarks should be relevant to the speaker's own.

Taking talk to the next level

Over the course of time, small talk—apparently light and inconsequential conversation—builds relationships and creates a pleasant, trusting atmosphere in the workplace. This itself is ample reason for small talk. However, some conversations that start off as small talk assume greater consequence:

- You may find that you really hit it off with someone.

- A topic of great importance may be raised.

- An intriguing idea may be born.

- An important issue or problem may be brought to light.

Don't let opportunity die. If you have time to expand a small-talk conversation on the spot, do so, suggesting, perhaps, that you move to your office to continue the talk. If the time is not right at the moment—you or the other person have something else to do—set up a lunch or some other meeting to continue: "Mary, this is an important issue that's been on my mind, too. I have to get to my two o'clock appointment right now, but can we con-

Watch Out!
Never correct people's grammar, word usage, and pronunciation, unless asked to do so. Your conversation partner may say "thank you" for pointing out that "irregardless" isn't a legitimate part of the English language, but secretly he will resent that you corrected him, especially if you do it within earshot of others.

tinue this conversation? Would four o'clock in my office work for you?"

Don't try to force every small-talk encounter into something more than it is. But be aware that a great deal of an organization's most important business gets done not in formal meetings or conferences but in casual hallway encounters. Prepare for them, and be prepared to take them to the next level.

Just the facts

- Done right, small talk is not a waste of "business time," but a valuable aid to business.

- The chief benefits of small talk include building a friendly, efficient, trusting team feeling in the workplace, and helping you learn about the needs, wants, and feelings of those you work with.

- Small talk is so valuable that you should take time to prepare for it, stocking yourself with good openers and effective conversation topics.

- The most powerful conversational tool you own is your ability to listen attentively and sensitively.

GET THE SCOOP ON...
Setting objectives and building an agenda ▪
Choosing meetings and selecting participants ▪
Using meetings to generate ideas ▪ Leading a
meeting ▪ Coping with disruptive people
▪ Arriving at a meaningful conclusion

Meaningful Meetings— Not an Oxymoron

Chapter 6

I f you ever want to see a group of eyes roll in unison, just walk into a room full of business people and ask them to tell you about the last meeting they attended. And after you get tired of seeing the eyes roll, just say two words, "productive meeting," and you will get a new reaction—laughter.

Not only do all too many business meetings waste time and effort, but people go into them actually *expecting* to waste time and effort. The business meeting is a prime example of the principle of the self-fulfilling prophecy.

The savvy office politician cannot be satisfied with the typical business meeting. She has to learn how to be a useful participant in meetings. What's more, she needs to learn how to take a leadership role, making meetings useful, productive, and meaningful. Meetings provide career-building opportunities to acquire power in the form of information and connections, to delegate power, and to

❝

Try skipping a
meeting if you
want to find out
how important
it is.
—Robert
Townshend,
*Further Up the
Organization*
(1984)

❞

demonstrate power—especially if you have a say in
who is invited to attend and in setting the agenda.

Why good meetings go bad

There should be an ancient Arabic proverb addressing the failure of the typical American business
meeting. Something like this: "It is easier to count
the grains of sand in the desert than to number the
reasons behind a bad meeting." The factors contributing to the failed meeting seem to be innumer-
able. But certain causes are especially common and
serious.

Meetings can be dull and unproductive for two
main reasons: the way participants approach them
and the way they are *dis*organized by their leaders.
Let's take a closer look at each.

Individual problems

There are six main problems related to individual
attitude and approach:

- **The self-fulfilling prophecy.** In many organizations, people enter a meeting already expecting
  to have a miserable experience. The result is a
  miserable experience.

- **Knowing all and telling all.** Some people walk
  into meetings confident that they already know
  everything and determined to "share" with the
  meeting's participants everything they know.
  Being subjected to one person's stream of consciousness can induce unconsciousness in others.

- **Whining.** Some people believe meetings are
  essentially gripe sessions. This creates an
  oppressively negative tone for the meeting.

- **Daydreaming.** Many meeting attendees are
  unwilling to devote any attention to the issues

on the table. They quickly grow bored, give up, and zone out. Call them *empty suits.*

- **Being fearful.** A certain number of those present in the meeting will say nothing because they are afraid to speak. Some fear getting shot down, while others are uncomfortable speaking in public. The worst aspect of being fearful in a meeting is that when a person is concentrating on his fear, he cannot pay attention to what's going on around him.

- **The disenfranchised.** Many junior-level employees don't feel entitled to participate in meetings, even though they are required to attend. The causes of this attitude range from their own subjective feelings and insecurities to the interpretation of mixed messages from their seniors. The results of this attitude range from simple inattention to hostile resentment.

Organizational problems

As if individual attitude and approach problems weren't enough to torpedo the typical corporate meeting, there are also the more collective problems of poor organization:

- **Purposelessness.** Few meetings have specific, stated objectives. As a result, participants are often confused about why they are there, when the conversation is going well or not, and what marks a successful conclusion.

- **Winging it.** Few business meetings have an agenda, a document outlining the plan for achieving the objectives.

- **The gang's all here.** In many organizations, attendance at meetings is indiscriminately mandatory. The result is that each meeting

Watch Out!
If you are in charge of a meeting, avoid the trap of inviting too many people. Many of the effective tools we'll discuss in this chapter simply can't work when groups are unnecessarily large.

Timesaver
Before you call a meeting, ask yourself whether the purpose of the meeting could be accomplished by a simple conversation, a telephone call, an e-mail, or a memo. As a rule of thumb, whenever possible, use these simpler, less time-consuming procedures in preference to a meeting.

includes people who could be doing something else somewhere else, and doing it more productively.

- **Oh, I'll just stand.** In many meetings, no forethought is given to personal comfort issues such as adequate seating and a supply of fresh air. As a result, people may feel ill at ease and restless and pay less attention to what's being discussed.

- **Anything goes.** Many business meetings have no ground rules relating to behavior. To be sure, these don't have to be spelled out; however, it must be clear that profanity, intimidation, shouting, and the like are not acceptable. If participants don't feel confident of courteous, professional treatment, they are less likely to participate productively.

- **The ambush.** From time to time, emergencies and opportunities will arise that call for an impromptu, short-notice, no-notice, or last-minute meeting. Such meetings should not be routine, however. When meetings are not planned in advance, participants have no time to prepare, and they may also enter the meeting with a heightened feeling of dread, rather than expecting anything positive to result.

- **The secret club.** Most meetings don't have to be top secret. When nonparticipants are kept in the dark, as happens too often, they assume they are being purposely left out of the loop. The result is resentment and damage to group cohesiveness, damage to the sense of communal enterprise, and loss of team spirit.

What's the use?

Considering all that's wrong with them, why continue having meetings? Although it is true that, in most organizations, the number of meetings can probably be reduced, it is also important for various groups and task-oriented teams to get together to exchange information, make plans, and discuss problems. Just as it makes no sense to hold meetings only for the sake of holding meetings, it also makes no sense to eliminate or reduce meetings arbitrarily. There are three main steps involved in holding successful meetings:

1. Determine which meetings are absolutely necessary.

2. Determine which meetings are absolutely necessary for *you* to attend.

3. Take steps to make those meetings as productive as possible.

The importance of the agenda

All meetings should have a defined and stated objective or a *manageable* set of objectives. Once these objectives are defined, an agenda can be drawn up; this is simply a list of topics or issues that must be addressed to attain the objectives.

If you are responsible for the meeting, you have the authority and the responsibility for defining the objectives and setting the agenda. Even if the meeting has been called by someone else, however, you can take steps to elicit a statement of objectives and an agenda. Find the person who is calling the meeting, and ask:

■ "What issues are we addressing in this meeting?"

■ "Can I get a copy of the agenda? I need to plan my time, and I want to make sure that I'm fully prepared."

■ "What do I need to do to prepare for the meeting?"

Watch Out!
Just as calling meaningless meetings can become a destructive habit, so can habitually dodging meetings. Before you excuse yourself from attending, be absolutely certain that your presence is unnecessary. Don't cut yourself out of the loop, and don't make yourself look like an unwilling member of the team.

■ "What would you like from me at this meeting?"

Note the tone of these questions. Although you are largely acting out of self-interest—you don't want to waste your time at an unproductive meeting—you're asking the leader how you can contribute more effectively. This approach makes it more likely that he'll give you useful answers. If you cannot get answers to these questions, consider counting yourself out of the meeting: "Frank, I have other commitments at that time. Are you sure you need me to attend?"

There are many objectives for calling a meeting, but they fall into four major categories:

1. Presentation or informational

2. Idea generating and problem identification

3. Problem solving

4. Motivation

If you cannot classify a meeting into one of these categories, it is almost certain that the meeting will serve no worthwhile purpose.

Once the objectives have been identified, plan the agenda:

1. List the topics you need to cover.

2. Poll participants for topics. Be certain to ask them how much time they need to present their topics.

3. Assign at least approximate lengths of time to each topic.

4. Based on the time allotted to each topic, set a time limit for the meeting. Open-ended meetings produce anxiety; participants feel like they'll never end. Open-ended meetings also make it difficult to plan the rest of the workday.

Bright Idea
Any single meeting should address a manageable number of objectives. If you find that you have a jumble of objectives, more than one meeting should be planned. Ideally, any one meeting should have a single purpose; however, up to three main objectives are usually still manageable.

In planning agenda timing, consider the following:

- **If the meeting is primarily informational,** consisting largely of a presentation, allot 75 percent of the time to the presentation. The remaining 25 percent should be set aside for questions.

- **If the meeting includes a presentation,** but is open to general discussion, limit the presentation to no more than 50 percent of the time scheduled.

- **If the meeting will go beyond 90 minutes,** schedule a break of at least five minutes about half-way through. Make sure that the break is part of the agenda. Don't skip the break to save time.

Roll call

As important as deciding what will be covered in a meeting is determining who should be there. If you clearly state the objectives of the meeting, it should be relatively easy to decide who to invite (if you are the leader), or whether you should attend (if you are a participant). Remember: The more people, the more complex the meeting; the more complex the meeting, the longer the meeting.

Size counts

If you are calling the meeting, you may be tempted to assume "the more the merrier." After all, the more people who come to your meeting, the more important you must be! Just remember, though, that the more people who come to your meeting, the greater the cost in time and person hours, and the more complex (and longer) the meeting will be.

Among other factors, the size of your meeting depends on the size of your organization,

Bright Idea
If you are trying to get input from a number of different people, choose an informational meeting. You can productively invite more people to such meetings without risking an excessively long or chaotic session. In contrast, problem-defining or problem-solving meetings are typically most effective when attended by a small, carefully selected number of participants.

department, work group, or team; so there are no hard-and-fast rules. However, here are some rules of thumb for how many participants to include:

- **Presentation or informational:** Fewer than 30 people is best.

- **Problem identification or review and evaluation:** Fewer than 10 is best.

- **Problem solving:** Fewer than 5 is best.

- **Motivation:** The more the merrier!

Invitation etiquette

Invitations to formal meetings should be made at least a week in advance. The written invitation—it may also be e-mailed—should include:

- Time, place, and duration of the meeting.

- Purpose of the meeting, including a short list of objectives.

- The agenda. If possible and appropriate, invite the attendee to comment on or add to the agenda.

- A personalized statement of why it is important for the invitee to attend: "Katherine, we really need your input, especially on the troubleshooting issues."

- The name of the person to contact with pre-meeting questions.

Less formal meetings—and even spur-of-the-moment meetings—should also be preceded by invitations, although these will probably be verbal with, perhaps, an e-mailed confirmation. Try to convey to the invitee most of the information just mentioned. Emphasize why it's important for the person to make time to attend.

In the case of formal meetings, there may be some people you want to alert to the meeting, but who you feel do not necessarily have to attend. The courteous thing to do in this situation is to distribute an agenda to them with a note like the following: "Bob, you don't have to attend this meeting, but I thought you'd like to see what we'll be discussing. I'll send you a follow-up memo after the meeting."

Certain people in every office think the stars and planets revolve around them, and they resent any meeting that isn't scheduled to meet their needs. Obviously, you must be prepared for scheduling flexibility if you must have a certain person in your meeting. But if the person's presence is not crucial, and you've scheduled a meeting convenient for the majority—and doing so leaves someone out—just be as diplomatic as possible. A note like the following is effective: "John, I'm sorry you'll be out of town, but it's important that we get this meeting done as soon as possible. I'll make sure you get a full follow-up report when you return."

Bright Idea
One of the problems with impromptu meetings is that important people may be left out. To avoid this, ask each invitee to think of anyone else who should be asked to join in. Also, be sure to send reminder e-mails or notes. People like to feel that they would be missed if they were absent.

Making space for flexibility

Agendas are important in all meetings, including those intended to identify or solve problems or to generate ideas. However, don't let overly strict adherence to an agenda kill the meeting's spontaneity. After all, whenever two or more people come together, there's a chance that *new* ideas and *fresh* insights will be produced. On the other hand, don't leave spontaneity to chance—prepare for it. Here are three good approaches.

Problem polling

In problem polling, bring the participants into a room with a blackboard or the equivalent. Ask those present to call out the problems and issues of greatest concern to them. Have someone write them on the board, but don't discuss the problems or issues, and don't analyze them. Do nothing to interrupt the flow of issues until the flow stops; however, realize that some people can talk a topic into the ground. Be aware of how much time has passed, and, if necessary, gently suggest moving on to the next topic.

When the flow does stop, look at the blackboard and go through one point after the other, restating each concern in *positive* terms. For example, "I'm worried about quality control" becomes "Our objective is to improve quality control." Then the meeting can elaborate on this positive point: "Our objective is to improve quality control in order to reduce returns by 15 percent." By clearly formulating the objective in this way, the discussion can proceed in a highly focused manner, even though it began with great spontaneity.

66

Getting ideas is like shaving: If you don't do it every day, you're a bum.
—Alex Kroll, quoted by Roger Von Oech, *A Kick in the Seat of the Pants* (1986)

99

Brainstorming

This time-tested method for generating ideas works best in small peer groups, usually of five or fewer participants. Define an issue, then ask for ideas. Your objective is quantity of ideas rather than quality. Don't discuss the ideas generated, and don't allow any judgment, criticism, or expressions of praise.

Have someone write each of the ideas on a blackboard. After the flow of ideas tapers off, begin to analyze them, focusing on how to establish criteria for judging the value of each one. In this way, you should be able to winnow a mass of ideas down to a few viable ones.

Break it up!

For the purpose of generating ideas, larger meetings may be broken up into small discussion groups of, say, four participants each. Each of these groups is assigned a particular problem or issue to discuss. Each group should have a leader, whose job is to keep the talk focused on the assigned issue. Another participant should record the results of the discussion.

After a period of time, reconvene the smaller groups into a larger group, and ask the recorders to share the results of the individual discussions.

Stoking the furnace

If you are leading a meeting, make the most of the opportunity. This does not mean that you should seize the moment for self-aggrandizement. Rather, make certain that you lead the meeting to maximum productivity. Don't direct the focus to yourself, but keep it on the issues.

Be clear

One of the most important things a leader can do is to be certain that the participants are aware of and agreed on the objectives of the meeting. To ensure this, always state—or restate—objectives at the outset, then briefly explain why each objective is important.

If necessary, in the course of the meeting, stop discussions that drift from the objectives. Also remind participants of the objectives whenever necessary.

Manage time

Start the meeting on time. Be proactive. Remind participants of the starting time (and location) the day before the meeting.

If key people are not present, you will have to delay the start of the meeting. If they are still not

Timesaver
List the objectives on a flip chart or blackboard. This not only serves as a reminder throughout the meeting, but it will help latecomers get up to speed without the necessity of verbal review.

Bright Idea
If you know that a certain participant is habitually late, put his presentation high up on the agenda. This may compel the person to show up on time.

present after five minutes, however, you might have to proceed without them.

Keep an eye on the time as the meeting progresses. If you are following a timed agenda, enforce the time limits:

- In presentation-type meetings, enforcement of time limits should be strict.

- In idea-generation, problem-identification, and problem-solving meetings, the leader should be more flexible in enforcing time limits. If the meeting is moving along productively, hesitate before you interrupt the flow of ideas.

- Enforce economical use of time by discouraging irrelevant interruptions or discussion of tangential issues. "John, I think that's a subject for another meeting. We have two more major agenda items to get through before lunch."

- Try this technique to keep a meeting moving without getting held up on a tangential point: Put the tangential item up on the board in an area labelled "the parking lot." The participants agree to "park" that issue and address it later. In this way, the person who raised the issue is not immediately shot down, his problem is still up on the board for all to see, and the meeting leader can address the "parked" issue at the end of the meeting, after all the more immediately relevant points have been addressed.

Reflect and facilitate

The leader should both *reflect* and *facilitate* the discussion. *Reflection* consists of an ongoing summary and paraphrasing of major points: "So, it is clear that XYZ, and not ABC, is the big obstacle to quality control." *Facilitation* helps the group make logical, productive transitions from one point to the next. For example, after reflecting that "XYZ, and not ABC, is the big obstacle to quality control," the leader might continue: "Let's focus on XYZ. How can we attack this set of problems more effectively?"

Facilitation and reflection also serve to "bring out" hesitant participants or those who don't make themselves quite clear. For example, you might say: "That's an intriguing idea, Bill. Are you saying that . . ." Your restatement will not only help clarify matters for others; it might actually help the participant see more clearly in his own head what he is trying to say. If, on the other hand, he feels that you haven't heard him correctly, he will at least understand better how he's being heard, and this will help him state his position more clearly.

Keep an eye on the body language of participants. If someone looks like she has something to say, but remains silent, offer encouragement: "Sarah, you look like you've got something to say."

On power

Meetings are opportunities to demonstrate power. But what is said of comic-book villains applies as well to participants of meetings: "If only he used his power for good instead of evil!"

Many people bluster and bluff in meetings, throwing their weight around in an intimidating, bullying manner. That is using power for evil. Using it for good not only enhances a person's prestige and position within the organization, but does so by benefiting the entire organization.

Power seats

The first manifestation of power is blatantly territorial. If you can, occupy one of the power seats in the meeting room:

Watch Out! Don't try to shame non-participants into speaking up ("Come on, don't be bashful!"). This might lead them to feel even more resistant to participating. Instead, encourage and invite them.

- If you are the leader, try to sit farthest from the door. If you are seated at a conference table, sit at the head of the table.

- If you are a meeting participant, you should still try to sit as far from the door as possible. At a table, try to avoid sitting immediately next to the leader. Most authorities believe these are inherently weak positions (though some favor a position to the leader's left).

- When you sit, remember what your mother told you: Sit up straight. Do, however, lean forward slightly from time to time to show interest.

Power plays

Whether you are a leader or a participant, your greatest source of genuine *and* perceived power ultimately comes from two sources: how effectively you listen and respond to the ideas of others, and how effectively you champion your own ideas.

In responding to what others say, try to focus on how the ideas presented are relevant to the issues at hand. Show that you are listening both sympathetically and critically. Whether you are a leader or a participant, *reflect* what others say:

> What John is suggesting—that we increase communication between Sales and Customer Service—should help Sales address customer needs more fully. After all, Customer Service is down there in the trenches, in the front lines. They get a lot of valuable customer-generated information. I think we should come up with some ways to strengthen the links between Customer Service and Sales. Of course, this will require some extra work, and we'll have to decide just how much of that we can afford to invest.

The person who defines and redefines the ongoing issues in a meeting is seen as the power that drives the meeting.

When it comes to presenting and promoting ideas in a meeting, whether they originate with you or with someone else, the key is to become a *champion*—the person who wholeheartedly sponsors and supports the idea, who makes it happen.

To garner support for an idea, you must get the participants in the meeting to invest in it, to claim their own stake in it. This requires freely sharing rather than jealously guarding the idea. Use meetings to recruit "investors" in it.

Power ploys

Creative listening and active championing are genuine and valid power plays in any meeting. However, you will also almost certainly encounter the bogus bluster of certain power ploys:

- **Dominators** are not content unless they can dominate the meeting. As a leader or a participant, you should avoid confronting such people directly. Instead, respond to the dominator by giving him credit for whatever is contributed to the discussion. Then take the ball out of the dominator's court by asking others for their reactions to whatever was stated. Try to move the discussion away from its source and to the reactions.

- **Commentators** try to assert their power through side conversations, often in a derisive, sarcastic, or know-it-all tone. If you are the leader, intervene. Look directly at the people who are holding the side conversation. Don't scold. Instead, ask them if they have any questions. If necessary, restate the particular meeting objective

> 66
> The very essence of all power lies in getting the other person to participate.
> —Harry Overstreet, quoted by Zig Ziglar, *Secrets of Closing the Sale* (1984)
> 99

Bright Idea
Even if you are
not the leader,
you should feel
free to defuse
the "commenta-
tors" if the
leader fails to
intervene. Just
remember to do
so in a produc-
tive way, without
attacking the
individuals.

under discussion and emphasize the need to stay in focus. "Bob and Joan, you seem to have some questions. Do you?"

- **Naysayers** make it their business to shoot down ideas. A good way to stop knee-jerk naysaying is to ask the person for an explanation of her objections and, perhaps, for an alternative. This should not be phrased in a provocative way, but as a genuine request: "Sally, I'm not sure I understand your objection to the plan. Can you break it down for me?" Or: "I agree that we can't be sure this idea will work. Do you have an alternative idea you'd like to discuss?"

- **Scoffers** tear down ideas by ridiculing them or, more commonly, by attacking the originator of the idea. The attack is often thinly veiled as "good-natured" humor: "Oh, Pete, you're the perpetual optimist!" Don't let the attack stand, but don't attack back. Instead, bring the discussion back to the issues and away from personalities: "Ed, just what in this plan won't work, as you see it?" Note that the speaker does not respond to the crack about his perpetual optimism. Instead, he focuses exclusively on the issues.

Dominators, commentators, naysayers, and scoffers practice negative meeting manners. Like most negatives, however, these nasty habits have their positive counterparts: good "meeting manners."

Meeting manners

Among the most effective ways of promoting productive and time-efficient meetings is to practice good meeting manners. Most of the following is common sense.

For the leader

The leader should do her job by defining meeting objectives and keeping the meeting focused on them. In addition:

- Begin and end the meeting on time.

- If necessary, introduce yourself and meeting participants or any guests.

- Reflect and facilitate.

- Draw out the hesitant; make it easier for them to participate.

- Go out of your way to include newer and younger participants.

- Stick to the agenda.

- In longer meetings, be sure to schedule breaks.

For the others

As a participant you should, above all, *be present.* This means that you should listen actively, ask questions, and work to develop good ideas, taking them as far as possible. In addition:

- Arrive at the meeting on time.

- Do your best to observe time allotments when presenting material.

- Make certain everyone at the meeting knows who you are. Introduce yourself, if necessary.

- Study the agenda and prepare for the meeting.

- Stay wide awake. ·

- Avoid sarcasm, naysaying, and other power ploys.

- Participate creatively.

- Stick to the agenda; avoid side issues.

- Avoid engaging in side conversations, or writing and passing notes.

66

A new idea is delicate. It can be killed by a sneer or a yawn; it can be stabbed to death by a quip and worried to death by a frown on the right man's brow.
—Charles Brower, in *Advertising Age* (August 10, 1959)

99

Watch Out!
Don't fidget in your seat. At a conference table, be sure to keep your hands visible at all times (this communicates openness and honesty). Be careful not to appear to be reading someone else's papers.

Conflict—it's not all bad

The purpose of a business meeting is not to have a pleasant social time, but to achieve a set of goals that will contribute to greater productivity, solve problems, increase profits, and so on. While conflict tends to spoil a social occasion, it is not incompatible with an effective business meeting. After all, people have different points of view and differing needs.

So, as a leader or participant in the meeting, it is not your goal to eliminate conflict. It *is* a goal of the meeting to create a climate and a forum in which people can disagree without becoming disagreeable. Here are three helpful guidelines to keep in mind:

- Keep disputes focused on issues, never on personalities.

- Try to see issues from others' point of view. Reject the notion that you must cling to your idea no matter what.

- Observe the principle that the sum is greater than its parts. That is, from two differing points of view, try to fashion a third point of view that is better than either of the original two. Use conflict as a creative force.

The call to action

Of all the complaints people have concerning meetings, the most persistent—and, often, most justified—is that they lead to nothing, that they are all talk and no action. Every meeting should conclude with a clear call to action. The call to action ensures that everyone is agreed on a conclusion to the meeting, and that the meeting results in *some* productive step.

A call to action may be a set of specific actions: "So, we've decided that we will implement A, B, and C." Or it may be a decision that another meeting is necessary: "We've defined A and B, but we still need to investigate C further. Let's meet on this subject next Wednesday."

It is unrealistic to expect that each meeting will solve all of an organization's problems, but it is important to insist that each meeting end with closure—not an ultimate answer, perhaps, but a decision on what will be done next. At the end of the meeting, the leader should review and restate all action items. She should make certain that everyone is agreed on them: "Is there anything I've left out?"

Each action item should be specific and should be assigned to someone at the meeting. Participants should walk out the door with assignments in hand. If possible, deadlines (or, at least, interim checkpoints) should be set for each action item.

The leader should end the meeting by summarizing:

1. Which objectives were achieved

2. Which action items were decided upon

3. Who is responsible for each action item

"It ain't over 'til it's over," Yogi Berra once famously pronounced. Well, even when the meeting is over, it ain't over. Leaders should follow up on the results of the meeting, particularly on the action items. Participants who are responsible for action items must be sure to carry out their assignments.

Having genuinely productive meetings requires considerable and vigilant effort, but it's far more satisfying and far less exhausting than experiencing,

Bright Idea
If you're the meeting leader, always thank all participants before the meeting ends. This concludes the meeting on a positive note and reinforces the idea that the participants have spent their time productively.

meeting after meeting, the frustration of business encounters that consume much time but generate nothing except dissatisfaction. Meetings can and should be opportunities for building your business and building your career. They provide a showcase for the best that is in you.

Just the facts

- Most meetings are unproductive because they are undefined, lacking clearly stated objectives and a firm agenda.

- When the objectives and agenda of a meeting are clearly stated, it becomes relatively easy to decide who should attend—and to decide whether you should attend.

- Use such techniques as problem polling and brainstorming to generate ideas from meetings.

- To achieve genuine power in a meeting, champion worthwhile ideas by persuading the other participants to "invest" in them.

- All meetings should end with a call to some definite action, even if that action specifies nothing more than what to do next.

Busy Signals

E-mail, the Internet, videoconferencing—all these high-tech modes of communication make the plain-vanilla telephone seem pretty old-fashioned. But in fact, no business tool, not even the computer, is more used and more necessary than the telephone.

It is also true that no business tool is more hated. For every vital and positive purpose the phone serves, it presents the possibility of a pitfall. While the telephone is the basic means of making contact with customers, clients, and colleagues, it can also be the means of putting them off, holding them at arm's length, and even alienating them. Used well, the phone makes it easier for you to give the people you work with the prompt and personal attention that ultimately gets *you* what *you* want. Used poorly or with little thought, the telephone is just a way of treating others like so many numbers.

This chapter tells you how to make the best career-building use of a basic business tool.

Chapter 7

Timesaver
Whenever you make a phone call, jot down the callee's name and keep it in front of you. Try to figure out the pronunciation before you make the call. If it's a difficult name, take a stab at it anyway—but ask for help. "Hello, Mr. Kosciuszko. Am I pronouncing your name correctly?"

Before you pick up that phone...

A successful phone call begins before you pick up the receiver. If you are the one making the call, plan what you are going to say. Begin by deciding on the objective(s) of the call. What do you want to accomplish?

If the call is especially important or involves even slightly complex issues, jot down a few notes before you dial:

- Purpose—objective(s)—of the call
- Points you want to make or questions you want answered
- Questions, issues, or problems the other person is likely to raise
- Responses to these questions, issues, or problems

If you're answering a call, be sure to have a pen and paper handy. Quickly jot down the caller's name as soon as she gives it; then, unless you can instantly answer the caller's simple question, take notes on whatever issues are raised. It's also a good idea to jot down useful issues the caller may not raise in the course of the conversation, but that occur to you. For example, a caller is interested in buying a widget with features A, B, and D. While you respond with this information, you jot down "feature C." After giving the caller the information she has asked for, you add: "Have you also looked at the benefits of feature C?"

Any business call, whether with a client, customer, colleague, subordinate, or boss, is an opportunity. A little preparation will help you to make the most of the opportunity.

PTA: what it is and why you want it

Before you pick up the phone, make sure that you are equipped with PTA. That's *positive telephone attitude.* It consists of three components:

1. A desire to communicate

2. A desire to be helpful

3. A belief that phone calls from those you work with do not interrupt your business, but are the *purpose* of your business

By cultivating these three qualities, you enable yourself to make every phone call a positive, career-building experience.

Famous first words

Okay, it's not always practical or even possible to prepare fully for each call. However, you can *always* have effective opening words at the ready in your telephone toolkit.

Here are two things you can *always* do when you answer the phone. First, answer within two rings. Most callers will hang up after four. Second, pick up the phone, put the receiver to your ear, and *then* speak. Obvious? Yes. But how many times have you called, say, the firm of Huey, Dewey, and Louie, only to be greeted with "... and Louie"? Don't talk until you have the receiver positioned.

In fact, there is a third step you can always take: Use a *rich* greeting, one that includes information. You don't have to be psychic to figure this out even before the phone rings. The caller wants to know something he doesn't yet know. Therefore, why not greet the caller by furnishing what's wanted? Instead of answering with a barebones "Hello" or "This is Carol," say "Good afternoon. This is Huey,

Watch Out!
What's the opposite of PTA? Why, BTA, of course! Like PTA, Bad Telephone Attitude has three components: 1) a reluctance to communicate; 2) an unwillingness to help; 3) a belief that all calls are unwelcome interruptions.

Dewey, and Louie. Carol Johnson speaking. How may I help you?"

Take a good look at this greeting. It is packed with powerful information that is immediately helpful to the caller and conveys that you are in the know:

Timesaver
Using an information-packed "rich greeting" creates a positive relationship between you and the caller even before the caller has begun to speak. It also saves you and the caller valuable time.

1. "Good afternoon" sends the message that you are civil and civilized. This further suggests that your company holds similar values. Such a message is very important to prospective and present clients and customers, but is also important when speaking to colleagues, subordinates, and bosses. It helps cultivate a climate of polite consideration in the office and makes it that much easier for you to do business.

2. Announcing the company name tells the caller that he has reached a specific place. This assures the caller that he has reached the right place—and it avoids wasting time over a misunderstanding if the caller misdialed.

3. Announcing your own name lets the caller know that he has reached a specific, real, individual human being.

4. The phrase "How may I help you?" is critical. It not only tells the caller that you are available and willing to help, it actually focuses the conversation from the very beginning. It is important to say *"How* may I help you?", not just "May I help you?" "May I help you?" invites only two responses, yes or no. The *no* is unlikely. (Obviously, the caller wants help.) In contrast, "How may I help you?" pushes the caller to furnish specific information, beyond a yes or no: "Well, I'm looking for a replacement for a model XYZ widget …"

Ugh! That voice

Okay, so you pride yourself on *not* being one of those shallow people who judges others on the basis of some physical attribute. Sure, Hank is overweight, but he's a wonderful guy. Susan has a bad habit of talking with her mouth full, but she's the salt of the earth. Bill mumbles and talks too fast, but just look him in the eye, and you know he's sincere.

The trouble is that, on the phone, you're just a disembodied voice. The person on the other end of the line has only your voice—one single physical attribute—to hang onto. He can't see the sincerity in your eyes, can't watch your gestures, can't "read" your body language.

Your message is all in your voice. Some people are naturally gifted with a good telephone voice, but *anyone* can develop one. Focus on three areas:

1. **Pacing:** You don't need a musician's sense of rhythm or the timing of a great actor for this one. Just slow down. Almost everybody speaks too fast, especially on the phone. *Think* first, then force yourself to speak more slowly than you normally do. Give each word full value.

2. **Depth:** It is a fact that lower-pitched voices are generally perceived as more pleasant, more persuasive, more truthful, and more authoritative than higher-pitched voices. For human beings, higher-pitched sounds tend to signal alarm (think of a scream), while lower-pitched sounds convey control and well-being. Perhaps you already speak in a deep voice. Congratulations. If not, concentrate on pitching your voice a little lower than what is normal for you. This applies to both men and women. Lowering your pitch will also help you slow down and pronounce each word more carefully.

3. **Pronunciation:** Be certain to give each word you speak its full value. Careful and correct pronunciation is not only critical to ensuring that you are understood, it also conveys intelligence, understanding, and care. Mispronunciation suggests a lack of smarts and telegraphs an attitude of carelessness. If you mumble or slur your words, you will irritate the person on the other end of the phone.

In 1971, the social psychologist Albert Mehrabian published his study of how listeners judge the persuasive content of a speech. He found that the most weight—55 percent—was given to visual elements: the speaker's facial expressions and body movements. "Vocal qualities"—tone of voice, voice pitch, and pace of delivery—counted for 38 percent. The actual words the speaker used counted for a mere 7 percent of what listeners found persuasive.

On the phone, that first 55 percent of persuasive content is unavailable. Your listener can't see you. That only leaves vocal qualities and the words you use, and, as Mehrabian showed, vocal qualities are actually more central to getting your message across than the words you use.

Stand up and smile (no one can see you)

Ever watch a little girl make a call to grandma? "I got a new kitten. Want to see him?" And she holds little Snowball up to the mouthpiece of the phone. Adorable, huh?

Actually, it's more than adorable. It's effective telephone communication. Unless you're on a videoconference, you know that the person on the other end of the phone can't see you. But that doesn't mean you should *behave* as if she can't see you. You can make your telephone communication more immediate, more personal, and more persuasive if you do two things.

First, stand up when you make an important call. Standing deepens your voice, making it sound more sincere and more authoritative. It makes you more alert and gives you greater confidence, and standing also gives a more powerful edge to what you say. Even though the other person cannot see you, your voice derives energy from your standing posture.

Second, be the "voice with a smile." A smile is primarily a visual signal, of course, but when people speak while smiling, they sound like they are smiling. And we know that a smile is universally interpreted as a welcoming, inviting, open gesture. We respond more favorably to messages delivered with a smile than with a frown, grimace, or even a neutral expression. Even if, at first, you feel a bit foolish doing so, smile when you pick up the receiver.

You own the call

Cincinnati-based Michael Ramundo, a marketing and customer service consultant, has developed a telephone technique he describes as "call ownership"; it's designed to ensure that customer service reps don't give callers the "he's-not-available-now" or telephone-tag runaround. Anyone—not just service reps—can give and get real benefits from Ramundo's approach.

You begin by learning a single Golden Rule: *If you pick up the phone, you own the call.*

Watch Out!
Although smiling is a good rule of thumb, remember to exercise common sense. Don't try to deliver obviously bad news in a "smiling voice." If the situation is serious, suit your verbal delivery to the situation.

Bright Idea
The worst thing
to have on a
radio show is
"dead air"—
silence. Listeners
immediately tune
out and start
changing sta-
tions. The same
thing is true
when you com-
municate by
phone.
Remember, your
caller can't see
you. If you have
to look some-
thing up in a
computer data-
base, *tell* your
caller in detail
what you're
doing. It keeps
him engaged
with you.

Taking possession

Owning the call means taking complete responsibility for the call. It means taking *possession* of the call.
So, if you can handle the caller's issue, you must do
so, immediately. Don't put the caller off. Don't hand
the caller to someone else.

But even if you cannot immediately address the
issue raised in the call, you *still* own the call. Your
objective in handling a business call is twofold: You
want to help the caller—to satisfy the "customer"—
and you want to make yourself look good by doing
this.

Here's what to do:

■ Do *not* fake it. Don't make up a response. Don't
pretend that you can handle the issue if you cannot.

■ Do whatever you can to put yourself in a position that will enable you to address the caller's
issue.

Perhaps you have to look up a file on your computer. *Tell* the caller what you have to do. *Tell* the
caller how long this will take. *Ask* the caller what he
wants to do. Try to offer a choice:

> Mr. Burns, I have to bring that file up on my
> computer. This will take just a minute or two.
> Can you bear with me? Or would you like me
> to call you back?

If what you need to do to address the caller's
issue will require more than a moment, tell the
caller what must be done and ask the caller's permission to put him on hold. Give the caller the
choice of a callback. If you'll be taking more than
several minutes, arrange a callback. Agree on a specific time. Also be clear about what you have to do.
Don't just say, "I'll have to get back to you on that";

instead, give the caller whatever information you have available:

> Jack, I'll have to talk to our warehouse people about that. I'll do it as soon as I get off the phone with you, and I expect to have an answer by this afternoon. What's a good time to call you back?

Selling the call

If it's clear to you that you are not the person who can best address the caller's issue, remember that you *still* own the call. You can't just send the caller elsewhere, and you can't just dump the call on somebody else.

Most people hate calling big companies because they are afraid they will be tossed from person to person like a hot potato. All too often, such fears are justified. It's up to you to show the caller these fears are unfounded.

If you know whom the caller should speak to, and you can connect the caller directly to that person, explain what you are about to do, give the caller the person's name and title, then ask permission to transfer the caller. If at all possible, avoid making the caller redial and seek the person on her own.

Remember, you can't just dump this call on the other person. If possible, do the following. First, assemble the key details that will help the other person address the caller's issue. Second, don't just transfer the caller. Get on the line and introduce the caller and her issue: "Mike, I have Mr. John Smith on the line. He has a question about a widget trade-in. I know you can help him with this." This is called *selling the call.*

Now, a situation might arise in which you really don't know how to address the caller's issue. Well,

Watch Out!
Keep your caller informed, but do not burden him with a long story detailing the problems you have with filling the caller's request. Deliver only information that is useful to the caller.

you *still* own the call. You'll just have to work harder at selling it:

1. Come clean. Tell the caller what you do know, but also what you do not know.

2. Quickly assure the caller that you—or someone else—will try to get the required information.

3. Assure the caller that you or someone else will call back. Set a definite callback time.

Now, do your best to find the person who can supply the information needed. Once you have identified that person, sell him the call:

- Give that person all the information you have.

- Make certain that the "sale" has been made—that the person will accept the call.

- Give the person the necessary callback information, including the time agreed on for a callback.

Rules for putting the caller on hold

Bright Idea
Remember: You don't have to be the person with all the answers. But you should make yourself the person who knows where all the answers can be found.

To many callers, the words *hold* and *ignore* are synonymous. Unfortunately, it's often necessary to put a caller on hold. This can strain relations with an outside customer and also annoy internal customers—your colleagues, subordinates, and bosses. The following rules will ease the pain:

- When you are talking to Outside Customer A, and your other line rings, say to him, "Will you hold, please?" Then switch to Outside Customer B: "Good morning. This is Huey, Dewey, and Louie. Will you hold, please?" and return to Outside Customer A. "Thank you for holding."

  Take a good look at the phrase, "Will you hold, please?" Note that it is a request rather than a command. Ask permission to put a caller on hold. Don't issue a command—even a polite one—such as "Please hold." Phrased this way, you offer the caller no choice, and that makes him feel powerless and, potentially, abused. What's more, you get the same result in either case, because almost no one will answer you with a "no."

■ When you're talking to an internal customer (a colleague, subordinate, or boss), and you get another call, you still need to ask permission to put the current caller on hold.

■ Once you've put the first caller on hold, talk to the other caller. Quickly find out what the issue is, and prioritize. If you can address the issue with a callback, arrange one: "Ms. Jenkins, I'm on another call. May I call you back in about five minutes?" Then get the caller's number. Do *not* forget to return the call promptly. If the second caller's issue must take precedence over the current conversation, ask the second caller's permission to put him on hold. Return to the first caller and explain: "Fred, I've got an urgent call from a customer. Should take 10 minutes. Can I call you back?" Then get back to the second caller.

Don't get flustered by multiple calls. You can handle it. Juggling them gives you an opportunity to demonstrate that you are in control.

You can also use "hold" to give you time to handle a caller's request. Be sure to ask permission before you put the caller on hold, explain what you are using the time for ("I have to get your file"), and give the caller an estimate of how long she will be on hold: "I need about two minutes." If that "two

Watch Out!
When we say "hold," we mean *hold*—you know, the button on a phone that ensures no sounds will get back to the caller. It is highly annoying, unprofessional, and potentially embarrassing to subject your caller to office noises, together with your own "Oh, man! I *really* didn't need this guy calling me right now!" Always use the *hold* button.

minutes" starts to stretch, get back to the caller: "I need another couple of minutes. Would you like to remain on hold, or should I call you back?"

Singed wires: coping with the irate caller

Maybe you'll get through your business career without ever having to deal with a genuinely irate caller. Maybe, on the other hand, your job is such that you count yourself lucky if you get through a single day without stumbling across such a caller.

The reasons for rage are many, and your outside customers typically have different reasons (say, the failure of your company's product) than your internal customers (like the report failing to reach the boss's desk on time). Some business-related rage factors you can control, to some extent. Others, which are not directly related to business, you cannot control: the fact that your customer just argued with her kid, or that your boss had a miserable morning commute in bumper-to-bumper traffic.

One factor you *can* get a handle on is your own rage response. Returning anger with anger will only fuel more anger. In contrast, a calm, businesslike, sympathetic response makes it difficult for the caller to maintain her rage.

You can do a good deal to regulate the stress in your own life. For example:

- Get more sleep. Fatigue reduces your patience and tolerance. You know that expression about "waking up on the wrong side of the bed." When we're tired, we're cranky.

- If possible, tackle difficult calls after you've had breakfast or lunch—not when you're hungry. Hunger tends to increase irritability.

- Think about cutting back on coffee. Caffeine heightens anxiety and rage levels—more than you realize.

- If you can, turn up the air conditioning, open a window, or do something to get fresh air circulating. Working in a hot, stuffy office environment is not only unhealthy, it's very aggravating.

- Do as much as you can to make your work environment physically comfortable. Does a clock tick too loudly? Get rid of it. Is your chair uncomfortable? Lobby for a new one.

So let's say you can control yourself. But what about controlling the other person? The phone rings, you answer, and your boss lets fly. What do you do?

- Nothing at all—other than listen. Let the caller vent. Doing nothing isn't as easy as it sounds. A lot of your buttons are going to get pushed, and you'll have to bite your tongue to keep from interjecting a defensive—or offensive—comment. But remember, rage is an explosion of pent-up energy. If you let some of that energy bleed off, the explosion may be less damaging.

   Never tell an angry caller to "calm down." That's a sure-fire way to make things worse. For that matter, avoid *telling* the caller to do anything. It's also very important to avoid telling the caller how to feel.

- After you sense that the initial rage has been spent, repeat and rephrase to the caller—as best you can—the substance of his message, but minus the outraged tone: "If I understand you correctly ..." Or: "What I hear you saying is ..." Or: "Let me make certain that I understand you ..."

Anger is never without a reason, but seldom a good one.
—Benjamin Franklin, *Poor Richard's Almanack* (July 1753)

- If you think you have a satisfactory response or solution to the caller's issue, now is the time to trot it out. Fast.

What if the problem has no easy, ready, or immediate solution?

- Put the burden on the caller. This isn't just passing the buck. It's a way of empowering the caller, and empowerment should help reduce the frustration that fuels rage. Ask: "How would you like to resolve the problem?" There's more than a psychological benefit to this question. The caller may actually suggest a very good solution.

- If you can agree to the steps proposed by the caller, take action accordingly. If you're not sure of the correctness or feasibility of what's been suggested, try not to raise objections just now. Instead, reply that you need a certain, set amount of time to think about it. Arrange for a meeting or callback *at a specific time.*

- If you realize that the proposed solution is utterly unworkable, it might be best to negotiate an alternative immediately. Don't just say no. Instead, offer: "We can't do that, but here's what I think we *can* do."

Bright Idea
Remember what was said in Chapter 4 about transforming an *I-versus-you* situation into a collective and collaborative *we?* You may defuse rage by transforming the *I versus you* into *We versus The Problem.* Get the two of you on the same side.

When you're dealing with an internal customer—a colleague, subordinate, or boss—who is readily accessible in person, it's usually best to suggest a face-to-face meeting. If the caller is your boss or a colleague, suggest a meeting in her office. If the caller is a subordinate, ask her to meet with you in your office.

Of course, a face-to-face meeting with an irate caller may be the last thing you really want to have. But the more fully the other person sees you as a human being, the more difficult it will be for her to maintain rage.

A way out of voice mail hell

A lot of people cling to the belief that the more inaccessible they are, the more powerful they appear to the world. Wrong.

The fact is that each time you are unavailable, you miss an opportunity for contact, and each such opportunity you miss makes you a little *less* powerful. If you are sufficiently inaccessible, you'll ultimately find yourself dropped right out of the loop.

But you can't be everywhere, and you can't always be immediately available. That's where voice mail comes in. Used correctly, it's a wonderful tool—an empowering tool. Used poorly, it can be the source of great frustration for those who need to communicate with you.

Dodging telephone tag

Telephone tag: It's a popular game that everyone hates. You make a call, leaving a message on voice mail; the caller calls you, leaving a message on *your* voice mail; you call back, leaving a message … Time, energy, and often the original purpose of the call are all wasted in the process.

Telephone tag is a game worth killing. Here's how: Always leave a specific callback time when you find yourself in someone's voice-mail system: "Sarah, this is John Williams. I want to talk to you about the Baker account. I'll be here between two and four. Please give me a call then. And I'll try calling you at two sharp."

Call screening etiquette

Most callers—rightfully—resent the suspicion that they are being "screened" by voice mail. "He *never*

> "
> *A soft answer turns away wrath, but a harsh word stirs up anger.*
> —Proverbs 15:1
> "

answers his phone!" Although you *may* sometimes be too busy to take every phone call, you shouldn't make call screening a habit. You'll risk losing new business, risk alienating customers and clients, and risk making those you work with feel bad, frustrated, or resentful. Moreover, while it may seem as if call screening saves you time, chances are that it actually costs you time. You have to review your calls, then make your callbacks—and what happens when those callbacks run up against the *other* person's voice mail? You've just begun a time-eating game of telephone tag.

If you must screen calls, you are at a great advantage if your telephone includes a Caller ID display, so that you can see who is calling you *before* the voice mail kicks in. That way, you can immediately answer some of the calls you know are particularly important.

The effective phone message

Voice mail—or some sort of answering machine—is a fact of business life. A lot of people don't like it but, let's face it, it's necessary. But it need not be a "necessary evil." You can transform your answering device from an evil into a tool by doing the following:

- **Use the device flexibly.** Record one message for playback during business hours and another for after hours. Your business-day message should greet the caller with the name of your firm and your name, followed by something like: "I am away from my desk …"

- **End your business-day message by asking the caller to leave a message.** Ask, don't just invite a message. "Please tell me how I may help you. Leave a message after the tone, including your

Timesaver
Whenever possible, leave a callback time on your voice mail message: "I'll be back in the office at three o'clock and can be reached from three to six." One of the great advantages voice mail has over old-fashioned tape-based answering machines is the ease with which you can frequently modify and update your own voice-mail greeting.

phone number and the best time to call. I will return your call as soon as possible." Remember, the word "how" is a very powerful act of communication. It focuses the response, coaxing the other person to help you help her. It substantially increases the odds that the caller will get what she wants—*and* it will save you the time and effort of a guessing game.

■ **Create a helpful after-hours message.** If you regularly receive calls from outside customers, your after-hours message should include a greeting, followed by a statement of normal business hours. Note that your message should not ask the caller to call back during those hours, but should *ask* for a message: "Please leave a message after the tone, and please include your phone number and the best time to call. I *will* return your call." Even if you don't regularly take calls from outside customers, some sort of after-hours message is a good idea. For example: "This is Peter Williams, widget inspector. My usual office hours are 8:30 to 5:00, Monday through Friday. Please leave a message at the tone, with your phone number, and I will return your call as soon as possible.

■ **Broadcast additional availability.** Depending on the nature of your job and your business, you may want to make it possible for callers to reach you after hours. If you have an after-hours number you can dependably be reached at, or a beeper, or an answering service, your after-hours message should provide the necessary information.

■ **Change your daytime message daily.** The message on your voice mail or answering machine is

Watch Out!
Updating your message daily is an impressive business communication technique, but it fails miserably and embarrassingly if you forget to update the message each day. Until you get accustomed to changing your messages and to switching from day to after-hours messages and back again, write yourself a reminder note.

contained in an arrangement of magnetic particles. It is not cut in granite—it is very easy to change. The trouble is that our arsenal of office machines make us complacent. Resist complacency by letting your callers know a breathing, *thinking* human being lives behind the machine they're talking into. Begin your recorded greeting by including today's date: "Hello. This is Sarah Smith at Huey, Dewey, and Louie. It's Monday, October 3rd, and I'm away from my desk at the moment. Please tell me how I may help you. Leave a message after the tone, including your phone number and the best time to call. I *will* return your call."

- **Use teamwork.** Work with a colleague or two to develop a buddy system in which you cover for each other when one of you is unavailable. Then include an alternative in your message: "Hello. This is Sarah Smith at Huey, Dewey, and Louie. It's Monday, October 3rd, and I'm away from my desk at the moment. Please tell me how I may help you. Leave a message after the tone, including your phone number and the best time to call. I *will* return your call. If you need immediate assistance, please call Mary Clark at 555-5555."

How to get your call through

We've just discussed how the savvy office politician can ensure that callers get their phone messages through. Now, what can you do to get *your* message through?

Name names

Sometimes, you make a call and actually speak to the person you want. Much of the time, however, a secretary, operator, or assistant answers. In this case, the most effective way to get your call through is to announce yourself and the name of the person you are calling: "John Smith for Jane Best."

- Keep it simple. Use your name and the callee's name. That's all.

- If you are returning the callee's call, say so: "Hello. This is John Smith returning Jane Best's call."

- If you feel the need to push the issue more urgently, say: "Hello. This is John Smith. Jane Best asked that I call."

If you must leave a message, provide the following information:

- Your name

- The name of your firm

- A brief statement of the reason for your call

- Where and when you can be reached, including the *best* time for reaching you

- The level of urgency, ranging from very urgent to "get back to me at your convenience" (be honest!)

Practice extra courtesy by repeating your name and phone number at the end of the message. This way, the callee doesn't have to listen to the message again to get the number if he didn't write it down the first time.

On hold? Don't agree to it

Resist the urge to automatically comply when your permission is asked to be put on hold. Unless it's clear to you that you will be put on hold for just a moment or two, consider replying "No, I don't have the time now. Please call me back. Is 10 minutes from now good for you?" Or "I'd rather not be put

Timesaver
Many, perhaps most, voice mail answering devices do not provide unlimited time for a message. You may well get cut off without warning. Save time by giving your name *and* telephone number first, then briefly launch into the substance of the message.

on hold just now. May I call you back in 10 minutes?"
Send the message that your time and attention are
valuable.

Use the call ownership principle

Remember the call ownership principle from earlier
in the chapter? Use it in reverse when you want to
ensure that your call is given the attention it
deserves. Don't let the person you call dump you:

> **The Other:** I'm afraid I can't help you.
>
> **You:** Please transfer me to someone who can.
>
> **The Other:** I really don't know who that
> would be.
>
> **You:** Transfer me to your supervisor. Maybe
> he or she can help.
>
> **The Other:** He's not here just now.
>
> **You:** What would you suggest that I do at this
> point?
>
> **The Other** *(after a pause)*: Let me get your
> name and number, and I will have someone
> from the warranty department call you.
>
> **You:** When should I expect the call ...?

And so on. Be persistent. Don't provide an easy
way out. Instead, furnish the other person with an
opportunity to help you. Don't become angry or
lose your patience. If you coax the other person into
investing time in you, your call will seem all the
more important, and you might actually get what
you called for.

Just the facts

- Business phone calls are important opportunities for conversation and should be prepared for
  with the same care you use to prepare for a face-
  to-face business conversation.

- With a little work, anyone can develop a positive telephone attitude (PTA) and an effective "telephone voice."

- Use the concept of call ownership to guide you in providing helpful and productive telephone communication.

- Used intelligently, voice mail can be an excellent business tool that will enhance your effectiveness in the workplace.

GET THE SCOOP ON...
The importance of good memo form ▪ How to
write the major memo types ▪ How to write a
human business letter ▪ Advantages of the
letter in the electronic age ▪ Letter forms and
formats ▪ Business letters: the major themes

Letters Perfect

Chapter 8

N ot too many years ago, people talked a lot about the "electronic office," a phrase used interchangeably with the "paperless office." The prediction was that electronic communication would pretty much replace paper.

Well, guess what? The electronic office is certainly here—but it's hardly paperless. American business in the age of the electronic office uses more paper than ever before: 775 billion pages of it per year, which is enough to make a stack 48,900 miles high!

Letters and memos—whether on paper or in digital form—are more important than ever in business. Because electronic communication is so readily available, the power and permanence of the written and printed word has assumed greater importance. Sam Goldwyn once declared that "verbal contracts aren't worth the paper they're written on," and much the same can be said for today's business communication. More and more, the people you work with appreciate "having it in writing."

For building your career through savvy office politics, effective communication on paper is at least as important as effectively presenting yourself face to face. This chapter tells you how to look very good on paper.

The memorable memo

The word *memo* is short for *memorandum*—a reminder, a written record, a written business communication. The word shares the same root as *memory*, and the effective memo is one that, once read, is neither ignored nor quickly forgotten. It invites attention and, in some cases, it prompts timely action in a desired direction.

Official junk mail

Having read what I just wrote about the nature and purpose of the memo, maybe you're thinking: "Yes, this is all true. On Mars!" But earthly American business has added an Eleventh Commandment to the decalogue with which we are all familiar:

Thou shalt cover your assets.

In obedience to this commandment, millions of us churn out millions of memos just "for the record." The result is information inflation, which threatens to reduce even important inter- and intra-office communication to the equivalent of junk mail. And the development of e-mail communication within most workplaces has only accelerated the growth of this pile of junk.

We're buried in information, much of which is not directly relevant to us. Load people down with a lot of useless information, and it becomes a major challenge to gain a hearing for your particular piece of information. What to do?

Good form

Getting a fair hearing for your memos is helped by two matters of form. The first is merely mechanical and conventional, the second is more creative.

First, adhere to the time-honored formula for opening a memo with the following straightforward information:

DATE:

TO:

FROM:

SUBJECT: (or SUBJ: or RE:)

Why stick to this format? Only because it works. It lets you telegraph the essentials in a usefully concise way. Do give extra thought, however, to what you put on the "SUBJECT" line. Make the statement both clear and provocative.

Take a closer look at the word *provocative*. The action you want to *provoke* is a reading of the substance of the memo. Strange as it may seem, you have to *sell* ideas and information to your coworkers and colleagues, just as you sell products and services to the outside world. Therefore, open with a statement that commands attention and appeals to your recipient's needs. For example, in a memo concerning changes in the rules about the employee parking lot, you could list as the subject "Parking lot changes," or "Changes in parking procedures," or even "Important changes in parking procedures." If, however, you really want to provoke your coworkers into reading the memo, put something like this on the subject line: "Getting a parking space," or "Getting the parking space you want," or "Parking made easier."

Bright Idea
When you want to interest your recipient in reading your memo, appeal to her. State the benefit of reading the memo right in the subject line: "Getting new furniture for your office"; "Speedier reimbursements." The reader will see it immediately and want to read the full memo.

This brings us to the second aspect of good memo form. In contrast to the heading, there is no single prescribed format for the body of the memo. But remember, the purpose of the memo is to sell your idea—your message—to others. Therefore, think of the form of the memo as a sales document.

In Chapter 4, we looked at the AIDA formula as a way to put yourself and your ideas across. Try thinking of the body of the memo in terms of AIDA:

- First, command the reader's **Attention.**
- Next, develop the reader's **Interest.**
- Then, cultivate the reader's **Desire.**
- Finally, prompt the reader to **Action.**

We'll see some examples of AIDA at work in the following discussion of the major types of memos.

A menu of memorable memos

We are about to discuss the five major memo types. But there is one thing all memos have in common. Call it a *voice*. Most business memos attempt to strike the Voice of Authority, like this:

> Non-exempt employees must report for work on Saturdays, during the non-holiday season, in rotation. Each employee shall take the rotation per the schedule issued by the Customer Service/Sales Manager.
>
> As commissions will be payable on Saturday sales, no overtime salary will be paid.

The problem is that the Voice of Authority typically seems less authoritative than harsh, even abusive. Certainly, it is heartlessly impersonal—not so much because of the message it contains, but because of the pronouns it lacks. Where is the "we" (or the "you" and "I," for that matter)? The message is that the directive comes not from a human being, but from that godlike entity known as The Company.

The Voice of Authority is alienating rather than engaging. Now, at the other extreme is the Voice of Your Pal:

> Okay, folks. Here's my traditional let's-please-work-on-Saturday memo. Look, I don't like working on Saturdays any more than you do, but give me a break.
>
> You won't get overtime, which is a bummer. But you do get commissions—just like on any other day.
>
> Please! Please! Please! Drop by, see me, and sign up.

While this memo is friendlier, it tends to undermine the authority of the writer through negative, low-energy, wishy-washy language and by making him sound captive to outside forces.

As is true of most important things in life, the best course lies between the two extremes. Try to strike a tone somewhere between hyper-authoritative impersonality and the be-my-pal overly personal approach. Find the Voice of the Human Manager:

> As we have discussed, Saturday work assignments will be made according to the rotation attached to this memo.
>
> I realize that Saturday duty is a hardship, but we're all agreed that the rotation is a fair way to spread the load. Although overtime compensation isn't an option, Saturday certainly offers opportunity for impressive commission income.
>
> I appreciate your cooperation and commitment to the sales team.

Watch Out!
Avoid using memos as a way of issuing impersonal commands from on high. Use them to convey the impression that you are inviting teamwork and trying to keep your coworkers informed.

❝

I have received
memos so
swollen with
managerial bab-
ble that they
struck me as the
literary equiva-
lent of assault
with a deadly
weapon.
—Peter Baida,
*American
Heritage*
(April 1985)

❞

You can be a person without groveling. The challenge is to write a message that appeals to the self-interest of the reader even as it achieves a corporate purpose. In short:

- Humanize memos by using personal pronouns and names.

- Use a friendly but precise vocabulary.

- Approach memos as team communication, not as directives issued from an impersonal authority.

- Thank your readers and express appreciation.

Light their fire

You've got a crowd of people in a theater. You want them to leave. You yell "Fire! Fire!" And they leave.

Without doubt, delivering a message of dire urgency is highly motivating. It's a message that won't bear repeating, however. Like the Little Boy Who Cried Wolf, you will quickly lose your credibility if you rely on panic as a motivator. Hysteria may motivate action once or twice, but it soon sinks into the background din of annoying noises that are best ignored.

To write an effective *action memo* that will motivate without seeming like overkill, set three objectives:

1. State the issue, goal, or problem realistically.

2. Illustrate clearly how the issue, goal, or problem relates to the team.

3. Propose or guide an action to address the issue, goal, or problem so that the team benefits.

Here's an example. The subject is "Making the break room more livable":

Opening our refrigerator should be a refreshing and appetizing experience. But our fridge is packed tight with food items that have been there for a very long time. Not a pretty sight—and the smell is even worse. We can all help make the dining experience more pleasant by ensuring that unused food is removed and taken home each Friday.

Thanks for your cooperation.

Don't falsely cry "Fire!" Light one. Avoid hysteria. Emphasize the positive results of a desired action, not the negative consequences of failing to perform the proposed action. And establish the relevance and benefit of the proposed action to the team.

Keeping everyone on the same page

The second type of memo we often write is intended to inform individuals or groups about changes in policy, plans, goals, the availability of products, and so on. These memos keep the members of an organization in sync.

Memos that announce new or changed policies and seek to coordinate action should include two parts: 1) an explanation of the policy or changes, and 2) an explanation of how the policy or changes affect the readers of the memo—what actions they should take.

What to say when things get ugly

In an urgent or crisis situation, calm, clear communication is important. Such situations are no fun while they're happening, but they can give you an opportunity to shine. As Patrick Henry said, "These are the times that try men's souls." Include women in the phrase, and you have an adequate description

Timesaver
Consider color-coding memos by printing them on colored paper. For example, red is reserved for urgent policy updates, yellow for a product availability advisory, green for price changes, and so on. Color-coding will trim the time it takes others to interpret a memo. Also, *always* keep the memo itself to one page (if necessary, attach backup material as another document).

of the challenge and opportunity presented by difficulty. If it falls to you to write a memo in such a situation, keep three objectives in mind:

1. Provide clear information and instructions.

2. Attack destructive rumors.

3. Keep the team together and the actions of individuals coordinated.

The tone of the memo is critically important. Avoid scolding and threats. Avoid playing Chicken Little, predicting imminent doom and a falling sky, but. at the same time, don't falsely minimize a serious problem.

Consider this example:

Bright Idea
Abe Lincoln said it: "Honesty is the best policy." Temper this advice slightly and create a memo that is as honest as possible while still producing a positive result. Without ignoring the negatives, do your best to emphasize the positives.

DATE: 8/01/00

TO: Sales Department Personnel

FROM: Joe Blow, Sales Manager

SUBJECT: Our survival and prosperity

I am relieved and thankful to report that last night's fire resulted in no injuries. It did, of course, cause damage to our equipment and inventory. Upper management is moving quickly to assess the degree of damage.

In the meantime, we must accomplish two critical tasks:

1. We need to get on the phones to our customers.

2. We need to recover as many of our files as possible.

Please give the Recovery Team whatever assistance they need. The faster and more thoroughly we can recover files, the faster we'll get back up to speed. Most immediately, each of you should call your customers. Please include the following in your calls:

1. Tell them what has happened.

2. Tell them that we expect a five- to ten-day delay in shipping current orders.

3. Tell them that we will resume accepting orders by 8/15.

4. Ask them what their concerns are.

5. Assure them that we will address all their concerns.

Folks, when speaking to your customers, don't minimize the seriousness of the fire, but do emphasize continuity of service. If we continue to deliver top-notch service, we will not only survive this crisis, we'll prosper.

Thanks for your cool, calm extra-mile effort in this difficult time.

Invitation to a solution

Too many of us narrowly think of memos as statements of fact, position, or policy. Actually, the only absolute requirement for an effective memo is that it must communicate. Consider writing a memo to explain a problem to an individual or a group and to solicit suggestions for a solution.

The problem-solving memo should include the following components:

- A request for help
- A concise explanation of the problem
- A request for input, including (for example) thoughts, advice, and guidance
- An expression of gratitude

Timesaver
Think a phone call is quicker than a memo? Not always. Unlike a phone call, the memo gives you an opportunity to spell out the nature of a particular problem. It also invites a written response, which minimizes the chances of time-consuming errors and mis-understandings.

Here's an example:

DATE: 2/25/00

TO: Alice, John, Pat, and Claire

FROM: Zelda

SUBJECT: We're being robbed!

Our department has a problem, and we need your help.

You've heard the talk about chronic employee pilfering. So far, it's nothing really big—but the problem is real, and it seems to be growing. I don't want to take this to upper management at this point and create a major security issue, which could damage morale.

Any ideas for addressing this issue while keeping it within the family? Please write or call.

Thanks for your time and consideration.

When you write a problem memo, focus on the problem, not on personalities. Moreover, don't seek agreement with and validation of your own ideas. Your object is to gather potential solutions. Finally, don't *demand* answers. Instead, invite advice.

Might I suggest...

A great way to climb the corporate ladder is to build a reputation as a source of good ideas. Ideas are too valuable to be merely spoken. Put them in writing.

Although a good idea memo will help you build a career, remember that the immediate purpose of the memo is the collective good of the organization. Don't let ego get in the way of the goal of the suggestion: to improve matters for the team.

The suggestion memo is a work of salesmanship, but it should emphasize the rationale for the suggestion rather than make an emotional appeal for its adoption. Structure the memo this way:

- State the subject of the suggestion.

- Explain the problem or situation that the suggestion is intended to address.

- Make your suggestion(s) and explain it. Be certain it's clear how the suggestion(s) addresses the situation.

- Close the "sale" by prompting action. "Action" includes calling for a meeting to discuss your proposal further.

Also bear in mind that the suggestion memo should include at least three components. First is the message that your suggestion is motivated by a concern for the organization and team rather than by self-interest. Second is a push toward action. Third is a recognition that, in many cases, "action" will consist of a meeting or discussion.

Here's an example that brings all these elements together:

DATE: 6/11/00

TO: Sam Warren, Director of Human Resources

FROM: Penny Lane, Assistant Manager, Customer Service

SUBJECT: Improving productivity with flex time

At the suggestion of Tom Peters, manager of this department, I'm writing to suggest that our company consider introducing a policy of flex time to stagger starting and ending times according to employee preference and departmental need.

Bright Idea
For your memo to be effective, you must emphasize the impact of the problem or situation on the organization. Simply mentioning a situation will not help people understand why the situation matters, or why they have any stake in resolving it.

As many corporations have found, the benfits of flex time include:

1. Empowering employees

2. Allowing employees to integrate their personal and professional time more effectively

3. Reducing traffic congestion at rush hours; this will go a long way toward relieving employee stress and ensuring prompt arrival

4. Maximizing use of the physical plant

5. Creating an additional employment perk—at no cost to the company

6. Improving employee morale, with a consequent increase in individual productivity

I propose that, under your direction, we set up a meeting to begin discussion of flex-time policies and to determine if such a policy will work for us here. What do you think?

Looking good on paper

Memos are powerful tools for everyday business, especially within the confines of your organization. Letters ratchet up the level of outreach and importance and are especially critical in communicating with your external customers.

The elements of style

The single most important secret about writing an effective business letter is to remember that you are engaging in communication between human beings. If you doubt this is indeed a secret, look at most business letters. Most business correspondence is stuffy, stilted, bled out, and utterly dead.

Why? Because the writer forgot that he is a human being and tried instead to be the embodiment of the Huey, Dewey, and Louie Widget Corporation. When you write a business letter, it's true, you are representing your company, but you aren't required to *impersonate* your company. Be human. After all, it's another human being, not a company, who will read the letter you write.

If you want to write business letters that reflect well on you as well as your organization, follow these guidelines:

- **Be human.** Don't try to impersonate some great, impersonal Voice of Business.

- **Know your correspondent.** People who make a living at writing do so by knowing their readers—who they are, what they like and don't like, what they need. Be sensitive to the needs and interests of your correspondent, and address them.

- **Take time to use the right words.** Decide what you mean, and be precise about the words you use to express your meaning.

- **Use real words.** These are the words most immediately connected to the *real* world—mainly nouns and verbs, rather than adjectives and adverbs. Try to use words that identify things, events, ideas, and actions. Wherever possible, avoid vague abstraction.

- **Transform "I" and "you" into "we."** This is the soul of persuasive communication. An effective letter reveals or creates a bond of common interest between the writer and the reader.

- **Be positive.** Even if you are exploring a problem, try to focus on paths to solutions rather than on the dire nature of circumstances.

Bright Idea
Often, the challenge in business correspondence is to respond quickly to a situation. Before you rush into words, however, pause to assess time constraints realistically. If possible, reread what you write a few hours after you've written it, then rewrite as necessary. The time away will give you a fresh perspective.

Watch Out!
The passive voice
is dull, evasive,
and phony.
Abandon it!
Many business
writers find it
hard to do so,
because they
think it makes
them sound
authoritative
(godlike, in
fact). It also
relieves them of
responsibility for
actions. When
you use the pas-
sive voice, things
"just happen"—
they aren't
caused, and no
particular person
is responsible for
them.

Inhuman words are not the only problems we find in many business letters. Look at this: "The report was reviewed by this department and found to be generally correct." Well, the writer is speaking English. Sort of. But what's missing is any evidence that a human being wrote the sentence. We find a "report" and a "department," but no people.

This sentence is a classic example of the passive voice. An English teacher would point out that the roles of object and subject are reversed. So let's try un-reversing them: "This department reviewed the report and found it to be generally correct."

An improvement. The sentence is now in active voice, with the emphasis on the subject rather than the object, on the initiator of the action rather than on the object of the action.

But we can do even better: "I reviewed the September sales report." Here we've put a human being in the subject position, and we've made the object more specific. Add some more "real" words to this, and you've got an effective—human—sentence: "I reviewed the September sales report, which showed that widget sales were up by 12 percent."

Who writes letters anymore?

There was a time when instruction in business-letter writing was part of any secretarial or business-preparation course. These days, in an age of electronic communication, this seems old-fashioned to some.

Maybe that's precisely the point. All our electronic aids to communication are valuable and, indeed, make much of modern business possible. Without question, they serve a purpose. But so does a paper cup. And while you might hand a valued friend a drink of water from a paper cup, you probably would not serve him your best wine in one. For that, a vessel of greater value is required.

Something similar holds true in business. When things of real value are being discussed, a letter—preferably a hard-copy, paper-printed, signed letter—communicates heightened value. It is a more precious vessel. In an age of easy and ephemeral electronic communication, the old-fashioned paper letter is of greater value than ever before.

Forms and formats

The reference section of any modest-sized bookstore offers any number of volumes on the formal "rules" for writing business letters. (My favorite is *The Complete Handbook of Model Business Letters*, by Jack Griffin, Prentice Hall, 1993.) Here's a quick rundown on general guidelines:

- If possible, limit business letters to a single page. (The "if possible" part of this sentence is important. If what you have to say truly requires more than a single page, use another page.)

- Type the letter, single-spaced, with double spacing between paragraphs.

- Keep the first paragraph short. It should succinctly state the subject of the letter, and nothing more. This will get the reader going and will point her in the right direction.

Decide on the visual style of the letter. To create a professional, sophisticated look, choose one of the three generally accepted business styles: block, modified block, or indented:

- In **block style,** text begins flush with the left-hand margin. Assuming you're using letterhead stationery, begin two spaces below the bottom of the letterhead and provide a one-inch

Timesaver
If your message requires more than two pages, it's best to put it in the form of a multi-page memo or a short report, accompanied and introduced by a very brief cover letter.

margin on the left and right, and end the letter a minimum of one inch from the bottom of the page. Because each element in the letter is flush left, the block style conveys a formal sense of order and a high degree of professionalism.

- The **modified block style** is identical to the block style except that the date (at the top of the letter) and the complimentary close, signature, and typed name below the signature (at the bottom of the letter) are offset. The left side of these elements is flush with the center of the page. The effect is a little less formal—softer—than the block style.

- **Indented style** is the least formal format for the business letter. The entire date is centered, not just the left-hand side of the date. Each paragraph begins with an indented line, as in the text of a book. The left-hand side of the signature block should be flush with the center of the page, as in the modified block style. The indented style looks friendlier than either of the two other business letter formats. If that's the effect you're after, use it.

Word processing software typically offers a range of typeface styles, or fonts. Avoid using outlandish fonts, especially those that emulate script or handwriting. For a traditional look, try a font like Times Roman. For a more contemporary look, use Helvetica, Arial, or another sans-serif font. (Serifs are the little overhangs and ornaments on printed letters; sans-serif fonts eliminate these.)

Envelope rules

An envelope should include your full return address in the upper left-hand corner. If the envelope is preprinted with the address of your business, you

Timesaver
The paper your words are printed on sends an important message. For business stationery stock, choose a crisp 24-lb. sheet. The heavier sheet conveys value and substance, and, to boot, is harder for someone to crumple. Communicating on good paper is the written equivalent of a firm handshake.

may want to write your last name above or below the preprinted area, in case returned mail needs to find its way through a busy mailroom and back to you. The name, title, company, and full address of your recipient should be roughly centered left to right, and the name line should begin about halfway down the envelope.

Hello and goodbye

The best way to begin a letter is with the recipient's name. If necessary, make a phone call to find out the addressee's name. Using it makes a more powerful connection than starting off with, for example, "Dear Office Manager." Address men as "Mr." (unless you know that another title such as "Dr." or "Rev." is called for). As a rule, address women as "Ms."—even if you know the correspondent's marital status. Obviously, if your correspondent expresses a preference for "Miss" or "Mrs.," kindly oblige.

In business letters, the salutation is always punctuated with a colon—"Dear Mr. Jones:"—whereas in personal correspondence, a comma is customarily used.

Many business letters address the recipient by first name. Do not presume to do this with a stranger, and if you have any doubts at all, use the surname. The savvy letter writer indicates a desire to move on to a first-name basis by signing the letter with first name only, above a typewritten full name. If you are answering a letter that addresses you by your first name or that closes with a first-name-only signature, it's appropriate for you to address the response with a first name.

How you say goodbye is as important as how you say hello. The best general-purpose "complimentary close" is a simple "Sincerely." If you want to create

Watch Out!
For business communication, it is absolutely necessary that the envelope and the paper match. Never put colored paper in a plain white envelope or white paper in a colored one. A makeshift combination of paper and envelope tells the reader that you are careless or, even worse, thoughtless. It suggests you just can't quite get it together.

Watch Out!
Avoid closing
with "Yours
truly" and "Very
truly yours,"
which are univer-
sally regarded
as hopelessly
old-fashioned.

greater warmth, choose from among "Cordially," "With best wishes," "Best personal regards," and the like.

Some major themes

The range of business correspondence is extensive, but let's focus on the four major themes that most commonly exercise the skills of the savvy office politician: apology, complaint, asking for favors, and giving thanks.

So sorry

Do you enjoy making apologies? I'm sorry—that's a stupid question. Forgive me. Actually, the answer is not as obvious as it would seem. Most of us admit our dread of having to apologize, but as I discussed earlier in this book, if we give the matter a little further thought, we discover that it is not apologizing that makes us cringe, but having made the blunder that necessitates the apology.

An effective letter of apology can turn a mistake or misunderstanding into an opportunity for creating a positive relationship between you and your recipient.

When you respond to a complaint, do so with the intention of creating a positive relationship between you and the correspondent:

- Begin with an acknowledgment that you have received the complaint or the returned product.

- Express sympathy for the person's problem or issue.

- Provide a solution. If you cannot provide an immediate fix, suggest a course of action—a conference, for example. Whatever you do, it's important to propose some specific and prompt action.

- Close by thanking the person for his patience and understanding.

To be most meaningful, a letter of apology requires sufficient information to respond with an assurance of prompt and appropriate action. If necessary, include in your initial response a request for more information. For example:

> Dear Mr. Johnson:
>
> I am very sorry to learn that you've had a problem with your Model T Widget. I want to resolve the problem quickly and to your complete satisfaction. To do so, I need some more information from you. Please take a few moments to answer the following questions.
>
> No need to write a response. Just give me a call at 555-555-5555.
>
> I appreciate your taking the time to help me help you. With your answers, I am sure that we'll resolve the problem to your complete satisfaction.
>
> Sincerely,

Nobody likes to be wrong, but there is one benefit to being wrong and apologizing for it: It puts the other person in the position of granting forgiveness, and this transforms that individual from a victim to someone with real power. Receiving an effectively written letter of apology can actually make your correspondent feel good about you and your organization. Be certain to include the following five components in the letter:

1. Begin by expressing concern and sympathy.
2. State that the problem, issue, or error is an exceptional occurrence.

Unofficially...
If a particular "product" you produce should happen to fail, you *still* have an opportunity to sell yourself— and, often, your firm—by sending the message that you regret the problem, that you care, and that you will make things right. A good letter of apology turns a damage-control mission into an opportunity for relationship building.

3. Take responsibility for the problem, and apologize forthrightly for it.

4. Propose corrective action—or, at least, some positive course of action.

5. Close by thanking your correspondent for his understanding and patience.

We've got a problem with that

Some people enjoy nothing more than "firing off" a letter of complaint. With righteous anger heated white-hot and a word processor dipped in vitriol, off the letter goes.

The result? More often than not, little or nothing at all. Before you sit down to write a complaint, think about your objective.

- Is it to make yourself feel better? To get something off your chest?

- Is it to make the other person feel bad?

- Is it to resolve the problem or issue at hand?

If either or both of the first two most accurately describe your objective, then by all means fire at will. But if your object is to resolve a *problem*, focus on the problem rather than on feelings, people, and personalities. Emphasize facts—things and events—rather than emotions. Structure your letter this way:

- State the problem. Focus on the facts, not on causes, motives, or fault. Accuse no one. Include such details as the duration or frequency of the problem or error, as well as the *actual, material* impact of the problem or error.

- Propose—don't demand—the remedy you want. Issuing a non-negotiable demand is just as likely to provoke a defensive response as to produce compliance.

Bright Idea
Whenever possible, quantify the impact of a problem or error on the company: "Late shipments this month have cost us more than $1,900." This gives people a better sense of the gravity of the situation and the pressing need to resolve it.

- Close by transforming "I" and "you" into "we." Make it clear that you want to work *with*—not against—your correspondent to improve the situation, correct the problem, or rectify the error.

Here's an example:

Dear Mr. Burns:

We received order number 1234 yesterday. Of the 64 items shipped, 8 were damaged in shipment.

Mr. Burns, we realize that accidents will happen. But this is the third of five deliveries we have received from you in which goods arrived damaged.

I am very pleased with the quality and pricing of your merchandise, and I am gratified by the prompt attention with which you have made adjustments for damaged goods in the past. Nevertheless, the repeated delays caused by the nearly routine arrival of damaged goods costs us significantly in cash and time. Certainly, it must cost you even more heavily.

Let's work together to correct this situation. Please call me with what you propose to do to prevent shipping damage in future deliveries. I have a few suggestions that I am more than willing to share.

Sincerely,

Please help

If few people enjoy apologizing, an equal number don't look forward to asking for a favor. Most of us don't like the feeling that we are asking for something in return for nothing. This is understandable, but it is, after all, only a feeling. In truth, when we ask for a favor, we aren't expecting charity. We are giving the other person an opportunity to create good will; moreover, we are paying the other person a high compliment and an empowering vote of confidence.

It is, then, easier to ask for a favor if you think of it in positive terms as a kind of *quid pro quo*. Still, the most difficult step remains the first one: broaching the subject. Begin by laying a foundation for the request: "We've worked together for so long that I feel comfortable asking you for a favor."

This should put both you and your correspondent in the right frame of mind. Now, continue:

- State clearly what it is you want.

- Explain how the favor will benefit you. It's important to provide your correspondent with the means of estimating the positive impact her effort will create.

- Express gratitude.

Consider this example:

> Dear Frank:
>
> We've been colleagues now for so long that I actually look forward to asking you for a favor. I need a brief letter of recommendation to the Acme Widget Company to help us secure an important contract with them.
>
> Here's the opportunity: We've been asked to bid on supplying them with full widget-maintenance services. This would be a very significant piece of business for us. It would be most helpful if you could make the following points about your experience with us as a supplier:

Watch Out!
In expressing gratitude, don't use such phrases as "thanking you in advance," which implies that you take your correspondent's compliance for granted. Not only is this offensive, it may prove embarrassing.

- We supply high value.

- We furnish a high level of client support.

- We offer instant-response emergency service.

Frank, the schedule is tight, so I'd need this letter to go out by April 5. The letter goes to:

Ms. Catherine Pressboard
General Manager
Acme Widget Company
1234 56th Drive
Industry City, NY 02345

Please call me if you have any questions. As always, I appreciate your effort on our behalf.

Sincerely,

The magic of thanks

Finally is the most enjoyable—and rewarding—type of business letter you are likely to write: the thank-you letter. Here is where you should really strive to express yourself.

Include the following elements:

- **An expression of thanks.** Do this in a straight-forward manner. Make certain that there can be no mistaking the purpose of the letter.

- **An explanation**—with facts—of how valuable the favor, the service, or the help has been.

- **A reiteration of your gratitude.** Close the letter by thanking the reader again, emphasizing your feeling of good fortune in being associated with her.

Here's an example:

Bright Idea
When writing a thank-you letter, don't be afraid to let your personality and personal voice show through. The more you can personalize it, the greater impact it will have on the recipient.

Dear Anne:

Many thanks for your note to my supervisor, Ed Williams. The greatest feeling of satisfaction I get from my job is when I do it well enough to earn a kind word from one of my customers. When that kind word is directed at my boss—well, it makes me not only feel great but look great, too.

I look forward to working with you again— soon. And, again, many thanks for your thoughtful remarks.

Sincerely,

Such a letter requires perhaps five minutes to compose. It is the most valuable five minutes you will ever invest, and you should get into the habit of writing letters of thanks for just about anything and everything—not just the big things. Thank-you letters are great ways to keep in touch with your circle of business associates. They create a network of good feeling.

Just the facts

- Written communication has taken on greater, not less, importance in the age of the electronic office and digital communications.

- Memos serve purposes of self-protection as well as communication, persuasion, and motivation; how you write them will have great impact on your visibility and position within the workplace.

- The great flaw of most business correspondence is its lack of human presence. A business letter *can* be both professional and human.

- Expressing major issues in the form of a letter (versus a phone call or even an e-mail) underscores the value of what you have to say.

Chapter 9

Getting off the e-mail treadmill ▪ Getting your
e-mail message and fax read ▪ E-mail versus
face-to-face talk ▪ Making e-mail messages professional yet personal ▪ E-mail security ▪
Effective cover pages

Putting Yourself Across Online

" **Y**ou can take out every one of the 300 to 400
computer applications that we run our company on, and we could continue," Scott
McNealy, CEO of Sun Microsystems declared, "but if
you took out our e-mail system, Sun would grind to
an immediate halt."

That's a powerful statement about a technology
that few companies and even fewer individuals had
10 years ago. The word *revolution* is overused, of
course, but it's certainly applicable to the advent of
e-mail in the American workplace. This chapter suggests how you can make the best use of e-mail (and
fax) to build your climb up the corporate ladder.

The e-mail challenge

Let's assume that you clean and keep your own
house or apartment. You're thankful for such modern conveniences as the vacuum cleaner, automatic
dishwasher, clothes washer and dryer, and so on.
Certainly, you don't want to swap places with the

homemaker of a hundred years ago, whose technology was defined by a broom, a washboard, and a sink.

Today's "labor-saving devices" clean more thoroughly, more efficiently, and more quickly than the implements of old. Right?

Well, yes and no. A vacuum cleaner (for example) is faster and more thorough than a broom, but it—together with the other "labor-saving devices"—has raised the standards by which we judge a clean house. In the old days, cleanliness was defined by what a broom could do. Now, a house only counts as "clean" if it's thoroughly vacuumed. So the vacuum hasn't really proved to be the timesaver it was supposed to be. Although a vacuum cleaner can get a house "broom clean" faster than a broom can, it's likely that a broom will get that same space "broom clean" faster than a vacuum cleaner will get it "vacuum cleaner clean."

Much the same is true for our expectations regarding the cleanliness of clothes and crockery. By raising expectations, our so-called labor-saving devices may well have created more, not less, labor.

Now, consider e-mail. The technology makes it very easy for many people to reach you, and you them. It invites instant messages and invites—or demands—instant replies. Often, it saves a lot of little time-consuming steps:

- You don't have to dig out stationery and load it in a printer.
- You don't have to format a formal letter, with the address and so on.
- You don't have to sign the letter.
- You don't have to fold the letter, hunt for and seal the envelope, and put a stamp on it.

- Often, you don't even have to look up an address—especially if you are replying to a message. You just hit the Reply button.

No one can deny that e-mail technology is a labor-saving device—at least for any given message. The availability of e-mail, however, generates many more messages to you, together with the expectation of a reply. Additionally, we are all expected to use e-mail to "keep in touch." A business associate who never expects you to write a letter and may be content with the occasional phone call is likely to be sorely disappointed if e-mails from you fail to materialize.

Thus e-mail technology typically creates at least as much labor as it saves. And it puts an even greater pressure on us. The very speed and ready accessibility of e-mail communication that saves us so much time also places demands on our time. More precisely, the arrival of an e-mail demands or at least tempts an immediate response. Often, we are left with little time for thought. E-mail has speeded everything up—not just the mechanics of communication (which is good), but the thought processes that should go along with it (which is not so good). An indispensable tool, e-mail also presents us with formidable challenges.

E-mail etiquette

In many ways, the great weakness of e-mail is that it makes sending messages *too* easy, especially since "sending messages" is not always the same as "communicating." Typically, we think harder before we pick up the phone to make a call—and certainly before we compose a letter—than we do when we send an e-mail.

Timesaver
Consider using the "address book" function on your e-mail, if your server offers one. It will help you access addresses more quickly.

Bright Idea
Consider compos-
ing your e-mail
messages offline.
Read and edit
them before
going online to
send them. If
this saves you
from making
costly or embar-
rassing errors, or
even if this
makes your writ-
ing more clear
and correct, you
will save time
and effort.

Most e-mails are dashed off in a single draft. Often, the sender doesn't even read the message before clicking the Send button. The result is a message that, if committed to paper, would look like the work of a marginally literate or mentally deranged person. Capitalization is often erratic, syntax tortured or incomplete, and spelling downright embarrassing.

For generations, freshman composition teachers have been drumming into their students the following rule: Writing that can be read the fastest and the easiest typically takes the longest time and the most amount of effort to create. Conversely, writing that is dashed off often must be deciphered, with the reader making up for time the writer didn't invest.

Well, 'fess up. When is the last time you really labored over writing an e-mail message? The technology and the medium invite us to give little or no thought to what we say. The single biggest step we can take to increase the effectiveness of e-mail communication is to stop and think. Don't succumb to the temptation of careless speed just because the blinking cursor is panting to accept your message. Approach e-mail communication as you would any important business conversation or business letter. Remember your teacher's rule. The mental energy you fail to put into your message will have to be compensated for by the reader's effort. What does this mean?

- You'll make a poor impression on the reader.
- The reader will resent having to struggle with your message.
- The reader may misunderstand your message if you didn't make yourself clear.

The lesson is simple. The ease of e-mail communication is seductive. It tempts you to act before you think. Don't feel obligated to answer e-mails instantly, or to send off your very first thought. Write your message, but regard it as a first draft. As with a memo, delay sending your e-mail until you have read it over and edited it.

This is just to say—*we're drowning!*

When the lengthy classic *Moby Dick* was reissued in the 1920s, the hyper-sophisticated literary wit Dorothy Parker wrote a one-line review in *New Yorker* magazine: "Herman Melville has told us more about whales than we care to know." In many organizations, much the same is true about e-mails. We get more than we care to have, and they often concern things we do not care to know.

E-mail messages have become a digital knee jerk. We can't help doing them. And that creates problems:

- Too many e-mails take too much time to sort through and read.

- Dumb e-mails bury important e-mails.

- Drowning in a sea of e-mails, we stop paying attention altogether.

Practicing deft office politics usually requires that we do certain things. In the case of e-mail, it requires that we *don't* do something—namely, that we don't send unnecessary messages to people who neither want nor need them. Here are three pieces of e-advice:

- Think before you write. Is this message necessary?

- Think before you send. Does the recipient really need to have this message?

Unofficially...
Computer Associates International found that its managers received over 200 e-mails every day. This overload consumed time and created a climate in which people used e-mails even when a short conversation would suffice. Management responded by shutting down e-mail from 9:30 a.m. until noon and from 1:30 p.m. until 4 p.m. The result? Managers wasted less time, and people started talking to each other.

- Think before you "cc" (send copies to) additional recipients. Do *all* these people really need to receive the message?

Who's in *this* loop?

"
A memorandum
is written not to
inform the reader
but to protect
the writer.
—Dean Acheson,
*The Wall Street
Journal*
(September 18,
1977)

"

In days of yore, sending "cc" copies—carbon copies or courtesy copies—required real work. You had to duplicate paper memos, writing in each recipient's name. And because it took work, it was used only when truly necessary. With e-mail, however, sending a single message to multiple recipients is as easy as a few extra clicks. The result is a lot of unwanted messages. Like memos, the great majority of these are of the "cover-your-assets" variety, intended less to inform than to leave an electronic trail of documentation to protect the sender if something goes wrong later and he is blamed for it.

Curbing cc's would be a major stride toward cutting down on e-mail overload. Decide who should be in the loop for any particular message. Yes, it's better to err on the side of inclusiveness, but don't routinely send all messages to a list of everyone you can think of. With each e-mail, take a few extra moments to ask yourself who should get copies. In general:

- Copy anyone who, according to company procedures or policies, must receive a copy.

- Copy all those who will be in any way affected by the content of the message.

- If the message concerns a particular project, copy all members of the team responsible for the project.

More e-mail abuses

Two more e-mail abuses are common and highly destructive to effective office politics. First, some supervisors and managers use e-mail as a vehicle of terror. They send critical, nasty, or intimidating e-mails instead of calling a face-to-face conference to discuss problems. E-mail is a great message medium, but it is not well-suited to discussion. If you have an issue to discuss, make a phone call or, better yet, have an in-person meeting.

That brings us to a second e-mail abuse. Many people, managers and staffers alike, use e-mail as a means of *avoiding* meaningful communication. Perhaps they are uncomfortable with face-to-face conversation. Perhaps they want to avoid confrontation. Perhaps they are just fundamentally lazy. Whatever the reason, e-mail technology offers a tempting hiding place.

Don't yield to temptation. Climbing the corporate ladder requires that you be *seen* as well as heard. No form of communication is more powerful than live communication directly between people. The more sophisticated technology that comes between two would-be communicators, the truer this statement becomes. In an electronically mediated business environment, real-live conversation is more compelling than ever.

Oops! Can I take that back?

We've become so comfortable with e-mail that we readily abandon all standards of good business communication. Not only do grammar and syntax tend to evaporate, as discussed earlier in the chapter, but we also say things on the spur of the moment which cannot be retracted once the Send button is clicked.

If people are most careful about what they say in letters, and somewhat less guarded in conversation, they are downright careless and indiscreet online. There is a certain feeling of informal intimacy and privacy as we sit before our computer screens, typing away. Occasionally, we are lulled into letting

Watch Out!
Before you click
the Send button,
double-check
that the message
is being directed
to the person for
whom it is
intended. The
consequences of
a misdirected
message can be
annoying,
embarrassing, or
even career-
busting.

down our guard, and we dash off a remark we regret. Or perhaps we misstate, understate, or over-state a fact.

To be sure, e-mail does give us an opportunity we don't have in conversation. We can write what we want, and then we can delete or change it. But only *before* we click Send! The lesson? Take the time to reread your message before you send it.

Greetings and felicitations

Most e-mail programs insert in each message a beginning part called a *header*. This consists of the following information:

- A description of the electronic path the message took to arrive at its destination
- An electronic message ID
- The content type of the message (usually text)
- The date and time the message was sent
- The e-mail address of the sender
- A "To:" line
- A "cc:" line
- A "From:" line
- A "Subject:" line

The key line you must fill in is the subject. Most programs allow only a certain length of subject entry and will truncate any subject message that exceeds this length; therefore, keep the subject statement concise and provocative. You want to "sell" the recipient on reading your message.

The standard e-mail header, with its "to/from/subject" lines, is certainly useful, but rather cold.

You will probably want to personalize your greeting. E-mail etiquette discourages imitating the conventional opening of the paper letter—"Dear

John"—but welcomes using the recipient's name in the body of the message: "Bob, are you available for a meeting tomorrow morning?" If you want to be a bit friendlier, add "Hi": "Hi, Bob. Are you available..."

If the message is being sent to multiple recipients, try something like this: "Widget Project Team, please make yourselves available for a meeting ..."

The header feature is standard in most e-mail programs. Many programs also provide the option of adding a signature. This is not a script signature, but a collection of information that automatically appears at the bottom of any e-mail message the sender transmits:

Timesaver
For a discussion of how to write provocative and inviting subject lines, check out the discussion of memos in Chapter 8.

John Doe,	jdoe@widget.com
Sales Manager	Phone: 555-555-5555
Widget Wonders, Inc.	"Fine Widgets for Every
1234 W. 5th Street	Need"
Acme, NY 12340	

If your e-mail software doesn't provide the option of a signature, you can create a copy-and-paste file with this important information. Again, you may want to personalize the close of your message. Do so within the body of the message: "Bob, I look forward to seeing you at the meeting!"

Telegraphic or conversational?

E-mail brings out two opposite tendencies in people. Some emphasize the *electronic* part of "electronic communication" and write in a staccato telegraphic style: "Joe: Meeting 2 pm 5/22/00—my office."

Others are drawn out by the casual intimacy of e-mail and become quite conversational: "Hey, Joe, we're having a meeting at two in the afternoon on Wednesday. Love for you to be there. Can you make it? My office."

Which one is best?

■ As with any business correspondence, match the
style and tone to the purpose and the recipient.
If you are transmitting a single piece of simple
information, be brief but clear. Complete sentences are preferred. If your message is more
complex, take the space and words you need.
The tone you adopt with your boss will doubtless be different from the tone you use with a
colleague who is also a friend.

■ Small talk, as we discussed in Chapter 5, is an
important business activity. E-mail, however, is
not the place to engage in small talk. Don't use
e-mail to shoot the breeze or pass along personal notes. Save small talk for actual conversation in the break room or while waiting for the
copy machine.

■ You *can* strike a friendly, human tone without
yakking on and on. In general, keep e-mails as
short as possible, without sacrificing important
information or detail.

Watch Out!
Although e-mails
may be conversa-
tional in style,
they are still
written speech.
Avoid vagueness,
and don't ramble.
Keep your mes-
sage brief and to
the point.

Room for style?

Increasingly, people are equating e-mail correspondence more closely with conversation than with
paper memos or letters. For this reason, there is not
only *room* for style in e-mails, but the *expectation* of it.
Here are some guidelines for injecting style into
your e-mail messages:

■ In e-mail communication, informality is both
expected and tolerated to a greater degree than
in telephone conversation, and to a *much*
greater degree than in business letters.

■ Although spelling and punctuation errors are
more readily forgiven in e-mail than in other

written correspondence, take the time to proof-read and correct yourself. If your e-mail messages seem both spontaneous *and* correct in grammar and spelling, you will come off as an accomplished wit indeed.

■ You may find it helpful to picture your correspondent when you write an e-mail. You may also find it helpful to speak out loud when you compose an e-mail. This will help you write more naturally.

While it's a good idea to strike a mildly conversational tone in e-mail communication, don't abandon what you know about letter writing, either. Take a look at the discussion of structuring business letters in Chapter 8. These same structural principles can serve you well in creating effective e-mail messages.

Meet the emoticons

Veteran e-mailers aren't content with mere language to convey emotion. Those who regularly communicate via e-mail have developed a handy visual vocabulary for adding emotional expression to their messages. You must judge whether these "emoticons" (emotional icons) are appropriate to the corporate culture where you work, but they're worth knowing about.

Emoticons are used to express the emotions that are normally conveyed in voice communication but often lost in the cold phosphorescent print of the PC screen. Emoticons require no special software or equipment. They use nothing more than the basic (ASCII) characters found on your keyboard. There's only one proviso: Most emoticons must be viewed at a 90-degree angle—that is, sideways. Just tilt your head to the side and start reading (see accompanying box).

Bells and whistles

Emoticons were invented back when personal and corporate computing was pretty much limited to ASCII text—the basic characters you find directly represented on your keyboard. Some corporate e-mail systems still have this limitation, but most are now capable of supporting messages that include fancy graphics and even allow you to attach sound and video clips.

Should you personalize your e-mail with such bells and whistles? The short answer is no. In *most* business contexts, such electronic doodads are perceived as unprofessional at best, and downright offensive at worst. It is possible, however, that the culture of your particular office encourages decking out your e-mail with various digital ornaments. If so, be creative—but you still need to be careful to avoid potentially offensive graphics, video, or sound clips.

Safe and secure...right?

When e-mail works right, it's easy—easy enough (as we've seen) to promote some bad communication habits, and easy enough to lull users into a false sense of security.

Despite any number of software safeguards your company may use, e-mail is inherently vulnerable. It is not secure in the same way that ordinary postal mail ("snail mail") is. Other people can read the e-mail you write and the e-mail you read. You should always keep this in mind when you send an e-mail message —and when you are tempted to use BCC (blind carbon copies) to covertly copy a message to people other than the named addressee. The "blind" addresses are actually quite easy to see, and

Watch Out!
Avoid animated graphic e-mail signatures. Appended to an otherwise ordinary text e-mail message, these are typically perceived as annoying, childish, and unprofessional.

E-MAIL EMOTICONS AND THEIR MEANINGS

:-)	Humor (smiley face)
:-) :-) :-)	Hah, hah, hah!
:/)	Not funny
;-)	Wink
(@ @)	You're kidding!
:-"	Pursed lips
:-V	Shouting
:-W	Sticking tongue out
:-p	Smirking
<:-O	Eeeeeeeek!
:-*	Oops! (covering mouth with hand)
:-T	Keeping a straight face
:-D	Said with a smile
=|:-)=	Uncle Sam
:-#	Censored (or expletive deleted)
:-x	Kiss, kiss
:-(	Unhappy
:-c	Very unhappy
:-<	Desperately unhappy
(:-(	Even sadder
:-C	Jaw dropped in disbelief
:-l	Disgusted
:-?	Licking your lips
:-J	Tongue-in-cheek remark
:-8	Speaking out of both sides of your mouth
(:-&	Angry
||*(	Handshake offered...
||*)	...and accepted
(-_-)	Secretly smiling (This and the following are the only emoticons that require no tilt of the head to read!)
@%&$%&	Curses!

it can be very embarrassing to have your "real" recipient discover that a piece of confidential and exclusive communication is neither confidential nor exclusive.

E-mail systems are also vulnerable to crashes and other failures. Some failures are obvious, such as when the entire system in your company goes down. Other failures are more subtle. Most of the time, the e-mail message you send halfway around the world or just down the hall gets to its destination in a matter of minutes. Sometimes, however, it's passed from network to network, and if something in one of these networks fails, the message either is delayed (perhaps for days) or simply vanishes.

Take the following precautions:

- Check your incoming mail for returned messages. Most of the time, undeliverable messages will bounce back to you. If one does, you'll know the intended recipient didn't get it. (Note: This may take minutes, hours, or even days.)

- Make a backup copy of any e-mail document you consider important. It *could* get lost. (Many e-mail servers automatically save copies of any mail you send.)

- Large messages—for example, those with large graphic or video attachments—are especially vulnerable to delivery difficulties. Consider using such software as WinZip© to compress big files, or, if possible, break up large files into smaller components.

- If you've sent a critically important e-mail to someone, go ahead and confirm receipt by phone. You won't sound *too* paranoid doing so. Some e-mail systems let you attach a receipt to the e-mail, letting you know when the recipient

Bright Idea
Take time to find out about your company's policies regarding e-mail, including what kinds of communication are appropriate and how secure the messages are. In general, confidential information should not be transmitted via e-mail.

receives it, and creating a time-stamped record that the message was indeed received.

Finally, e-mail software and hardware has become so sophisticated that we take its flawless functioning for granted. Don't. Your network may be modern and fancy, allowing you to do just about anything. But your *recipient's* network may be old and stodgy. The most common compatibility problem from one network to another is the tendency of some networks to chop off lines of text that exceed 80 characters. Be safe. Set your e-mail composer to limit outgoing line length to 80 characters. Many networks also limit the overall size of incoming messages. Usually, these limitations aren't severe. America Online, for example, limits incoming messages to 102,400 characters, which is well over 10,000 words. Even the windiest e-mail messages rarely approach this limit; however, attached documents or graphic files may be too big to be accepted.

Big Brother lives

As we've noted, e-mail messages are vulnerable. Others can read them—for example, computer hackers and industrial spies. But not all electronic eavesdroppers are criminals; some are your employers, acting legally. Numerous court decisions have upheld an employer's right to monitor all e-mail going in and out of the network and equipment the employer owns or controls. Indeed, all e-mail generated by employees on employer-owned or controlled equipment is considered the sole and exclusive property of the employer.

Assume that everything you send and receive via the company's e-mail system is being read by management. Management also has the right to access

Watch Out!
Although it is good *ethical* policy for an employer to tell employees that their e-mail may be monitored, the employer is under no *legal* obligation to do so. Assume your e-mail is being read by your boss.

unsent e-mail (or other documents) that may be on your hard disk. Keep these cautions in mind:

- Don't use the company's e-mail system to send personal messages.

- Don't use the company's e-mail system to conduct non-company business (such as freelance work).

- The bottom line: Don't write anything you wouldn't want your boss, subordinates, or colleagues to read.

Bright Idea
Consider making copies of all e-mails you originate, if your system doesn't already do it for you. You can periodically review e-mails from a given period and delete those you don't need.

Keeping copies

You should keep a copy of any e-mail that you regard as rising to the level of business correspondence. Don't depend on the recipient to keep a copy. While you probably won't need a copy of everything, it's sometimes helpful to be able to reconstruct correspondence, especially if you're dealing with people who are prone to lose or accidentally delete their e-mails.

Deleted—or not?

You may be tempted not to worry much about others seeing the e-mails you send and receive. After all, you can always delete them. Or can you?

Deleting files from a computer hard disk does not erase the file. It merely makes the file inaccessible by ordinary means and allows other files to be written over it. Even if the file is overwritten, however, it does not completely disappear. Determined experts can recover many supposedly deleted files. Networked company-wide backup systems retain copies of your files, even if you use special methods to "wipe" the files from the hard drive on your computer. You may be able to obliterate a file from your own hard drive, but you cannot get at the network backups.

If you are handling sensitive material, be certain that you know your company's policies and procedures on how to delete files permanently so they cannot be recovered. If you have sent or received e-mails that are embarrassing to you or harmful to your career, be aware that they may well be recoverable. The best course? Don't write questionable e-mail messages, and discourage others from writing them to you.

Just the fax

The fax machine shares many of the advantages of e-mail. It's easy and accessible. As with e-mail, this advantage is also its pitfall. Faxes pour into offices and threaten to bury your message. How can you make your fax's presence known?

Getting it there

The main reason so many fax messages go astray or are simply ignored is that the sender didn't know what and when to fax. The fax machine is a powerful communications tool, which combines some of the benefits of a phone call and a letter. But it is a substitute for neither. Here are a few tips for sending faxes successfully:

- Unless you know that the recipient has her own dedicated fax machine, don't substitute a faxed message for a phone call. She may never get it. If you're sending an important fax, alert the recipient by telephone first.

- Try to keep your messages brief—a single page, preceded by a separate cover sheet. This will avoid tying up a client's fax line.

Timesaver
Not all unso-licited faxes are unwelcome. You might use the fax to announce a new product or service. Just make certain that you target clients and customers who are likely to benefit from the information. And don't send dozens of pages unsolicited. Provide just enough information, on a single page, to invite interest and inquiry.

- Avoid sending "junk mail" via fax. A few years ago, when fax machines were becoming more affordable and were beginning to proliferate in offices, many businesses saw them as ideal advertising tools. As with telephone solicitation, access was easy, but—here was the advantage—the prospect couldn't hang up. So fax "spamming" began. Advertisers transmitted loads of unsolicited material. The FCC acted to curb such transmissions, but no law was really necessary. The general ill will generated by fax junk mail soon sent its own message: "Tie up our fax line with garbage, and we will not give you our business—ever."

Cover page basics

There's an odd touch of nostalgia about fax machines. In most larger offices, they are reminiscent of the phone in the hallway of an old-fashioned boarding house. As the roomers shared the phone, so office workers share the fax, which is typically stationed in a more-or-less public area. As a result, you need to take steps to ensure that your fax reaches the intended recipient. That's where the cover page comes in.

The principal purpose of the cover sheet is to serve as a shipping and routing label—and as a kind of "cargo manifest." The cover page should include:

- The recipient's name and the name of his company, as well as the recipient's fax number.

- Your name and company name, as well as your address, fax, and voice phone numbers.

- The number of pages included in the transmission; make it clear whether the total listed on the cover sheet includes the cover sheet.

Watch Out!
Because fax machines are usually shared, never send confidential or sensitive material by fax without making a confirming voice call first. Get your recipient's permission to send the fax, and alert him to its arrival just before you transmit.

Cover sheets don't have to be fancy or especially eye-catching. In fact, it's better to avoid attempts at clever or humorous cover sheets. Just provide, clearly and in large type, the information specified above.

Between you and me

Misdirection of a fax is bad enough, but misdirection of a confidential or sensitive fax can cause great damage, including damage to your career.

It is certainly *dishonest* for a company or individual to make use of confidential material received by accident, but it may not always be *illegal*. Lawyers have successfully argued that sending material via fax is, in effect, the equivalent of publishing it, and the sender automatically relinquishes exclusivity as soon as the Send button is pushed. To counter this argument, include a confidentiality statement on your cover sheet. This declares to anyone who may see your fax message that it is private and confidential and that, even though you have in effect "published" the material electronically by faxing it, you do not intend to make the material public and you do not give permission for anyone else to do so.

The confidentiality statement asserts your ownership of and right to the material. It need not be a complex legal document. A statement this simple will work well:

> THIS FAX MESSAGE CONTAINS PROPRIETARY INFORMATION INTENDED FOR THE ADDRESSEE ONLY. IT MUST NOT BE USED FOR ANY OTHER PURPOSE. IF THIS MESSAGE REACHES YOU IN ERROR, PLEASE CONTACT SENDER IMMEDIATELY.

Bright Idea
You may want to include the following line on your cover sheet, in full capital letters: "If this fax reaches you in error, please forward it to the number above or contact sender at the number listed above. We appreciate it!" This will help reroute the fax if it goes to a wrong number.

Of course, the best way to avoid problems with confidentiality is, whenever possible, to avoid faxing confidential or sensitive material. Use a private courier service or an expedited delivery service. The savvy office politician makes wise use of electronic communication, and that includes knowing when to use non-electronic alternatives to e-mail and faxes.

Just the facts

- While e-mail has revolutionized business communications, greatly empowering individual employees, it also makes new demands on our time.

- In many offices, the volume of e-mail is overwhelming; take time to create concise, powerful messages that will stand above the mountain of incoming mail.

- Don't use e-mail as a substitute for a letter, a telephone conversation, or a face-to-face meeting when these are more appropriate to the situation.

- E-mail and fax communication present security issues which can lead to embarrassment—or worse.

- Fax messages are easily misdirected or buried; don't use them in place of phone calls, and do alert recipients by phone before you send an important fax.

Dealing with (and Being) the Boss

PART III

GET THE SCOOP ON...
Giving your boss the "right feelings" ▪ Relating
to your boss adult-to-adult ▪ Boss types and
how to deal with them ▪ Bonding with your
boss ▪ Negotiating a raise or promotion ▪
Selling ideas to your boss

Who's the Boss?

Cutting-edge management theory is all about redefining the role of the boss. Those in upper management today are supposed to be "facilitators" rather than taskmasters. The assumption is that today's workplace is driven chiefly by knowledge rather than material resources. In the old days, so this story goes, the boss held all the keys to the material resources; today, however, knowledge is distributed among the workforce. In many areas, it's acceptable—and even expected—that staffers know more than the bosses. Today's manager, then, must work with, not push or pull, her staff. Managers still lead, but what they lead is a collaborative effort.

That's the theory, anyway.

Doubtless, it may even be substantially true—in practice, in some places. But even the most enlightened, contemporary, and collaborative manager harbors a place somewhere within himself that is 100 percent unvarnished and unreconstructed *boss*. After all the management theory is shoved aside, she

Chapter 10

believes herself to be *numero uno,* the big cheese, The Boss. For some bosses, that fact feels good. Maybe it's a real ego trip. For others, however, it's intimidating and even scary. However your boss feels about being a boss, you have to deal with that person and those feelings, regardless of company policy or management theory. The good news? It's not an impossible task.

Setting the tone

> **"** Despite all you hear about participative management, the chief executive still casts a long shadow.
> —Joel E. Ross and Michael J. Kanti, *Corporate Management in Crisis: Why the Mighty Fall* (1973) **"**

Let's get one fact straight from the start. Whatever else you say and do, and no matter how skilled you are at the art of office politics, there is no substitute for knowing your job and doing it well. Even the most easygoing and humane boss won't tolerate incompetence for long. Regardless of the staffer's social skills, if he consistently produces unsatisfactory results, there's no way that mere office politics can make matters right.

Generations of parents have told generations of offspring that the world is not always fair. So the following should not come as big news: While incompetence will get you nowhere (at least, nowhere you want to be), there is no guarantee that knowing your job and doing it well will automatically earn you the rewards you deserve. Some bosses are great; some are horrors. All are human—all too human. To satisfy them consistently, you should plan on giving them not only top-level work, but also the right feelings about you and what you do.

R-E-S-P-E-C-T

As anyone who has spent more than 15 minutes making a living knows, whoever said "Flattery will get you nowhere" was dead wrong. Unfortunately, the reverse—"Flattery will get you everything"—is not true, either. Giving your boss good feelings about herself and the things she does is important, and we'll talk about this in a moment. But it's even more important to give your boss good feelings, the right feelings, about *you*.

Psychologists of every stripe—professional, pop, and amateur—will tell you that for others to have good feelings about you, you must have good feelings about yourself. But this observation can be taken too far. There's no denying that self-confidence is an asset for relating to others effectively, but it is not a prerequisite. After all, you can't put off a conversation with your boss until you've got five years of self-esteem training under your belt. It's far more practical to learn how to act as if you feel great about yourself. How do you do this? Begin by reviewing the discussion of body language in Chapter 2. Pay particular attention to your voice. Remember, people tend to respond more positively to a deep voice than to a higher-pitched one.

And keep an eye on your "voice of fear." Observe what happens when you're nervous—or downright scared—and you try to talk. Your voices comes out thin, tight, quavering, high-pitched, and completely unpersuasive. Does something like this happen to you when you have to speak to your boss? Unfortunately, there's probably little you can do about feeling scared, but you can prevent that fear from announcing itself through your voice.

Here are three tips:

- **Practice using the lower register of your voice.** Push your voice lower than normal. This advice applies equally to men and women.

- **Slow down.** This doesn't mean you should make your conversation excruciatingly slow, but be certain that you give each word weight and pronounce each word carefully.

Bright Idea
Slowing down your speech not only makes you sound more intelligent and articulate, it tends to lower your voice, and it allows you to breath more comfortably.

■ **Breathe!** Speaking requires us to control breath-ing. If we are excited or frightened, we breathe more rapidly and less deeply. The result is that we find it harder to speak—we sound "breathless"—and this unmistakably telegraphs fear or, at least, the absence of confidence. Take a few deep breaths before talking to your boss. Focus on your breathing. Slow it down. Make it deeper. The result? You will present yourself as far more self confident than you may feel.

Regarding body language, make certain that, visually, you put yourself across as an adult. In deal-ing with your boss, this may sound easier than it is. Some years ago, a psychotherapeutic technique called Transactional Analysis (TA) was a popular alternative to traditional psychological counseling. TA was based on the assumption that we all have within our personalities aspects of an "adult," a "parent," and a "child." Ideal communication between two people takes place when their "adults" connect. Unfortunately, interaction with different people tends to bring out different, less complete components of their personalities. For many people, a conversation with the boss becomes a conversation between a "parent" and a "child." Without getting into the details of this type of psychotherapy, you can make good use of the following suggestions taken from TA. These tips will ensure that you con-nect with your boss, adult to adult, by avoiding putting yourself across as a child:

■ Make eye contact.

■ Use hand gestures to underscore verbal points, but don't fidget.

■ Keep your hands away from your face—especially your mouth.

- Keep your hands out of your pockets.

- Stand still. Don't shuffle your feet, and don't rock from side to side.

Here's another childish trait to kill: overeagerness. Be sensitive to the rhythm of the workplace and the workday.

- Is there a good time to have a conversation with the boss? Or, more to the point, is there a bad time? Keep your eyes open and see for yourself. Exploit the good times, and avoid the bad.

- Generally, Mondays are not favorable days to raise issues that can be put off until Tuesday.

- Avoid important conversations immediately before lunch or quitting time.

- Avoid bringing up potentially adverse subjects just before a weekend or just before your boss is going on vacation. You don't want her stewing on account of you.

- Avoid shoe-horning in a conversation when you know the boss really doesn't have time: *You:* "Can I talk to you?" *Response:* "I'm off to a meeting. Will this take more than a minute?" *You:* "Well, I wanted to discuss my promotion . . ." Bad idea. Arrange to put time on your side.

The natural rhythm of a conversation is give-and-take. If you extend this a step farther, you have the essence of negotiation: asking *and* giving. When you approach your boss to ask for something, do not do so as a beggar, expecting something for nothing. Approach all requests as negotiations, a promise to return value for value. This is not for your boss's benefit, but for yours. We naturally find it more difficult to be persuasive if we feel that we are taking without giving. It feels much better to walk into a

Timesaver
Invest a few minutes at home in front of a mirror—a full-length mirror, if possible. Imagine yourself talking to your boss in various situations— discussing a project, asking for a raise, delivering bad news, and so on. How do you come across? You don't need a body-language textbook to tell you what works and what doesn't. *Look and learn.*

store with a full wallet than an empty one. Similarly, don't walk empty-handed into any important conversation with your boss.

And don't walk in empty-headed, either. When in doubt, learn something. You wouldn't wing a major client presentation, for example. So don't wing an important conversation with your boss. No law says conversation has to be spontaneous. How can you be an overnight success? Prepare overnight for success the next morning:

- Plan what you have to say.

- Consider making a written outline.

- Consider rehearsing the conversation—either by yourself or with a friend.

Pressing the right buttons

Now that you've thought about your own feelings, it's time to stop focusing on yourself and start thinking about your boss. Think about what he needs and wants—and what he needs and wants to hear. Think of yourself as a salesperson. You may desperately want to make the sale. You need that commission to pay your rent. But if you focus on *your* needs instead of your customer's, it's a pretty good bet that the sale will slip through your fingers. In the same way, the boss is your customer, the person to whom you're trying to sell yourself or your idea. So prepare for conversations with your boss by asking yourself what it is he needs and wants:

- What good news can you bring?

- What issues (that matter to the boss) can you raise?

- What problems (that matter to the boss) can you solve?

And what words does the boss want to hear? Consider some of these candidates:

advise	effective
expedite	helpful
improved	increase
productive	profitable
reasonable	smart
terrific	thanks
valuable	vigorous

All are active, positive, and inclusive, and all imply productivity. In contrast, you can be sure your boss doesn't want to hear words such as the following:

cannot	collapse
demand	fault
guess	loss
lost	mistake
overloaded	unreasonable

Your boss doesn't want to hear about limits, closed doors, and irreversible errors. Don't distort reality, but do exercise your imagination to express it in positive, active terms. Don't hide problems, but do try to show them as opportunities—if nothing else, as opportunities for leadership and team building.

Bright Idea
Do you like to doodle during idle moments? Why not try verbal doodling. Jot down as many positive, boss-pleasing words as you can think of. Get this language into your head. Make it a habit.

A guide to bosses

The ideas and techniques we've just discussed work well with all kinds of people in charge, provided they're more or less grown-up and reasonable. Unfortunately, not all bosses are reasonable, and even the most grown-up people in charge, when put under sufficient pressure, fall into destructive patterns of behavior from time to time. The following are six of the most familiar adverse and unpleasant patterns.

Tyrannical types

The British historian Lord Acton put it most famously: "Power tends to corrupt, and absolute power corrupts absolutely." For some people, it's hard to be in charge without becoming a tyrant. The tyrant boss acts like a punitive parent—not a father or mother, which are roles that imply love and nurturing, but your *parent:* a figure of absolute authority, whose authority it is not your place to question.

The "leadership style" of the tyrant makes you feel like a child in the narrowest and most negative sense of the word: a little person who is entirely dependent on the parent and who is quite incapable of making decisions.

- The tyrant relies on monologue and avoids dialogue.

- If the tyrant asks questions, it is not so much to gather information as it is to keep you feeling unstable, unconfident, and inferior.

- The tyrant likes a big desk with a chair that's always higher than yours.

- The tyrant routinely makes threats. They may be blatant, or they may be couched in language such as "you'd better," "get a handle on," "get on top of," "get on the ball," and "get on the stick."

Clichés like the phrases just mentioned are important to the tyrant. Indeed, you may get the feeling that your tyrannical boss is acting out a script. That's because, in a sense, he is. The tyrant operates from a rigid self-image, a crudely drawn schematic of what he thinks "The Boss" should be. Acting from this image, the tyrant boss really doesn't see *you*. Playing a role, he expects you to respond by playing yours. If the boss's role is the person in charge, yours is the worker, the drone, the dependent.

Are we overstating the case of the tyrant boss? After all, you might say, few bosses have *absolute* power. But in fact, not having total power may actually make the tyrant even *more* difficult to cope with. The manager who occupies a niche midway up the corporate food chain has power to wield as well as pressure to bear. Just how hard this middle manager comes down on you is the product of his power multiplied by the pressure on him. The equation is simple: If the boss's boss knocks him, he's liable to pound you.

So much for the bad news. The good news is that the tyrant can be dealt with effectively, and you need not be at his mercy.

1. First, put your boss in perspective. What can he actually do to you? Does this boss have the power to fire you? More important, has this boss fired a lot of other people?

2. While you are cutting the boss down to size, play a little game with yourself. Try to identify all the things about your boss that make him look ridiculous. Wears loud ties? Ugly shoes? Bad hairpiece? Makes grammatical errors? The more petty you can be, the better. Make this hunt for the ridiculous a daily imaginative activity.

3. While you are concentrating on his or her foibles, find something to compliment your boss on. Make your boss feel good about something,

Watch Out!
Don't be too quickly over-whelmed by your boss's bluster. Chances are, much of your boss's apparent tyranny is just noise. Look beneath the surface and assess the reality.

anything—his choice of necktie, the color of her jacket. Then imagine what these articles of clothing would look like with nice, big food stains on them. The idea is to put yourself in control of an encounter with your boss. You are accustomed to thinking of yourself playing the role your boss has cast you in: the victim of a tyrant. Now turn the tables by allowing your imagination to tyrannize over your boss.

Having taken these steps to reduce the tyrant to a more vulnerable, human level, use *your* power to empower him. Make your boss feel important by doing some of the following:

- Asking for advice

- Finding something to genuinely admire—some accomplishment or idea; offering a compliment

- Generally treating your boss as if he were your mentor

This last step may be quite difficult, but the point of it is to stop reinforcing your boss's favorite image of how the two of you relate—as master and slave—and to shift the perception of the relationship to one that still empowers the boss, but elevates you as well: mentor and student (or even protégé).

Here's a final trick: If you can't beat 'em, join 'em. And one person you usually can't beat is a boss. So if your boss attacks you, instead of responding defensively, why not try joining in?

> **Boss:** I'm disappointed in you. Sales in your territory are way below par.
>
> **You:** I'm disappointed, too. Sales are below what I had projected. I am calling a meeting of the reps, and I was about to come to you for your take on the situation. I also think it

would be helpful if you participated in the meeting. Can I sit down with you before the end of the week to clarify some of the details of the issues and hammer out an agenda for the meeting?

Dealers in guilt

The full-blown guiltmonger is the mirror image of the tyrannical boss. Instead of towering over you, she endeavors to prove to you that you are tearing *her* down by your unwillingness to "go the extra mile." The guiltmonger doesn't make direct threats, but will from time to claim that, unless you do more, the business will collapse.

The guiltmonger does not explicitly direct you to put in extra hours, but she will look up from her desk at 5:30 p.m. and say something like, "Oh, no, don't stay late. You have more important things to do, like having dinner with your family. My family has gotten used to my working late by now." Just as the tyrant lives by certain clichés, so does the guilt-monger—using such passive-aggressive one-liners as:

> Don't trouble yourself.
>
> Think nothing of it.
>
> No, really, we'll manage without you.
>
> I understand what it means to have a family.
>
> We'll find somebody to do it.
>
> I guess we'll manage.

While it is true that the tyrant boss can cause great anxiety, it is also possible to cope with the tyrant and walk away from an encounter feeling pretty good. But you *never* come away from a trans-action with a guiltmonger feeling good. The best you can hope for is to escape outright manipulation.

Bright Idea
Don't go overboard reacting against a guilt-mongering boss. If doing extra tasks fits in with your job and your own ambitions, feel free to "go the extra mile." Just be sure that you are motivated by what's in your own interest.

In dealing with the guiltmonger, adhere to the following strategy:

- Separate your commitment to your job, the company, and your career from your relationship to your boss.

- Distinguish between the unavoidable demands that come with your job and the emotional demands that come from a manipulative guiltmonger.

- After you have successfully distinguished between necessity and emotion, help your boss to do the same.

Let's discuss this last point. You might try two tactics to help your guiltmonger boss see the light. First, if an unreasonable demand is made on your time and you have a legitimate excuse, use it. "Normally, I could work overtime, but today's our anniversary," or "I wish I could change my day off, but I have a medical appointment that would take months to reschedule," and so on. This approach works when you have a good excuse, but because guiltmongering is a chronic affliction, you will quickly run out of legitimate excuses; if you start fabricating excuses, you will be perceived—quite rightly—as uncooperative.

So try this: Administer a calming dose of reality. "Well," your boss says, "I suppose I'll just stay here and work on this report myself." You reply, "Are you sure you have to? You know, I'll be available to do it tomorrow. I could rough out a draft by noon, and you could review it."

The object is to assure your boss that you will do the necessary work, but at a time and in a manner that is convenient for everyone and (this is very important!) that is most likely to result in a job well done. For, as you can point out, it is not a good idea to rush through a critical task at the end of the day.

Dealers in blame

Few work situations are more infuriating, frustrating, and threatening than being unreasonably and undeservedly blamed. Unfortunately, there are bosses who make the casual distribution of blame a habit.

Difficult as it may be, try to remember that bosses are human. On occasion, you may be blamed for something that is not your fault. The best approach in such a situation is not only to defend yourself, but to offer to pitch in to correct a problem that you did not cause.

But we're not concerned right now with the boss who occasionally assigns blame where it doesn't belong. The "blamer" boss habitually and routinely doles out blame. For this type of boss, blaming is an article of management style.

Whenever you are blamed for something, take a deep breath and stop yourself from loudly protesting your innocence. Instead, do the following:

- Get the facts. Don't deny anything before you have the full story. By collecting the facts, you will accomplish two things. You will calm your boss down by shifting her focus from personalities to events. And you will acquire the opportunity not only to demonstrate your blamelessness, but perhaps to help resolve the problem.

- Once you have the facts, turn your focus—and that of your boss—on them. In an emotionally charged situation, it is always advisable to draw attention to the facts of the situation rather than to the feelings and personalities involved.

Watch Out! Make certain that you can distinguish between those times when you really are at fault and those times when you are not. If you've goofed, own up to it, confront it, deal with it, and repair it.

- Confront the events rather than the accusation. It's difficult to respond reasonably and constructively to confrontational, angry words. So don't try. Just dodge them, and deal with the situation.

When you are dealing with a habitual blamer, it can be frustratingly difficult to get the facts you need in order to defuse and remedy the situation. Because the blamer's chief objective is to shift responsibility from herself to you, the last thing she's interested in is any facts that may make such a shift difficult.

What can you do?

When you are unjustly blamed, counter with a demonstration of your willingness to accept responsibility—but not blame. Make it clear that, although the situation is not your fault, you are prepared to accept it as your problem and will work to resolve it.

If you respond to blame by merely challenging your boss, the result may well be an escalation in hostile feelings. Your offer to help resolve a problem, however, is far less likely to be rejected or met with anger.

The most satisfactory outcome possible in dealing with a blamer is to avoid being defeated by accepting wrongful blame by offering to help resolve the problem—allowing her to feel as if she has won.

Timesaver
Trading accusations and affixing blame wastes energy and time. You do your boss, your company, and yourself a service by focusing the discussion away from issues of blame and directly on resolving the problem at hand.

The impractical leader

A significant minority of bosses subscribe to the popular myth that great ideas are born from the merest sparks of chance inspiration. An apple dropped on Isaac Newton's head, and he formulated the theory of gravitation. Someone knocked on Beethoven's door, and he wrote the *Fifth Symphony*.

Obviously, inspiration does play a role in creativity. So why is this a "myth"? Well, it leaves out the other side of the equation. You need that spark, all right, but you also need the smarts to work that spark into a flame. Newton and Beethoven were geniuses. They also had the practical know-how to make the most of their inspiration.

Alas, the impractical boss typically has nothing more than the spark: "I was driving in this morning, and I got a brainstorm." Pretty soon, you find yourself unwillingly swept away in whatever direction your boss's stream of consciousness takes you.

This is not to say that you should dodge every idea your boss comes up with:

- Your boss may be competent.
- Your boss may be gifted.
- Your boss is, after all, your boss.

In any case, you may have little or no choice about whether to act on whatever assignment your boss hands out. Depending on your position and the way your company is organized, you might not even be in a position to offer an opinion. But if you are confronted by a harebrained idea, you owe it to yourself, your company, and—yes—your boss to employ some of the following verbal strategies to return the impractical boss to reality:

- First and foremost, *avoid* delivering a verbal slap in the face. Responses such as "It'll never work" or "We can't do that" will only provoke hostility (not good for you) or stubborn insistence (not good for anyone).

- Unless you are pressed for an opinion, withhold verbal judgment. Instead, respond to the mechanics of your boss's request or instructions: "What kind of priority do you want me to

Watch Out!
Never tell your boss you don't have time to act on the idea just offered. This dismisses both the idea and the person behind it. Instead, point out what will have to be sacrificed to act on the idea. This will put the idea in perspective, while taking some of the pressure off you.

give this?" Or, "Should I put such-and-such on hold and get to this right away?" Or, "Such-and-such is due tomorrow. Do you want to postpone it?" The idea is to respond in a way that tends to return your boss's focus to day-to-day reality.

- Don't hesitate to exploit whatever standard procedures your company has in place for dealing with new ideas, concepts, and programs. If there are forms to fill out and reports to write, get your boss involved in this. This may head off the development of an unworkable idea.

- Finally, play for time. "Can you give me some time to think about this? I think I'll have lots of questions for you." Take up the task, but don't leap onto the bandwagon.

The incompetent leader

To an outsider looking in, an incompetent, bumbling boss can appear to be a rather endearing character—the proverbial absent-minded professor. So what if she forgets appointments, lets details slide, waffles when decisions are called for, and isn't very good with money? She's only human!

But this kind of behavior gets old fast to those who actually work for the incompetent. While it's true that the tyrant may cause more raw anxiety, the guiltmonger more grinding grief, the chronic blamer more frustration and resentment, and the impractical boss more useless work, no one can top the incompetent for generating a low-level state of chronic panic. "Follow your leader"? To *what?*

Approach the incompetent with careful verbal strategies:

- Resist the temptation to express your exasperation.

- Resist the temptation to bad-mouth this boss to others, inside or outside of the company.

- When you talk to the boss, be sure to confirm instructions and correct errors. Avoid a mocking or patronizing tone.

- Communicate by e-mail or paper memos; get as much as possible in writing.

- Be helpful. If you can educate this person, do so.

The emotional volcano

Another category of bosses is the boss who just periodically explodes. By definition, the emotional volcano is a poor manager. His explosive personality puts people off and discourages communication. While it's true that fear of the boss is a great motivator, *what* it motivates is passivity and the avoidance of confrontation. And ultimately, it motivates employees to seek alternative employment.

There are effective ways of dealing with this type of boss. First, think through your own fear reaction. What intimidates you about the boss's temper? If you really think about it, you'll probably find that much of your fear is unrealistic—a natural but unthinking response to being yelled at.

You *can* cope with being yelled at. Here's how:

1. When the volcano erupts, just let the lava flow around you. Difficult as it may be, listen to the tirade. If possible, stand, arms at your sides. It won't be easy, but try to maintain eye contact, as if you were having a regular conversation.

2. Wait for a lull in the storm. At this point, inject a note of calm. This doesn't mean that you should tell your boss to calm down. Telling an angry person what to do or how to feel will only make him angrier. Instead, after the boss has

Bright Idea
If you are genuinely afraid that your boss will fire you, you should begin looking for another job. No one should have to work under such conditions.

had an opportunity to vent for a time, acknowledge him: "I can't blame you for being angry, but . . ."

3. After the "but," begin to introduce alternatives to the fulminating tirade to which you have been subjected: ". . . but I need to talk this through with you. Would it be better for me to come back and discuss this later, or do you want to sit down and go over it now?"

4. Give your boss choices, alternatives. In this way, you empower him and you also invite him to *think* rather than just *feel.*

5. Do not meekly submit to abuse, but don't join in a shouting match, either. If you are both yelling, no one is listening.

Anger can be hard to let go of. If the volcanic flow won't shut off, the most effective move you can make is *out.* Separate yourself from your boss. Excuse yourself: "Excuse me, Mr. Vesuvius. I can appreciate how angry you are, and, because of that, I think it would be best if I went down to my office for a while. Please give me a call when we can sit down and talk about this problem without yelling at one another." Sometimes the best remedy for anger is to use your feet—for walking, not kicking!

How to bond with your boss

The good thing about bosses who act like jerks is that the vast majority of them don't *always* act like jerks. Much of the time, they're decent enough, well-rounded human beings with a job to do. They are not always problems to be "dealt with," but coworkers you should bond with. Unfortunately, the line between "bonding" and "sucking up" is sometimes difficult to see and all-too-easily crossed. So read on.

Watch Out!
Anger is a powerful emotion. If you ever feel physically threatened, walk away *immediately*. If a physical threat is made against you, remove yourself from the situation and seek help. If necessary, call the police. Don't put yourself in danger.

Accepting a compliment

Effective leaders are more liberal with praise than with blame. Behavioral psychologists have known for years that positive reinforcement is far more effective at creating and maintaining desired behavior than punishment is. Besides, it feels good to praise others.

How you respond to your boss's compliment determines just how good it feels. Your boss is trying to give you the right feelings, and this is a golden opportunity to build a relationship. Don't blow it.

If you have a hard time accepting a compliment, you're not weird, and you're not alone. Most of us have grown up to the tune of "be modest" and "don't get a swelled head." The result is not true modesty, but an inability to take a compliment. It's a skill most of us have to learn. And it's important. Learning to accept a compliment is not only an opportunity to feel good, it's also a chance to make your boss feel good by giving her the pleasure of having bestowed recognition where it is deserved. Accepting a compliment with appropriate grace will give your boss the satisfying feeling that she has acted correctly and is wise in placing confidence in you.

Fortunately, learning how to accept a compliment can be as simple as saying "thank you" when you're told you've done a good job. Now, just dress that up a bit, but turn the compliment on your boss: "Coming from you, that really means something."

The rules for accepting a compliment are straightforward:

- Express thanks.
- Express pleasure.

Bright Idea
When you receive a compliment, share the praise with others who deserve it. Be sure to name names; give your colleagues and coworkers the credit they deserve. You will look *great* doing so.

- Express surprise, if the compliment really is unexpected.

- Use the opportunity to express your high regard for your boss.

It's just as important to avoid saying the wrong things as saying the right. Don't "confess" unworthiness: "I really don't deserve this." And don't deliver a long speech.

Apologizing

We all dread making mistakes, but, in fact, most mistakes are not fatal or beyond fixing. Usually, the bigger problem is the feelings that mistakes create— feelings that are often more destructive than the mistake itself.

When you make a mistake, it's important that you start communicating. Effective communication should help to rectify the problem, even as it serves to minimize bad feelings. Best of all, it creates the opportunity for forgiveness. While it's true that some bosses get satisfaction from fixing blame, far more feel good about forgiving, especially if the apology is accompanied by a plan for correcting the problem.

Here is the basic formula for apologizing:

1. Acknowledge the error.

2. Let your boss know that she would be justified in getting angry.

3. Thank your boss for being patient and understanding.

4. Offer suggestions for remedying the situation.

When an error occurs, report it as soon as possible. The bad news is better coming from you than if your boss discovers it on her own. Avoid rushing to your boss in a panic, however. First take the time to assess the nature and degree of the error and to formulate some alternatives for controlling and repairing the damage, *then* report the problem.

In reporting an error, observe the following guidelines:

- Deliver factual information. Be objective.

- Don't shift blame to someone else.

- Don't heap blame on yourself. Report facts. Come up with solutions. Don't wallow in guilt. Your guilty feeling really doesn't interest your boss. How you feel should not be the focus now. Assessing and repairing a mistake are the tasks to which you should devote your energy.

Watch Out!
Don't tell you boss how she should feel about you. Apologetic remarks like "You must think I'm a real jerk" invite the boss to start thinking in just that way.

Typical scenarios

Now it's time to put some of this theoretical knowledge about communicating with bosses to work. Let's look at four common scenarios—salary reviews, promoting yourself, promoting an idea, and extending a deadline.

Salary review

From your boss's point of view, it's a salary review. From your point of view, it's asking for a raise. "Why do you need a raise?" Stupid question. *Everyone* needs a raise. There are cars to be bought, mortgages to be paid, children to educate. Your boss doesn't care about any of that. Or, at least, she doesn't care about your needs nearly as much as she cares about *her* needs. So here's the two cardinal rules of the salary negotiation. First, don't bring your needs into the discussion. Second, focus on what your boss needs.

Prepare thoroughly for the salary discussion. You'll need to do some homework, so you can enter the discussion armed with two sets of facts: a verbal resume hitting the highlights of the year's accomplishments; and facts about what others, in similar jobs, get paid (assuming, of course, it's more than you get now).

The most important thing to remember is that you are not *asking* for a raise, but *negotiating* for one. Your aim is not to get something for nothing, but to get fair value for all that you bring to the table.

Play this scenario as a negotiation of value for value. Remember these tips:

Bright Idea
Determine your worth on the job market. How? Good, persuasive, and objective sources for this information are compensation surveys published by trade organizations in your field. This information will not only help persuade your boss, it will enable her to make a decision by providing an objective basis for that decision.

- Good negotiators don't lay all their cards on the table.

- Do sufficient research to form a firm idea of how much more money you can reasonably expect, but do not begin the discussion by stating a dollar amount. The pitfall here is not that the initial number will be too high, but that it will be too *low*, and you'll get stuck with less than you might have bargained for.

- Elicit an offer from your boss. Use that figure as a basis for further negotiation.

Promoting yourself

Talking to your boss about a promotion is similar to negotiating for a raise, because your task is to persuade your boss of your value. You are negotiating a deal, not demanding something for nothing.

Which is harder, getting a raise or securing a promotion? This is really a variation on the classic question: Is the glass half-empty or half-full? The pessimist will tell you that it is more difficult to get a promotion because you are asking for two things: more money *and* more authority. Of course, the same pessimist might also tell you that it's harder to get a raise, because you're asking for more money without doing anything more for it. An optimist, on the other hand, may believe that a boss is more likely to yield on money than on power. Or the optimist will tell you that a boss is more likely to tie a raise to a promotion because she feels she is getting a better deal—paying more, but also getting more.

So don't debate the pessimist-versus-optimist question. Just discard pessimism and embrace optimism. It's the only viewpoint that will do you any good in a negotiation. Follow three simple steps:

1. Begin by deciding what you want: a raise or a promotion.

2. If you opt for the promotion, bear this rationale in mind: You are willing to take on more responsibility.

3. Always go into the discussion armed with a menu of your accomplishments. Your point is that if you did so well in the lesser position, think how much more you can accomplish in the greater position.

Promoting an idea

Query: "How did the idea go over?" The mournful reply: "They shot me down in flames." Look at that metaphor. An image of violent and fiery death is a dramatic indicator of the strength of the bad feelings associated with rejection and humiliation.

As unpleasant as rejection can be, however, it's not really as painfully final as "getting shot down in flames" suggests. Bad feelings are only feelings, after all. Most dissappointments are temporary, and you don't want to miss out on other opportunities because you can't let go of a past rejection.

To promote an idea successfully, you need to make your boss see himself as your partner in the

Watch Out!
If you are undecided whether to go for a promotion or a raise, remember: If you are turned down for the promotion, you are still in a position to negotiate a raise in your present position. If, however, you begin by asking for a raise, you cannot fall back on a bid for a promotion.

project. Get your boss to take an ownership stake in the idea. Try using phrases like, "As you look through the proposal, you might want to take special note of how I incorporated your thoughts . . ." or, ". . . what I did with the concepts you and I discussed last month."

Extending a deadline

Nobody likes to hear excuses, and bosses are certainly no exception. When you miss a deadline, you might well be able to get your boss to accept your excuse, but you will never be able to get him to like it.

The solution? Stop making excuses. Recognize that extending a deadline is buying time, and as with anything else you might buy, the buying of time is a matter of negotiation.

- Persuade your boss to sell you more time in exchange for value received: "To do the best job possible on this, I'm going to need a week more."

- Don't whine about not having enough time. Instead, make it clear what the additional time will buy: a more thorough, successful result.

- When a time crunch threatens, tell your boss quickly—not at the last minute. Even if you have slipped a deadline, you want to demonstrate that you have a firm hold on the schedule. You are still in control.

- Offer alternatives: "I can get x done by Wednesday, y by Friday, and z by early next week." Or, "If I postpone x, I can get you y and z by the original deadline."

The last point is really the key to creating the best possible relationship with a boss, in all sorts of scenarios. You empower and give good feelings whenever you can offer a choice and alternatives rather than a take-it-or-leave-it situation. The creative office politician always looks for the alternatives she can offer.

Just the facts

- Nothing is better for your career than a record of successful performance; however, producing tangible results is not always sufficient to advance a career. Learn to give your boss the right feelings about you and what you do.

- Think of all major interactions with your boss as negotiations, an offer of value for value received.

- It can be very helpful to identify distinctive patterns in your boss's behavior, so you can anticipate and avoid problem scenarios.

- You *can* create positive bonds with your boss without resorting to empty flattery and other "suck-up" behavior.

GET THE SCOOP ON...
Teaching yourself how to be a leader
■ Credibility ■ Effective communication ■
Defining goals and objectives ■ Delegating and
motivating ■ Giving critical feedback and com-
municating praise

On Loyalty and Leadership

Chapter 11

If you accept as absolute truth clichés like "So-and-so is a born leader," or "Leaders are born, not made," there's no reason for you to read this chapter. Indeed, there's no reason for you to read this book, and I apologize for having waited until Chapter 11 to reveal this to you. But let's set aside folk wisdom and catch phrases and, instead, tackle the truth.

It's true that some people probably are, in fact, "born leaders." That is, through a combination of genetics and early childhood experience, they have a natural gift for instantly establishing their credibility in the eyes of others. And it is credibility that is at the core of leadership.

But just because some people are born leaders does not mean that the rest of us cannot work hard, acquire the ability to convey credibility, and thereby *learn* to be leaders. This chapter will guide your leadership learning and practice.

Listen to some leaders on leadership

Learning how to be a leader is not as difficult or mysterious as it may seem at first. Just begin by listening to what leaders say about leadership. You might begin by reading. Many of history's great leaders have left us memoirs, autobiographies, and other opinions on leadership. Other authors have collected such pronouncements. In Appendix C, I've listed several of the most valuable collections.

Once you get your nose out of a book, try actually talking to some of the leaders you work with and admire. Seek them out. Talk to them about what it means to be a leader.

Take another look at the word *admire*. Managers and bosses get hired, rise through the ranks, or maybe are lucky enough to own the company. Not all managers and bosses are leaders. Many volumes have been written in an effort to define leadership and the nature of a leader. But most of us can make do with a simpler, shorter definition: The qualities and traits we generally attribute to leaders are identical to the qualities and traits of the people we most admire.

The credibility blueprint

Think about the people you admire, whether they are bosses, colleagues, family members, or friends. What gives them charisma and credibility? Study those you admire. Learn from them. And while you are studying and learning, bear in mind three elements that are essential to establishing the degree of credibility that is the foundation of leadership:

- **Know what you know and what you don't know.** Leaders are typically self-confident and sure of themselves. Some people are lucky enough to be born confident, it seems. But you don't have to be born that way. Confidence and self-assurance come from knowing your job, knowing your facts, knowing the basis for your own decisions and opinions, and—just as important—knowing what you *don't* know and understanding the limit of your knowledge. The Bible tells us that the foolish man builds his house on sand. Conversely, the wise person builds on bedrock. Intelligent self-assurance, a key to creating credibility, is built on the bedrock of solid knowledge. There is no substitute.

- **Persuade with your ears.** The most convincing speakers and charismatic leaders listen much more than they speak. When you do speak, don't fritter away credibility with idle words. Listen, learn, then choose your own words carefully.

- **Avoid defensiveness.** Express yourself with self-assurance, then listen to all responses, including criticism. Don't try to shout down your critics. Learn from them. Make it clear that you are open to all points of view. Not only will you gain valuable insights, you will also project strength and confidence.

Lay it out

By definition, leadership involves a leader and one or more followers. Any time more than one person is involved in an enterprise, effective communication becomes crucially important. Most of the rest of this chapter concerns such communication, but let's start with communication at its most basic level: how you lay out the task at hand.

66

Leaders are people who do the right thing, managers are people who do things right. Both roles are crucial, but they differ profoundly. I often observe people in top positions doing the wrong thing well.
—Warren Bennis, *Why Leaders Can't Lead: The Unconscious Conspiracy Continues* (1989)

99

Charisma, confidence, persuasion—all are important aspects of communicating a sense of leadership, but there is something even more basic without which all the other apparatus of leadership is empty window dressing.

The effective leader consistently communicates clear objectives and goals, and that begins by understanding the difference between objectives and goals: Goals are long-term achievement targets, while objectives are short-term steps necessary to attain those long-term targets.

The ability to separate objectives from goals and, even more, the ability to decide which objectives are necessary to achieve those goals, are marks of a leader. The truly effective leader not only understands these things herself, but can communicate them clearly to her subordinates.

Bright Idea
Whenever possible, link some form of evaluation to each objective. It's always best to be able to measure the degree of success with which each objective has been attained. Quantifiable evaluation is the simplest and most direct; for example, a particular objective may be defined as achieving a certain sales figure by a certain date.

When you delegate a task, be certain that you and your delegate or delegates agree on goals and objectives:

- Communicate what's to be done.

- Communicate when it's to be done—the deadline.

- Communicate all relevant specifications, limits, budget constraints, and other requirements.

These three items are all dimensions of the objectives of a particular task. Next, give your delegate the big picture. Many leaders covet and hoard information, meting it out to subordinates on a need-to-know basis. Generally, it is more effective to share sufficient information to show how the delegate's task fits into the big picture—how the objectives you have defined advance a project, a company, or a department toward a greater goal.

No one likes the feeling of working in a vacuum. Most people enjoy a sense of accomplishment. An effective leader injects greater meaning into the lives of those he leads.

Think of the example of Rosa Parks, an African American seamstress. In 1955, in Montgomery, Alabama, Parks boarded a bus after a hard day's work. At this time, as in most of the South, public transportation was segregated. African American riders were supposed to confine themselves to the rear of the bus. On this particular day, Rosa Parks decided instead to sit down in front. Told to move, she refused, and she was arrested.

A horrible event, but, in an Alabama town in 1955, an ordinary one. Martin Luther King, Jr., a Montgomery clergyman at the time, saw the big picture of which this event was a part. He had the leadership genius to make others see it as well, and Rosa Parks's courageous action was injected with greater meaning, becoming the "ordinary" event that launched the great civil rights movement in America.

If the prospect of trying to emulate Martin Luther King, Jr. seems both daunting and presumptuous, just remember that what you're after is the *essence* of leadership, and that is giving people a vision. In King's case, it was a vision of the most sweeping, profound, and epoch-making kind. In the case of the average manager or supervisor, it may be a vision of what great customer service means, or of how saving one or two steps in a repetitive process will contribute to greater overall efficiency, and ultimately, the welfare of the entire company.

Choose carefully

Not all leaders have the opportunity to choose their followers, but to the extent that you have a choice of delegates for a particular task, choose carefully. Matching the right person to a given task is a major part of leadership. After all, you are judged by the performance of your subordinates. What's more, choosing the right people saves you worry and time. It allows you to keep your focus on the bigger picture.

Watch Out!
Avoid calling "emergency" meetings, if at all possible. Project meetings should be scheduled in advance. You want to deliver a positive message to your delegates, and unscheduled meetings suggest that you are unhappy with their performance.

Choosing the right person does not, of course, set you free from the responsibility of monitoring the progress of a project. While you don't want to micromanage, do keep tabs on each project. Your bosses expect you to "be on top of" what your subordinates are doing. Also, build in a schedule of meetings for purposes of monitoring projects. Schedule these meetings as far apart as possible while still retaining the possibility of fixing any problems that come up.

Empowerment

No leader routinely delegates more tasks and authority than a military commander. Here's a quick lesson on delegating from General George S. Patton: "Once, in Sicily, I told a general, who was somewhat reluctant to attack, that I had perfect confidence in him, and that, to show it, I was going home."

For many managers, the most difficult aspect of leadership is delegating, and the hardest part about delegating is doing so in a way that empowers the subordinate. Here are some tips to make delegating easier:

- Avoid the sink-or-swim approach. Ease the subordinate into progressively greater levels of responsibility. This is leadership by mentoring.

- Try to allow the leeway to let the delegate perform at least some aspects of the task his own way. Encourage creativity—*well-monitored* creativity.

- Start by delegating repetitive and routine tasks. This not only frees you up, but is the best opportunity for the delegate to gain experience and practice.

- Be there to help, but don't offer help too quickly. If the delegate asks you to determine a course of action, try not to respond with *the* answer. Instead, review with the delegate the various possibilities. Leave as much of the actual decision-making to the delegate as possible.

- Don't be in a hurry to bail out a floundering delegate. First consider adding another member to the team. *Delegate* that person to help.

- Resist routine pressure to do the subordinates' work for them by pointing out your other high-priority work. Assure the delegates that you have full confidence in them.

Giving the right feelings

We have all heard a lot of talk about "management style"—one of those buzzword phrases that seems so full of mysterious meaning. In reality, there's nothing very mysterious about management style. It's the professional or business equivalent of personality. It is, if you will, the *personality* you choose as a leader.

Think about the importance of personality in everyday life. Our moods and emotions change from one day to the next, or even from one hour to the next. But for the most part, the personality we present to the world is perceived as fairly consistent. Our friends and family can be far more tolerant of mood changes than they would be of a change in personality. *That* would be scary. An inconsistent personality makes other people very uncomfortable.

Now translate this situation to the workplace. Your subordinates (as well as colleagues and bosses) may take in stride momentary changes in your mood or emotions, but they will be quite disturbed by an inconsistent management style. So it's best to establish a management style early on, practice it, and stick with it.

66

Leadership, like life, can only be learned as you go along.
—Harold Geneen with Alvin Moscow, *Managing* (1984)

99

But just what style is best? Some managers think of themselves as dictators. Combining limited choices with unlimited threats is actually effective— in the short term. Results are immediate, but not always what is desired. Dissatisfaction among employees is great, and turnover high. Dictatorial managers rarely create successful teams.

At the other extreme is the loosey-goosey leader who gives little direction. With the right team assembled, a laissez-faire management style can work rather well, but you'll need a lot of luck. It's usually difficult to develop a team in a laissez-faire manner, and in a crisis, passive management typically leads to frustration or even panic, for you and your staff.

All things being equal, today's most effective managers resemble the legendary Notre Dame football coach Knute Rockne more than either a dictatorial Mussolini or a let-it-be Gandhi. Such managers aren't afraid to lead, but they do so by example and inspiration rather than by fear. They coach team members to discover and use the best within themselves. They ladle on plenty of positive criticism and encouragement.

The Rockne-style leader creates loyalty and dedication not by delivering a cock-and-bull story about how they work for a great company, but by persuading them that their personal professional goals mesh with those of the company. They consistently paint the big picture, showing how personal success depends on the success of the corporate endeavor.

For the long term, demonstrating the connection between personal objectives and company goals works well. In the short term, however, it is even more important to create in staffers a sense of personal loyalty and responsibility to you. You can do this primarily through effective communication. Always convey the following:

- Your accessibility
- Your willingness to hear—and respond to—grievances and complaints
- Your adherence to absolute clarity about expectations
- Your generosity with positive feedback
- Your equal generosity with helpful and constructive criticism
- Your passion and good humor in every directive and instruction you issue

Motivating ASAP

Management style has an additional dimension. It is not just about deciding whether to be dictatorial, easy-going, or taking a coaching/mentoring approach. Another important element of management style is general attitude and demeanor. How you behave, how you exhibit your prevailing emotions, will rapidly percolate down through your organization. Organizations, whether small departments or entire companies, take their attitude and demeanor from the person in charge.

Bright Idea
While it's important to develop and maintain a consistent management style, you do *not* have to be stuck with an unworkable style just for the sake of consistency. Decide what changes you need to make, then phase them in gradually, one change at a time.

Do you want a grim, depressed group? Project those vibes, and that's what you will end up with. Is the only alternative to walk around with a happy-face smile frozen across your lips? No, unless you want to produce an organization that looks as if it stepped out of *Invasion of the Body Snatchers.*

The effective leader communicates neither unrealistic gloom nor unrealistic cheer. Instead, she consistently projects *enthusiasm.* Getting the best from your team requires that you develop and nurture your own enthusiasm, then convey this to others.

Enthusiasm is a fairly fragile commodity. It is easily killed by insensitive supervision or reckless cynicism. The truly inspired manager circulates among the team, infusing it with enthusiasm by doing the following:

- Talking with team members regularly
- Working closely with the group
- Suggesting new approaches to stubborn problems
- Expressing empathy in difficult situations
- Consulting, coaching, and empowering

Enthusiasm doesn't just happen. It has to be created through informal conversation, through the example of the leader, and through regularly scheduled meetings and brainstorming sessions in which the leader does a lot of listening, but also takes a positive, active role. The effective leader shares information and observations, reinforces positive achievements and attitudes with sincere praise, and continually corrects the team's direction and focus as required.

Critical feedback

The operation of the most technologically sophisticated robotic systems is based on continuous feedback and self-correction. The effective leader can apply this level of cutting-edge technology to the everyday tasks of management. Truly exceptional leaders give effective feedback:

Watch Out!
As a manager, share only as much information as you safely can. If trade secrets or corporate confidences are considerations, exercise appropriate restraint in painting the "big picture"!

- They focus on actions and the results of actions, not on personalities. By placing emphasis on action rather than attitude, they avoid either sugarcoating their criticism or using it as a bludgeon of attack.

- They are specific. They avoid blanket statements or wholesale judgments. Instead, they cite specific actions and discuss them in detail, if possible using objective data such as quantities, costs, time, and sales figures.

- They are supportive. Effective leaders recognize that any criticism, no matter how constructive, provokes anxiety. They balance criticism with praise. They emphasize what can be done better next time rather than what was done poorly this time. They convey confidence in the staffer's ability to create satisfaction.

The role of critical feedback in leadership is so important that it merits a closer look. Consider the following guidelines:

- Approach the task of criticism as a mentor or a coach, not as a cop or a judge.

- Make your loyalties clear. You want to convey that your commitment is not only to yourself and your company, but to the development of the staffer as a member of the team and as a future leader.

- Although criticism should be delivered in a timely fashion, think before you pounce. Be certain of the need to criticize. And stop yourself before you use criticism as a means of venting frustration, anger, or irritation. If what you are about to say is not likely to improve the situation, just don't say it.

- Be certain that the cure will not be worse than the disease. Decide if the problem is worth the risk to a vulnerable ego. Choose your battles wisely.

- Ask permission to criticize. Many leaders find this difficult to do because they believe it conveys weakness. But the contrary is true: Asking permission before you offer criticism enhances the effectiveness of your remarks. Instead of approaching a staffer with something like, "We have to talk about how you're handling so-and-so," begin with "We have a problem with so-and-so. May I speak with you about it now?" You won't be refused, and the staffer will feel that he has not relinquished all control.

Bright Idea
Critical feedback must be given soon after the event. Criticism is most useful when an action is fresh in your mind and in that of the staffer. Also, delivering timely feedback increases the chances for remedying a situation effectively. Finally, if you criticize "ancient history," you will give your subordinate the feeling that you are ambushing her.

- Be discreet. Never criticize someone in front of others. Take the person aside, subtly. Find appropriate privacy.

- If possible, avoid criticism first thing in the morning or at quitting time. Criticism is not a good way to start the day, and it is typically of no benefit to give somebody something to fret about at home.

- Keep your sense of perspective. After all, you and the staffer are on the same team. So be friendly and constructive.

- Criticize only what can be changed. Don't criticize a subordinate for something over which she has little or no control.

- When a cabinet member suggested to Civil War president Abraham Lincoln that the United

States should declare war on Britain, the President calmly replied, "One war at a time." Follow Abe's example. Address one issue at a time. Avoid overwhelming the staffer with a cluster bomb of problems.

Meaningful praise

The business world is still clogged with a number of spare-the-rod-spoil-the-child managers who protest that "grown-up" employees don't need and shouldn't expect praise. Isn't the opportunity to earn a living enough, they ask?

One look around shows just how wrong-headed this belief is. Our world is full of rewards, awards, and ceremonies of public recognition. Positive reinforcement is not a new-fangled leadership theory— it's as old as ancient history, and its usefulness is a matter of plain old common sense.

Not only should you go out of your way to praise staffers for good work, including the same level of specifics you include in criticism, you should also consider establishing a regular program of reinforcement meetings. Make such meetings totally positive and upbeat. Serve refreshments, or just share a funny story or two. Greet attendees with kind words. Tell everybody how great they look this morning. Share the specifics of what you are praising. Talk about results.

Team talk

Ever wonder why we remember little or nothing from babyhood? Most psychologists believe that we remember little because we lacked the language necessary to translate experience into memory. To a great degree, it is language that constitutes our reality. That's why it is so important to use words that

Timesaver
One of the most enjoyable aspects of a reinforcement meeting should be brevity. Hold it to a half-hour or less. Provide just enough time to cite, in some detail, several positive examples. Don't lecture. Make the reinforcement meeting interactive.

create a team reality in the workplace. Use the language of team building, and you will make it much easier to fulfill a leadership role.

Fifty team-building words and phrases

Consider the following words and phrases. Make every effort to work them into your workday vocabulary. They are part of the language of team building:

Bright Idea
Whether dealing with an external customer or an internal one—a colleague, subordinate, or boss—remember to ask "How may I help you?" rather than "May I help you?" The *how* coaxes the other person into focusing her needs, which increases the odds that whatever you communicate or transact will have a satisfactory result.

advice	future
advise	get your input
analyze	give guidance
ask your advice	glitch
assist	hear your take on this
build on this	help
collaborate	How may I help you?
consider	How do you want to proceed?
consult with you	improve even more
control	invest
cooperate	join the team
cope	lead
counsel	learn
create satisfaction	lesson
create progress	make progress
determine	manage
discuss	navigate
Do you understand?	perspective
evaluate	plan
excel	procedure
expedite	realize our goals
formulate	reconsider
full cooperation	

rethink   What would you suggest?

revise   What part is unclear?

team effort

Twenty-five words and phrases to avoid

Just as it is important to use the right language, it is vital to avoid destructive language, the words that attack self-confidence and tend to tear down teams. Avoid these 25 team-killers:

Bright Idea
There is an easy way to avoid team-killing language. If you catch yourself talking like a parent, bite your tongue. The language you use should be adult to adult, not parent to child.

better shape up	foul-up
blame	hopeless
can't do it	impossible
catastrophe	know what's good
crisis	for you
demand	mess
destroyed	misguided
disaster	must
don't worry about it	no choice
don't ask	not allowed
exploded	you wouldn't
fault	understand
figure it out yourself	you'd better
force	

You could add to this list any words that border on the abusive or the coercive. They will not help you to lead.

The next chapter puts into practice the principles of this chapter and discusses leadership and team building day-to-day and situation-by-situation.

Just the facts

- Although some people do seem to be "born leaders," leadership is a skill that can be learned, practiced, and honed.

- Two very important elements of leadership are *credibility* and the capacity for *communicating* that credibility to others.

- The effective leader provides those she leads with meaning and direction by discretely defining goals and objectives.

- Delegating tasks and authority requires both courage and a mentoring spirit.

- It is important to develop a consistent management style that includes plenty of feedback in the form of creative criticism and generous praise.

GET THE SCOOP ON...

Creating motivational speech ▪ The importance
of optimism and enthusiasm ▪ Encouraging creative thinking ▪ Progressive discipline ▪ How
effective managers say no ▪ Leading by example

Using the Carrots and the Sticks

Chapter 12

No subject is richer or more varied than that of human motivation. Why people do what they do is the focus of the behavioral sciences, religion, ethics, and literature in all its many forms. We are fascinated by what makes people tick . . . and perhaps also intimidated by the subject. After all, something so vast and profound must be mysterious and complex, a subject for a Freud, a Tolstoy, or at least a highly paid management guru.

Well, there is a long way around the subject of motivation, a twisting route winding through the secret places of the mind and heart. But there is also a shortcut. Here it is: People are driven by a desire to survive. Period.

Anything that enhances survival—ranging from a big bonus check to an encouraging word from the boss—contributes to motivation. If you add to this some guidance and instruction, you stand a good chance of persuading your staff to do what you want and need them to do.

An organization with a liberal but fair policy of compensation—bonuses, salary raises, and other perks—is the ideal setting for generating motivation. You may or may not have any control over such policies at your company. But one thing you *can* do, apart from handing out cash, is to say the right things to create the right feelings to motivate the right actions to achieve the desired objectives and goals. In this chapter, we'll look at some suggestions.

Motivational speech

The extremes of motivational speech are praise and criticism, and the effective manager gives plenty of both. But between these extremes, your language need not be neutral. Everything you say can be positively motivating. Here's how.

First, take every available opportunity to express optimism. Pause a moment, though, to consider what optimism is *not*. It is not ignoring problems or exaggerating good results and neglecting warning signals. It is not calling poor results or poor performance "good." It is not misleading, and it is certainly not lying.

> **"** Perpetual optimism is a force multiplier.
> —Gen. Colin L. Powell, 1995 **"**

Optimism is seeing everything in the best *possible* light—with the emphasis on "possible." It is seeing the proverbial glass as half-full rather than half-empty.

Get into the habit of looking for truthfully positive messages to deliver. If you were looking for a 10 percent increase in sales and achieved only 5 percent, stress the achievement and talk about how it will "inspire us all to go on to another 5 percent." Don't complain that "we have achieved only 50 percent of our goal" or, even worse, that "sales growth is only half of what it should be" or "we've fallen behind in sales growth by 50 percent."

Don't ignore, avoid, or sugarcoat negative information, but do express it in positive terms. Let's take the example just mentioned. Try approaching it this way: "Sales have increased this quarter by 5 percent. Now, if each of us can reach just three more customers, we can notch that up another 5 percent, which will give us a 10 percent increase for the first half of the year."

The point is always to look for what *can be done,* not what didn't get done or what went wrong. Focusing on the absence of something is the most negative position you can take, unless you also focus on the past. Nothing is more negative than time that has been consumed. No matter how much you think about it, the past is, by definition, a negative quantity. You can worry about it. You can kick yourself on account of it. But you can't have it back. In contrast, focusing on the present and future is, also by definition, positive. It represents the potential for positive, productive action.

As always, watch your language. Again, don't sugarcoat and don't lie, but do find ways to substitute positive terms for negative ones wherever possible:

■ A *problem* can be called a *challenge*—maybe even an *opportunity.*

■ A *time crunch* can be called *accelerated production,* or something that is given a *high priority* or that is *expedited.*

■ A *criticism* can be called *feedback.*

■ A *cost* can be an *investment.*

■ A *lack of a particular skill* might be termed an *opportunity for professional development.*

Dress up your speech. A good way to convey optimism is to make your everyday speech as

Bright Idea
Become a collec-
tor of anecdotes
and bits of wit
and wisdom that
you can use to
drive home your
leadership direc-
tives and goals.
Clip good stories
out of newspa-
pers and maga-
zines, file them
away, and trot
them out as
needed.
Illustrative anec-
dotes and power-
ful analogies
humanize your
leadership style,
making what you
say more mean-
ingful to others.

enthusiastic as possible. If a project is nearing completion, say that it is *on the verge of completion* or *on the
threshold of completion*. If your company or department beat out the competition, tell your staffers that
we annihilated them. If your department wins an
award, make sure you describe it as a *prestigious
award*. Make events special with the language of
embellishment.

Information, please

Inspiration begins with information. Nothing is
less inspiring or *less* motivating than the feeling of
aimless activity and uncertainty of direction. Keep
the following points in mind:

- Be crystal clear in all of your directives and
  instructions.

- Set clear goals and objectives. (See Chapter 11.)

- Make schedules and evaluation criteria clear.

- Be certain that team members understand the
  benefits of accomplishing a particular task. Give
  them a reason to be doing what they're doing.

Whenever possible, quantify your instructions:
"We need to survey 10 clients by June 3rd." The
more concrete and immediate your instructions, the
more highly motivating they will be.

Of course, it's not always possible to quantify
your communications. In these cases, use metaphor
and analogy to make what you say as real and as
immediate as possible. For example, "We need to
make this sale" is clear enough, but not very motivating. Make it *real:* "We need this sale the way
Microsoft needed to sell IBM on buying its DOS
operating system back in the 1980s." To consider
another example, "If at first you don't succeed, try,
try again" is so trite, it hardly makes any impact. You

need to make your message *immediate,* concrete: "Thomas Edison tried more than 1,600 substances before he discovered a workable filament for the electric light. Keep plugging away. It *will* pay off."

Positive praise

Giving something good usually costs you something valuable—money, for example. But giving praise costs you nothing. In fact, it is *failing* to praise that, in the long run, costs you. No motivational tool is more powerful than praise. Its presence is keenly felt, and so is its absence.

There are six rules for using praise effectively to motivate your staff:

Rule 1: Always look for things to praise. Don't issue empty praise, but do praise absolutely everything that deserves it. It is up to you to go out of your way to identify praiseworthy events, acts, words, and ideas.

Rule 2: Praise whatever you want more of. Praise is positive reinforcement. If you want your staffers to be more attentive to customers, pounce on the next example of good customer service that you see. Praise it. Then find another, and praise it. Reinforce the behavior, and you'll produce more of the same.

Rule 3: Deliver praise in a timely manner. Behavioral psychologists learned long ago that it is important to associate positive reinforcement as closely as possible with a desired behavior. Any time lag between the behavior and the reinforcement greatly reduces the effectiveness of the reinforcement. The lesson here? Praise quickly. Don't put off kind words. Seize the moment.

Rule 4: Deliver praise as publicly as possible. There is certainly some value in taking an employee aside and praising him privately, but the value is multiplied many times over if you praise the person in front of his colleagues. This leverages your kind words. Not only do they come across more strongly and more satisfyingly to the target of your praise, but they give others an opportunity to participate in the good news. Why do you think shows like the Academy Awards, Tony, and Grammy presentations are so popular? We like being praised and honored, but we also enjoy participating in the praising and honoring of others. This is all the more true when we are associated with them.

Watch Out!
Praise is free, but don't make it cheap. Avoid dispensing empty, meaningless praise. Always attach praise to something specific—an idea, an action, a good result.

Rule 5: Praise specific things. There is nothing wrong with telling someone that she is "doing a great job," but the praise is much more powerful if it's tied to specific accomplishments, actions, or events: "You did a great job handling the Smith account." If you can add even more, so much the better: "Thanks to you, it looks like they'll up their order by a dozen units." And maybe even more: "This will bring our third-quarter figures up by a full percentage point."

Rule 6: Look to the future. Praise is great, but it always relates to the past: what *has been* accomplished. Conclude your praise with a glance toward the future: "If you can keep satisfying customers like that, we ought to have one terrific year!"

Progress report

It would be great if you could deliver a motivating speech, add a few words of praise along the way, and just sit back and watch performance soar. Sometimes it almost works that way. Usually it does not.

Experienced gardeners know that, with some plants, you just put them in the ground, give them a little water, and let nature take its course. With others, however, you must provide careful monitoring and constant care. They are high-maintenance plants. Typically, these are the gems of the garden, well worth the trouble it takes to nurture them.

Usually, leading a team is like gardening these prized plants—a more or less high-maintenance endeavor.

- Begin by setting clear objectives and goals.
- Establish clear-cut criteria for measuring progress.
- Monitor progress. Keep a record of progress toward objectives and goals.
- Provide ample feedback. Discuss performance with your staffers. Provide helpful evaluation.
- Don't leave the people you lead in the lurch. If progress isn't what it should be, offer helpful direction and advice, and/or work with the employee to come up with alternative courses of action.
- As appropriate, suggest additional training, reading, or whatever else you think will speed progress in the desired direction.

Criticism without the crush

In Chapter 11, we looked at some strategies for creatively criticizing those who report to you. Let's take criticism to another level here. Let's take it beyond

Timesaver
Make sure that formal employee evaluation review sessions are interactive dialogues rather than monologues. Lecturing an employee is usually less time-consuming than having an actual give-and-take conversation, but, in the long run, time consumed in an interactive exchange is more usefully invested than less time spent on a one-way speech.

correcting a particular problem and toward more generally (and permanently) encouraging the kind of creative thinking that will maximize performance and minimize the need for criticism.

First, make objectives and goals clear from the beginning. Set unambiguous performance criteria.

Second, if improvement is needed, set realistic improvement objectives. Asking for the impossible will not create improvement, it will create frustration. Setting objectives you know are well beyond the reach of a particular staffer will not inspire that person to stretch and to achieve; it will create disappointment, frustration, and bad feelings all around.

Third, don't abandon the person you criticize. Coach her. Provide plenty of feedback. Monitor the achievement of objectives. Give praise.

Always be certain that the objectives, goals, and performance criteria you establish are meaningful to everyone involved. You need to provide and explain valid reasons for the performance objectives, goals, and criteria you set. It is not sufficient merely to set them. For example, you may have decided that each salesperson should average 10 cold calls per day. Why? Make it clear: "If each rep makes 10 cold calls a day, we can expect three additional sales per week. That alone will keep the department on track for the quarter."

Remember: Offering criticism creates a contract between you and the employee. Both parties are obligated. You cannot turn your back on someone whose performance you have criticized.

- Don't just talk—listen. Listen carefully. Do not censor what the employee says. Do not interrupt. Be patient.

- Don't just declare—ask questions. And don't just ask questions—ask questions that invite extended responses. Instead of asking simple "yes" or "no" questions, ask open-ended ones: "What would you do to make communication with customer service more effective?"

- Offer advice and direction. Ask for honest feedback to your advice: "Do you think this suggestion will help the situation?"

- Provide positive emotional support. Saying "If we can improve your performance in this area, there is no limit to what you can achieve" is far more effective in producing improvement than saying "If you don't improve in this area, you'll find yourself looking for another job."

Ethics of progressive discipline

There are situations in which you, as supervisor or manager, are called on to do more than coach improved performance. If poor performance or misconduct is serious enough or becomes routine, it's time to institute *progressive discipline.*

Progressive discipline is an orderly procedure of incremental warnings designed to send a clear message to an employee: Correct the situation or suffer termination. As a manager or supervisor, you cannot afford any of the following:

- Consistently subpar or destructive performance from an employee

- The needless loss of a potentially valuable employee

- Legal action from an employee who feels he has been disciplined or terminated unjustly

Subpar performance must be confronted aggressively and constructively. Do everything you can, as we have just discussed, to motivate the employee in the desired direction. If diligent coaching fails, you

Watch Out!
Don't confuse—and don't let the employee confuse—criticism with rejection. By criticizing an employee, you make a commitment to help that employee improve. Criticism is cultivation. Rejection is abandonment.

need to begin progressive discipline. Your career and the welfare of your company, as well as the well-being of the employee, hang in the balance.

Although it may not be immediately apparent, you are not doing the employee any favor by allowing him to continue misperforming or misbehaving. Through vigorous action, you may be able to correct the situation and salvage the employee. Even if this fails, it's better to terminate an employee who just cannot be persuaded or trained to work as required. Maybe he will do better in another job at another place. Maybe the experience of termination is precisely the wake-up call this person needs. In any event, there is no benefit to perpetuating failure or destructive behavior.

In the absence of stated company policy on progressive discipline, the following is a reasonable and ethical course of action:

- Before discipline or discharge takes place, warn the employee. The most important part of the warning is a precise description of the misperformance or misconduct.

- Be certain to follow any verbal warning with a written warning if the misperformance or misconduct is repeated or persists.

- Make certain that you are being reasonable. Is what you are asking of the employee feasible? Are you applying policy reasonably?

- Make certain that you are being fair. Never single out one employee for discipline if you wouldn't discipline others in the same way. Rules and standards must be applied evenhandedly.

- Discipline promptly. As we discussed earlier, very little time should be allowed to elapse

Timesaver
Many firms, especially larger ones, have clearly stated policies on progressive discipline. If any employees report to you, it is critical that you become thoroughly familiar with this policy and follow it to the letter. Adhering to such company policy will save time and grief for all concerned. And it may even save your career.

between the misperformance or misbehavior and the warning.

- Follow every warning with an employee conference. Take notes during the conference. Record the date accurately.

When you have to say "no"

Praise is fun to give. Creative criticism, given in the right spirit, can be quite a gratifying coaching experience. Progressive discipline is a delicate and demanding task, which many managers face with dread. Fortunately, it doesn't happen every day or even every week or month. But there is another delicate, demanding, and often distasteful task that does come around frequently and that every effective manager must master.

It's called saying "no."

Why is saying no so difficult for so many of us? The answer is that most of us make the mistake of saying no to the *person* who makes a request rather than to the *request itself.* The truth is that you can say no to the request without negating, denying, or rejecting the requester. Not only does this make your task easier, it makes the negative response easier for the other person to hear, too. In business, always focus on issues, not personalities.

Here are some steps to take to say no to a request, without alienating an employee:

1. Listen without interruption, unless you need a point clarified.

2. Engage in active listening by showing that you have understood the request by rephrasing and summarizing it.

3. If there's any part of the request that you *can* satisfy in some degree, begin with that.

Bright Idea
Many companies specify that an employee's record be purged if, after a certain period (typically 12 months), the problem cited does not recur. Consider adopting or encouraging the adoption of such a policy. It's important for employee morale.

Demonstrate that your priority is satisfying the employee, not denying his request.

4. Say no clearly and unmistakably, but gently. Do not hem and haw or beat around the bush. Do not offer false hope.

5. Express sincere regret that you cannot satisfy the request or that you cannot satisfy it completely.

6. Explain the reasons for not satisfying the request. This step is the most important of all. Never leave it out.

7. Try to put the request in proper perspective, and develop your negative response in the context of department or company needs and goals. These will ultimately benefit the employee. Help the employee to see the big picture and to realize his stake in that picture.

8. Express your wish that the refusal will create no great hardship or disappointment.

9. If possible and appropriate, suggest an alternative.

10. If you can, offer *rational* hope that the request may, at some time, be satisfied. Just make certain that there are conditions under which the request might be satisfied in the future. Be as specific as possible about these conditions and the time frame.

11. Acknowledge the employee's understanding, and thank her for it.

Bright Idea
When turning down an employee's request, shift the focus from what you cannot do to what you *can* do—even if this is substantially less than what you were asked for.

"I want a raise"

Perhaps the most frequent occasion for "no" is an employee's request for a raise. If you find yourself having to refuse such a request, follow the steps just outlined, and remember the following as well:

You can make the situation easier for you and the staffer by establishing clear guidelines and policies, including annual or semi-annual performance reviews. Firmly establish that raises will be considered only at the set review time. This will at least reduce the number of occasions on which you might have to say no.

Too often, we allow ourselves to be placed on the horns of a dilemma, limiting ourselves to an all-or-nothing response. Don't make the mistake of seeing salary issues in terms of an absolute *yes* or *no*. If you can't swing a requested raise in salary level, perhaps you can offer the following:

- A lesser amount
- Enhanced benefits or perks
- Additional paid vacation
- Flexible hours

Remember, stress what you *can* do, not what you *can't*.

"It's *my* turn"

Turning down a request for promotion may be even more difficult and demanding than rejecting a bid for a raise. The reason is that the dangers of offending pride, of injuring self-confidence, of implying that you don't trust the employee or appreciate her accomplishments, are intensified when the employee is asking to take on greater responsibility. Saying no to a promotion can erode morale and motivation.

It is critically important to avoid making the employee feel that she has reached a dead end and should seek opportunity elsewhere. Try responding with these four points:

Watch Out!
Don't use the phrase "company policy" to justify the refusal of a promotion. This will be taken for exactly what it is: arbitrary and inflexible—a cop-out.

1. Say no, but be certain to give a full explanation for the response.

2. If possible and appropriate, provide hope for the future. Be as specific about this hope as you can honestly be. Outline the conditions and performance expectations under which a promotion might be made in the future.

3. Agree on steps that may be taken to make the promotion possible at some future time.

4. Don't promise any action you cannot take, but do at least try to set a firm date for a new performance review.

Demonstrate your willingness to take all requests seriously and in good faith. Employees may be disappointed if they don't get what they ask for, but they will be enraged—and rightly so—if they feel that their requests are thoughtlessly dismissed by a boss who doesn't care to listen to them.

You as role model

Of the many clichés to which inept leaders habitually resort, perhaps the lamest, is "Do as I say, not as I do." This is lazy and destructive. Face it: The leadership role is a demanding one, and it requires a complete commitment. This means not merely giving direction, but leading by example. Consistently, the most effective way to shape the behavior of others is to present yourself as a positive role model. You want those who report to you to do as you say *and* do as you do.

To achieve this level of leadership, remember the following:

- Ensure that your words are not contradicted by your actions. If, for example, you demand that your staff treat one another with respect, consistently demonstrate respect in your dealings with them.

- It is not enough that your words and deeds do not conflict. They must positively support and reinforce each other. If you tell your staff to deal with customers honestly, go out of your way to demonstrate a high degree of honesty and integrity in your dealings with staff and customers.

- If you stress the value of character, present yourself as a model of character. Avoid cynicism, irony, and sarcasm.

Do you want to cultivate loyalty and a work ethic in your staff? Exhibit these qualities in the way you relate to them, to colleagues, to customers and clients, and to bosses. Above all, present a model of professional behavior, consistently working hard, demanding excellence, and expressing yourself in positive, optimistic terms. Whether you like it or not, your personality—or, more precisely, the personality you project in the workplace—will be reflected in the attitude, words, deeds, product, and performance of the people who report to you. The things your subordinates say and do *are* your career.

Just the facts

- Motivation is a full-time leadership job; motivational words should be a part of the language you speak in the workplace.

- Cultivate realistic optimism, the habit of expressing yourself in terms of what can be done rather than what went wrong or what is impossible to do.

- Leadership requires establishing clear objectives and goals, monitoring progress toward these, and providing ample feedback about this progress.

- Effective leaders are generous with meaningful praise.

- It is essential to effective leadership that you learn to say no, when necessary, without alienating the person whose request you decline.

- Ultimately, the most effective leadership tool you have is yourself: Lead by example.

Let the Games Begin

PART IV

GET THE SCOOP ON...
Office politics: liabilities and benefits ▪ The art
of ethical manipulation ▪ Becoming influential ▪
Killing destructive gossip ▪ Disarming the back-
stabbers ▪ Looking beyond your office: building
a network

The Good, the Bad, the Ugly

Chapter 13

Y ou've now read the chapters in this book about working with bosses and subordinates, and you've read a tome or two on management. What's more, you actually know your job, and you're actually good at what you do. So what does your boss do? She goes ahead and gives the promotion to the person down the hall, the one who couldn't manage a hamster and has no idea of what he's doing about anything.

Infuriating? Yes. Unfair? Yes. Unusual? Not at all. Welcome to the world of office politics.

You can run, but you can't hide

Most people find out about office politics when they become its victim. How do you know you're a victim? Look for these telltale signs:

- You expected and deserved a promotion, but a less-deserving inferior coworker got it instead.

- You find that you are dropped from a certain e-mail routing list. You no longer routinely receive management memos.

- You are criticized, way out of left field, at a meeting.

- You are no longer asked to attend certain management-level meetings.

- You aren't invited to the boss's birthday party.

- You discover that you are the subject of office gossip.

- You are scapegoated—blamed for things that aren't your fault.

- You can no longer rely on the cooperation of colleagues.

"
Sharks have been swimming the oceans unchallenged for thousands of years; chances are, the species that roams corporate waters will prove just as hardy.
—Eric Gelman, *Newsweek*, October 1, 1984
"

These are some of the negative impacts of office politics. If you've suffered any of these, take them as a wake-up call. You need to get in touch with the political situation that, like it or not, you happen to be in.

But despite the negative connotation of the phrase, office politics is not all bad—especially if you don't wait until you are victimized to become aware of politics around you. Office politics is a set of strategies people use within an organization to further their careers. When other people use these strategies against you, office politics is a dirty, rotten business. But when you use these strategies to your benefit, it's savvy business.

Ethical manipulation

Just about every office has at least a few—and sometimes more than a few—Machiavellian types. Perhaps you remember Niccolò Machiavelli, the 16th-century Italian political theorist who wrote a book arguing that a determined ruler could and should act with complete moral indifference. For some people, politics, whether in the office or in government, means using what President Nixon's men called "dirty tricks"—and the dirtier the better. As some see it, where careers are concerned, all's fair.

In some offices and industries, ruthlessness does pay off. People climb a corporate ladder fashioned out of the knives projecting from the backs of their colleagues. Do you want to prosper this way? Can you live comfortably with yourself if you do? No one's listening; you can answer honestly. And if the answer is yes, just consider that the karma of the corporate world is typically pretty thick. What goes around comes around. Wield a long knife, and you're likely to get cut. After all, Richard M. Nixon was the only president in U.S. history who ever quit—or had to.

However you look at office politics—as simply evil, as a necessary evil, or as a set of positive strategies for advancement—at its heart is manipulation. Now that word definitely has negative connotations, often in connection with the word *underhanded*. But it doesn't have to be negative. It's very possible, and often desirable, to practice ethical manipulation.

Become influential

Ethical manipulation is based on the assumption that the more influential you can make yourself, the more powerful you become—and are perceived to be. The more powerful you are perceived to be, the more powerful you will become. This isn't a vicious circle. It's a very sweet one, as long as you make it work for you.

How do you make yourself influential? By selling your influence to others. The more ideas and initiatives of yours that others—especially bosses—adopt, the more influential you become. Begin one idea at a time.

Only the fittest will survive, and the fittest will be the ones who understand their office's politics.
—Jean Hollands, *Newsweek*, September 16, 1985

As usual, follow the power

Archimedes said of the power of the lever, "Give me a lever and a place to stand, and I'll move the world." An idea is a wonderful thing, but you can't do much with one unless you find the right lever. If you keep the idea to yourself, nothing will come of it. Of course, you can share your idea with a colleague. This might stimulate an interesting conversation. But, depending on the colleague, you might find that *your* idea has suddenly become someone else's.

Don't squander your idea. Identify someone in your office—it might well be your boss—who has power and influence. That person is the lever that allows the idea to be lifted. Win that person over, and you've multiplied the effect of your idea, just as a lever multiplies the effect of your arm muscle.

Watch Out!
The bandwagon strategy will fail if used on people who pride themselves on being cutting edge or who strive to be different. Always assess your target, and proceed accordingly.

But how do you sell your chosen "lever" on your idea? One, if it's a very good idea, simply present it as effectively as possible. Miracle of miracles, many good ideas, if clearly presented, go a long way toward selling themselves. Two, use the bandwagon strategy. In most businesses, nothing finds more favor than a "brand-new idea that's worked well in the past," a "time-tested innovation!" Try to demonstrate that other influential people, groups, or companies are using an idea like yours. Or make a strong comparison between your new idea and a time-tested idea that has already proven itself successful. Finally, use the we-don't-want-to-be-left-out technique: "Everyone is getting into e-commerce on the Web. We don't want to be left out."

Selling benefits

There are many other strategies for selling your idea. Perhaps the most straightforward is to stress the benefits of compliance with your idea or suggestion. The benefits you underscore must apply directly to the person you are trying to persuade: "Starting the special customer support group certainly will give you a greater voice with upper management." Don't hesitate to say how your idea will benefit the company, but put the main emphasis on the *personal* benefits your "target" will enjoy.

The undercut: a master stroke

In some situations, you can gain what you want by purposely undercutting yourself while you elevate your "target." For example: "I'm certainly not the expert on customer support in this specialized area. *You* are. That's why I came to you with this concept."

Bonding

Purists may fancy a business world in which ideas are promoted and implemented strictly on their merits. Good ideas just naturally float to the top, while the dregs, just as naturally, sink.

Doubtless this happens sometimes. But a lot of ideas get acted on because somebody in power likes the person who is promoting the idea. There's nothing new about business associates building friendships and then taking advantage of those friendships for business purposes. It's a given: You are better off *professionally* if people like rather than dislike you *personally*. And you are even better off if powerful people like you.

So why not work at being liked? Be friendly. Cultivate warm personal relationships with the people who hold the power and influence in your firm. Here's why:

■ It's easier for a top manager to trust the professional judgment of someone she knows socially.

- It's harder for that manager to shoot down a friend than it is to ax someone who just occupies the cubicle down the hall.

- A top manager is more willing to go the extra mile for a friend than for a mere subordinate or associate.

If you can't beat 'em, make 'em join you

You may get through your professional life making few enemies or maybe none at all, but even the most highly respected, successful, and best-liked people have their opponents on this or that issue. Often, the most effective way to cope with an opponent or potential opponent is not to avoid but to embrace him.

Bright Idea
Making an ally of one potential enemy often makes allies of other potential enemies; that is, this one ally leverages others.

Suppose you want to start a special customer support group, but you fear that Joe Schlub in sales will perceive this as an encroachment on his turf, and will therefore oppose the idea. To preempt this, you recruit Joe: "Hey, Joe, I really need your input on developing the special customer support group. I hope you have some time to serve on the Steering Committee." Recruiting a potential "enemy" is a fast and efficient way to gain his support.

Great idea!

Persuasion is always easier if the people you are trying to persuade become convinced that the good idea is *their* idea. Once you discuss your idea with the person you've identified as a key mover and shaker, start referring to it as "our" idea rather than "my" idea. Let's say, for example, that you've convinced Joe Smith to support your idea. Now you take it to Jane Doe: "Jane, Joe and I have been working on an idea for a special customer support group, and we really need your input . . ."

It takes a certain strength of character and self-confidence to let others in on the credit that should be yours and yours alone. But, then again, it does you little good to be given sole credit for an idea that fails to fly.

Bear in mind, however, that you have to show some flexibility. Suppose, for example, that you've become a savvy office politician. You approach a person you've identified as a real mover and shaker, a person you need to recruit in support of your idea. You trot out the "Great Idea!" strategy: "Bill, thanks for your input. I'm ready to take our idea to management."

"Now just a minute," Bill says. "*Our* idea? Are you trying to manipulate me?"

Busted! How do you get out of this one? Simple—just come clean: "As a matter of fact, Bill, that's exactly what I'm trying to do. I need your help to make this idea fly. Right now, it's just an idea. You can make it work, and I really think it will be good for all of us."

The rumor mill: don't be grist

Maybe this has happened to you. You send an e-mail to the guy down the hall, and he doesn't receive it until a half hour later. What's going on? Doesn't electricity travel at the speed of light? Well, if you want *really* fast communication *every time*, don't rely on e-mail. Start a rumor. It will get around in no time at all.

No office with more than two people is without gossip. The impulse to gossip is natural and inescapable—and, for that matter, it's not all bad. Good-natured gossip can be a sign of a healthy workplace. If people don't get along with one another, they tend not to talk with one another. If,

66
Gossip, unlike
river water, flows
both ways.
—Michael Korda,
1976
99

in contrast, they do get along well, they communicate freely. Some other benefits of business gossip:

- Grapevine gossip builds relationships among coworkers. It socializes the office.

- Grapevine gossip creates personal bonds that may facilitate professional working relationships.

- Grapevine gossip builds a sense of group identity.

- Grapevine gossip boosts morale, adding a bit of interest to the day.

But it is also true that gossip can be destructive, especially if you are the unwilling subject of it. It's important that you curb potentially destructive gossip and rumors concerning you. Use common sense here. Act and speak in a manner that provides little material for the gossipers. Be discreet; don't air your dirty linen in the workplace. And don't gossip about others' personal lives. This is an open invitation to others to gossip about you.

If you are approached with gossip about someone, make it clear—without being offensive or acting superior—that you're not interested in hearing the gossip:

> **Gossiper:** Did you hear about Ted and Alice?
>
> **You:** Mary, I have a report due out. I can't really take the time to discuss Ted and Alice just now.

That's as far as you need to take it. (And, yes, it does require a lot of self-discipline to deny yourself the guilty pleasure of hearing *all* about Ted and Alice.)

If you find you've become the subject of malicious gossip, don't ignore the situation in the hope that it will pass. If you can identify the source of the gossip, seek him or her out. Don't make any accusations. Instead, ask for help:

> **You:** Fred, I don't know if you've heard this story going around about Alice and me.
>
> **Fred** *(with obvious embarrassment)*: Uh, well, yes, uh, I've heard something . . .
>
> **You:** Well, you can be a real help to me. You know how destructive such gossip can be. There's absolutely no truth to it. I know how influential you are. You're very well-connected here. People listen to you. So I'd appreciate it if you could spread the word: There's just nothing to this gossip. I'd like to save Alice and myself needless embarrassment. Do you mind helping us out?

Sometimes, gossip is not entirely groundless, but a distorted version of the truth. There are two strategies for setting the record straight. First, use the air of confidence. Find old Fred again—the person you believe to be the source of the gossip. Talk to him about the matter in question. Use a confidential tone: "Fred, those rumors about what I'm doing with the Smith project are a riot! Have you heard what they're saying?" Then, as if in confidence, tell Fred the story you *want* people to hear. You can depend on Fred's spreading the word.

Second, in the case of a falsehood that you feel must be corrected immediately, consider distributing an e-mail to everyone in the office. You might begin: "It has come to my attention that a rumor is circulating to the effect that I intend to . . ." Summarize the rumor, then continue: "Misinformation like this can be very destructive. I owe you the truth, and here it is." Then give the correct

Bright Idea
Remember, not all grapevine material is bad! While you should demonstrate a complete absence of interest in personal rumors, don't discourage small talk or the informal exchange of professional information. But draw the line at malicious words.

version of the story. Avoid lecturing or any expression of anger. Just provide the facts.

What's that sticking out of your back?

Much gossip, even destructive gossip, starts out innocently enough. For many people, dishing the dirt just comes naturally. But there is another class of person who is truly malicious and will stop at nothing to damage you if she sees a way to profit thereby. Let's look at a few types in this section.

Dodging the schemers

Anyone cold-blooded enough to practice calculated back-stabbing may well be sufficiently skilled and practiced to catch you entirely by surprise. In fact, plenty of people never realize they've been victimized. Gradually, for no reason apparent to them, their career just goes south.

Generally, if you find yourself afflicted by some of the symptoms described at the beginning of this chapter—exclusion from meetings, a feeling that you're being cut out of the loop, a failure to get an expected promotion—you should suspect foul play. Also watch out for a colleague who is suddenly and inexplicably "nice" to you—overly concerned about your welfare, for example, or worried that something may happen to you. And beware if you enter a room, and all present go dead silent.

We'll talk in a moment about some steps to take if you suspect the work of a back-stabber, but, as with most bad things in life, the best cure is prevention:

- Cultivate good corporate karma. Be considerate of others. Make it your primary mission to be liked at work.

- Engage in creative small talk, as we discussed back in Chapter 5.

- Gather a few reliable allies. Don't wait until you're under attack to do this. Begin from the first day on the job.

- Don't engage in malicious gossip.

- Do your job very well indeed. Make yourself valuable.

Credit where credit is due

Perhaps the most common form of back-stabbing is credit-grabbing and idea-stealing. This does not mean that a colleague will rifle through your desk drawers in search of your top-secret documents. More typically, the idea thief will listen to you talk casually about an idea, then simply appropriate it, boldly presenting it as her own at a later time.

Of course, if you don't share your ideas at all, they never get known. And you often must share ideas with colleagues in order to gain support for them. So how do you strike a compromise between collaboration and paranoia?

1. Put your idea in writing before you discuss it. Distribute the written idea, dated, with a note that it is a draft, that you are seeking input, and that you intend to have the completed proposal ready by such-and-such a date.

2. Choose your confidants carefully. Don't trumpet your thoughts to everyone indiscriminately.

3. If the thief is bold enough to present your idea as hers in a group meeting, rise in challenge. Keep it simple: "Jane, that's the idea I presented to you on Friday, isn't it?" And if you get a denial, don't let up: "It isn't? Just how is the idea you're discussing now different from the one I discussed with you Friday?" This is no time to be shy or polite.

Watch Out!
Don't indulge a paranoia for credit-taking. You want to receive recognition for your work, of course, but if you are too hesitant to share your ideas with others, you'll lose a chance for help and good feedback.

4. Kill this form of back-stabbing whenever you encounter it, even if it doesn't affect your own idea. If you've been privy to Sam's idea and now Ed presents it as his own, call him on it: "Ed, that's the idea Sam discussed with me two weeks ago, isn't it?"

The smiling killers

Consider the colleague who's never been particularly friendly but who is suddenly *very* friendly. Your best bud. "Look," he says, "I don't like to talk behind anyone's back, but Hal in Accounting has been saying some pretty rough things about you. I think you should know about them." And he goes on to the details.

What you need to suspect is that your new "friend" is working a scheme to undermine your collegial relationship with Hal, or, perhaps, to undermine your self-confidence in general.

Here's another common ploy: "You know, I really like you and enjoy working with you. So I'd hate to see you go. You need to know something the boss said about you." Same motive—to undermine your relationships and self-confidence—only more so.

There's a good reason why hearsay evidence is inadmissible in a court of law: It's highly unreliable. Never act on the basis of hearsay. Go to the supposed source. Explain the situation—"So-and-so told me that . . ."—and talk it out. And before you even seriously consider a hearsay message, ask yourself: Why is this person suddenly so friendly and so willing to be helpful? Then go on to consider what he has to gain from helping you out. Think about your past relationship with the person and about his reputation.

Emotional manipulation

Yet another variety of back-stabber is highly manipulative—in an emotional and utterly unreasonable sense. She will appeal to you with an emotionally urgent reason for doing something: "You've got to back me up on this project or I'm sunk. I don't know what I'll do. You *can't* say no!" Any time a colleague tells you that you have no choice, you'd better begin to choose. The first choice? Whether or not you want this manipulative, clinging weight hanging around your neck.

People who make such inappropriately emotional appeals probably are not consciously back-stabbers. Quite likely, they just can't help themselves. But what does it matter? They can be dangerous. If they can't help crossing the line between business and whining, they might not hesitate to cross the line between persuasion and blackmail: "If you don't back me, I'll have to go to Mr. Chambers about . . ."

About what? The fact is that most of us have made mistakes from time to time, and we are vulnerable to threats of blackmail. Here's what to do:

- Choose not to become attached to the emotional manipulator. Do you really owe this person anything?

- If you don't have to work with her, don't. Steer clear as much as possible.

- If you are threatened with out-and-out blackmail, go to the boss—now, before the blackmailer gets there. If there really is an issue in the past, get it out in the open. Calmly explain the situation. You cannot be threatened with a secret that's in the open.

Unofficially... Don't assume that everyone in business acts from rational motives. At least 20 percent of any given population suffers from some form of mental illness, including illnesses that can disrupt typical rational thought. And a fair number of psychologically "well" people have thought processes you could never hope to figure out. For this reason, it's always best to deal with problems, actions, and issues rather than with personalities.

Removing the shiv

Often, the most effective way to deal with a back-stabber is not to deal with him at all, but to focus your efforts on cleaning up the mess he has made. If, for example, you are made a scapegoat—falsely blamed—fight back with the truth. If you are offered "help" from a smiling killer, don't accept the offer. If you are the target of a nasty rumor, work on broadcasting the truth.

But sometimes there is no viable alternative to confronting the back-stabber, especially if he is a repeat offender:

1. Begin by arranging a meeting—not a hallway confrontation, but a meeting. This will catch the back-stabber off guard.

2. If the problem is chronic, arrange for someone from Human Resources to attend the meeting as a neutral third party.

3. Confront the supposed issue, not the person: "I hear that you have some problems with the way I've been handling the Smith project. I'm not aware of any problems. Can you help me out?"

4. Avoid anger, sarcasm, or a "gotcha!" attitude. Focusing on the issues is actually the worst punishment you can inflict on the back-stabber.

5. After you have talked, assuming that the back-stabber doesn't fold, direct future behavior: "Fred, in the future I'll expect that you'll come directly to me if you have a problem with something I've done."

6. Don't tell the back-stabber that you've been offended or hurt by his actions. Don't hand this person a victory.

Watch Out!
If possible, avoid going to your boss about the actions of a back-stabber. Even if reporting the problem results in action against your antagonist, it may make you look incapable of handling the situation yourself. However, do not hesitate to bring in the boss if the back-stabbing escalates into physical threats, sexual harassment, or verbal abuse.

7. Conclude on a positive note, no matter how negative you may feel: "Fred, I hope that, from now on, we can keep the lines of communication open between us." Manage a handshake.

Network news

Do you think your cubicle is small? Well, the entire office is small, too. The savvy office politician does not confine her career to the space of a department or even a company. "Networking" was a hot-button word of the 1980s and early 1990s world of work. It's heard less often now, but it's still a valuable concept. As a theory, it's quite simple: Networking is getting to know people in your industry or line of work who can alert you to job opportunities in different departments, divisions, or companies.

The key to practicing effective office politics is to have as many options available as possible. Having to choose between a couple of unpleasant alternatives or among very limited possibilities is no choice at all. And to the degree that you are deprived of choice, you lack power. Networking opens doors beyond your immediate work environment.

Making connections

How do you go about putting together a network? First, consider which people you want to be in it. If you have those proverbial "friends in high places," by all means start with them. But all you really need are people who can serve as antennas, sets of eyes and ears alert to what's going on in your industry.

Stop now and make a quick list of all of your professional colleagues—everyone you know in your industry or field, including your clients and customers. The names on this list are all excellent prospects for membership in your network.

Now start contacting some of the people on your list. Keep it low-key. Ask for help, but don't demand it.

> Hey, Pete, I'm calling to ask you for a little help. I'm thinking about my prospects beyond Acme Widgets. I'm not job hunting yet, but I am testing the waters, and I was wondering if I could sit down with you for a half hour or so to have what, for lack of a better word, I'd call a networking meeting.
>
> I am *not* going to hit you up for a job. I just want to talk to you about who's who at your shop and anywhere else you might know about—who I should see—and I want to talk to you about the outlook for the industry in general.
>
> I can drop by your office at your convenience. But I would like to make it *your* office, since I'm not eager for anyone here to know that I'm "looking around."

Pete may have valuable information for you, and he may also be able to put you in touch with the person who matters most, as far as you're concerned—the person with the power to hire you. And if your network consists of three or four Petes, you have the start of a pretty powerful network.

Keeping doors ajar

Through one of your Petes, try to obtain an introduction to a boss, to someone with the power to hire you. Arrange an informal meeting with that person:

1. Begin with thanks for the meeting, and be sure to reiterate who recommended you. Remind the person of the reason for your visit. "I'm not looking for a job right now, but I would like to

Timesaver
When starting a networking meeting, avoid misunderstanding and resistance by making it clear that you are not sneaking in for a job interview. "I'm just trying to see what's out and about in our industry. Of course, if you know of any specific opportunities, I'd appreciate hearing about them. But I haven't come here with that expectation."

pick your brain about industry trends, growth areas, and specific people I should talk to."

2. Provide a thumbnail sketch of your background—no more than two or three minutes.

3. You've got the floor. Now ask your questions. Try to cover the following: the job market in your industry, specific job leads, and the outlook at this person's company.

Then invite this important person to talk to you about his or her experience. What advice does he have for you? What does he see as the smart move now?

Don't allow the conversation to go beyond a half hour, unless you are specifically invited to continue. When that time has elapsed, thank your host, leave him with a business card (if you have one), and depart.

Congratulations! You have conducted an informational interview—and you have added a brand-new "node" to your network. Do this two, three, perhaps four more times, and you will open doors beyond the confines of your office. This is the ultimate step a savvy office politician can take.

Just the facts

■ Office politics can be dirty, but "office politics" isn't a dirty phrase; at its best, it's a set of strategies people use within an organization to further their careers.

■ Positively considered, office politics can also be defined as the art of ethical manipulation.

■ The savvy office politician finds and exploits opportunities to make himself or herself increasingly influential.

Bright Idea
The evening after your meeting, sit down and write a thank-you note for the time this stranger has invested in you. Do not omit this important step.

- The nasty side of office politics includes malicious gossip and back-stabbing. These are real problems, but they can be effectively coped with.

GET THE SCOOP ON...
Conflict is inevitable—and not all bad
• Causes of conflict • Managing conflict
• Working toward mutual solutions • Managing
verbal and physical abuse

Office Diplomacy

Chapter 14

olitics is about building influence, and office
politics is no exception. One way to build
influence is to make yourself valuable and
admired by doing your job very well. But that isn't
enough. Another way, which we discussed in
Chapter 13, is to "sell" your ideas and opinions to as
many coworkers and bosses as possible. That's a big
step, but it isn't enough, either.

The savviest office politicians build reputations
as office diplomats, the people whose counsel is
sought whenever trouble rears its head or conflict
brews and boils over.

As the Good Book says, "Blessed are the peacemakers." In an office, peacemakers are always in
demand, for there is rarely a shortage of difficult
situations to be resolved, difficult decisions to be
made, and difficult people to be dealt with. This
chapter will help you handle all these difficulties,
not just because they *must* be handled, but also
because they present opportunities to practice
career-building office diplomacy.

Conflict is like death and taxes

There's no place for friction in high school physics problems. It complicates the math to at least a college level. Friction makes problems more difficult. And the same is true in the real world: Friction makes problems more difficult. But unlike in high school physics, you can't choose to ignore it; it *has* to enter into your calculations. Only two things are certain in this world, Benjamin Franklin said: death and taxes. He should have added friction as well.

> **"**
> Arguments are
> to be avoided;
> they are always
> vulgar and often
> convincing.
> —Oscar Wilde,
> *The Importance
> of Being Earnest*
> (1895)
> **"**

Of course, we're not just talking about the mechanical friction created when physical bodies rub up against each other, but the mental and emotional friction that results when two or more personalities rub together. Such friction is not an exception in business life, a rare occurrence, or an accident. It's a part of the physics of the workplace—inevitable.

Friction is conflict and vice versa. Just as mechanical friction can have results ranging from a slow wearing away to a sudden catastrophe, so workplace conflict can:

- Wear everyone down
- Slow everything down
- Make everyday tasks more difficult
- Generate enough heat to cause an explosion

But, friction isn't all bad. In fact, it's necessary. If we had to spend our lives walking across ice or oil slicks, we'd slip-slide around, but wouldn't get very far. It is through friction in the physical world—and conflict in the social world—that we move ahead.

In the workplace, the task is not to eliminate conflict, but to manage it. This means minimizing or resolving it where it is destructive and making effective use of it where it is productive.

Causes of conflict

Conflict can occur whenever two or more people don't agree on how to handle a situation. It's that simple. Since people don't think or feel in an identical fashion, because their needs and motivations vary, it is too much to expect perfect agreement on every situation. In fact, if each situation that arose in your workplace resulted in perfect agreement, you probably wouldn't stay in business long. Multiple perspectives are valuable. Remember, in resolving conflict, your object is not necessarily to erase disagreement, but to keep disagreement from escalating into destructive conflict. What can cause this escalation?

If two men on the same job agree all the time, then one is useless. If they disagree all the time, then both are useless.
—Darryl F. Zanuck (1949)

- **High stakes situations.** Disagreeing over what brand of coffee to put in the office coffeemaker is one thing, but disagreeing over whether to invest several million dollars in project A or project B is another. When the stakes are high, the pressure is on, and tolerance may shrivel.

- **Crisis situations.** All crises come down to a radical reduction of options. A situation arises in which we feel cornered or trapped. This is why a crisis is so hard on the nerves. Feeling trapped, we tend to respond in a primitive, unreasoning way. Emotions are raw, and the potential for explosive conflict is real.

- **Conflict of personalities.** If people were chess pieces, conflict might not be eliminated, but it would be completely predictable. If you're a pawn, you know that you'd better not line up against a rook. But people are people, and it's not always possible to predict in advance who will get along easily. Besides, it is the nature of the workplace that you may find yourself paired with a difficult person and may have no choice in the matter. You've got to find a way to make things work.

- **Conflict of objectives, goals, or needs.** Suppose that the Sales Department wants more advertising dollars, but Production wants those same dollars to go into adding features to the product. The dollars are limited. Who wins?

The conflict management concept

The Roman philosopher Publilius Syrus observed that "agreement is made more precious by disagreement." The first step in managing conflict is to learn to value conflict. As noted earlier, we move ahead by means of friction. And "two heads are better than one," as the cliché goes. Of course, two heads thinking *identically* is redundant. It's only when two heads have different points of view that one person can contribute something helpful and novel to another. So you should learn to value multiple perspectives, and coach others to value them as well.

Here's the core of good office diplomacy: When conflict arises, do not respond negatively to it. Do *not:*

- Try to stifle it
- Gloss over it
- Ignore it
- Admonish people to "grow up" or "behave"
- Bully one person into accepting the point of view of another

But *do:*

- Invite both (or all) sides to present their points of view

- Focus on the issues instead of on personalities

- Respect delicate egos, but try to keep them out of the conflict

- Encourage discussion

- Let people know that disagreement is healthy and creative

- Express thanks and gratitude for so many good ideas: "This is a lively debate. I think we're getting some really valuable perspectives on this problem."

- Remind all involved that you are working toward a common solution to a common problem for the common good

- Reinforce the idea of teamwork

Bright Idea
A general rule: Availability of options reduces conflict. Whenever possible, offer the people who work for you, with you, or above you more than one viable option.

Sometimes, management of conflict—good office diplomacy—is a matter of becoming a cross between a coach and a referee. Thinking of yourself as such can be a valuable aid to maintaining your perspective in a volatile situation. This analogy has its limitations, however. In a football game, the roles of coach and referee are clearly defined, and whatever else they may be, they are *not* the players. In business, however, although you may find it helpful to act as a coach or a referee from time to time, you are also, inescapably, a player. As such, there is ample opportunity for you to get sucked into a conflict.

How can you stop yourself from becoming part of the problem? Avoid reacting emotionally. In tense situations, when the stakes are high, when a crisis looms, or when somebody just rubs us the

Bright Idea
Fixing your attention on an object while regathering your wits is like the old trick of tying a string around your finger to help you remember something. There's nothing magical about the string. Similarly, there's nothing special about the object on your desk. It's just a reminder. Choose one now.

wrong way, we often respond without thinking. How can you remind yourself to think before lashing out? Look around your office or cubicle. Find some particular object on your desk. It doesn't matter what that object is, as long as it's always there. Now, tell yourself that whenever you are about to react without thinking, that object will remind you to stop, to hold your tongue, to listen, to think, and then to respond to the issues and not to the person.

Consider the example of management advisor Clay Carr (in *The New Manager's Survival Manual*, Wiley, 1995). Carr borrowed an idea from a colleague. He puts an eight-inch green foam ball on his desk. He tells his staff what the function of that ball is, so everyone knows that, before they lash out, they are to look at that ball and *think*.

Carr also borrowed an idea from Dean H. Shapiro, Jr.'s *Precision Nirvana* (Prentice-Hall, 1978). Instead of putting your reminder on your desk, Shapiro advises, keep it in your pocket. Shapiro suggests carrying around in your pocket a small counter, like the ones golfers use to keep their score. Whenever you find yourself tempted to react with reflexive negativity, punch the counter.

The idea is to do something to snap you back to awareness, and substitute thought for the mindless reflex arc of stimulus-and-response. The amazing thing is, it really works.

Now, once you get yourself thinking instead of simply reacting, think about this: Why should your objective necessarily be to defend yourself against an opinion, idea, or point of view that differs from yours? Maybe the other person is wrong. But maybe not. You have one brain, one imagination, one set of eyes and ears. Here is somebody offering you the benefit of another brain, another imagination, another set of eyes and ears. Why not thank him for the gift? "You know, Mike, I never thought about it this way. Let me give this some consideration, and let's discuss it further."

Baby steps

Now let's look at some specific steps toward managing—not eliminating—conflict. Each is a small step. But taken together, they make up a full toolkit for the effective office diplomat.

Label it

Writing about the ultimate form of conflict, warfare, the early-19th-century military theoretician Karl von Clausewitz created a concept he called the "fog of war." Combat is so full of movement and noise that obtaining and maintaining a clear picture of just what is happening can be difficult or even impossible. Often, Clausewitz wrote, the combatants are lost in the fog of war and fight without clear knowledge of objectives and effects.

All conflict, whether on the battlefield or in the boardroom, is subject to a similar "fog of war." In a crisis and when emotions are running high, it's often difficult to penetrate the sound and the fury and see the crux of the conflict. But you can cut through the fog somewhat. Use that object on your desk to remind you to think before you react. Then start thinking. Take a deep breath and try to define the conflict. What is it about, really? What are the real issues involved? Be as specific as possible.

Defining—labeling—the conflict is an important step, not only for resolving the issues more effectively, but for averting emotional escalation of the conflict. Before emotions boil over, say to the

"
There cannot be a crisis next week. My schedule is already full.
—Henry Kissinger, 1969
"

other person or people: "Let's stop a minute to think about what exactly is at issue here. Bill, why don't you go first? What do you see as the main problems?"

Let Bill talk. Don't interrupt, and don't let others interrupt: "Now, Mary, let's hear Bill out. Then we'll get your take on this. I need to understand this thing from all sides."

Pick your fights

Who says you *have* to get involved in any given conflict, anyway? True, sometimes a conflict comes to you, and when this happens, you can't just walk away. But you don't automatically have to intervene in every conflict you run across, and you don't have to fight every battle that comes your way. When you see a conflict brewing, ask yourself:

- Are the issues worth expending energy on?

- Has the other person made up her mind?

- What happens if the other person wins? Can you live with the results?

- If you let the other person win now, will this give you bargaining chips for next time?

- Does this particular problem have to be attacked at this particular time?

A time and a place

Avoid ambushes. Don't pick a fight with someone in the hall, and conversely, don't let yourself be dragged into a public argument. Once spectators figure into the picture, issues recede into the background, and egos come to the fore. It's one thing to feel that you have to save face in the eyes of one other person, but quite another when a dozen pairs of eyes and ears are watching and listening.

Conflict should not be a spectator sport. Do all you can to arrange for the discussion of potentially volatile issues in private and at a time that is convenient for everyone involved.

One at a time

One of the particularly unpleasant aspects of disputes with one's spouse or "significant other" is the tendency of one or both parties to begin with one issue and then dredge up a host of complaints, so that they all start to run together in one ill-tempered blur. The same thing can happen in the office. To avoid this, try to focus on a single issue. If you must address multiple issues, separate them and deal with each one separately.

Speak specifically

Frequently, disputed issues are lumped together under some vague category: "Your department is always late." Such blanket statements are usually unfair, rarely helpful, and almost always provocative. Break it down, and be specific: "Your department was a week late with the numbers on the Smith project. Before that, on the Blake project, the deadline was missed by four days. Let's try to figure out what's going on here."

Defining specifics not only reduces the destructive emotional impact of a dispute, it also sets up the conditions that make finding a solution much easier. Defining a problem is at least 50 percent of solving a problem. Why not give the other person a head start reaching the solution you both want?

Address issues, not people

If any technique can be called a panacea for avoiding the emotional escalation of disputes and even for resolving them, it is the practice of addressing

Bright Idea
When you're dealing with conflict, your first impulse may be to seize the home-court advantage by arranging to have the meeting in your office or cubicle. However, this may merely put the other person on the defensive. Consider finding neutral ground, such as a conference room.

the issues rather than the people behind the issues. Keep these points in mind:

- The issues are what you want to resolve.
- It is far easier to create change in issues than it is to create change in people.
- An issue has no ego. A person does.

Watch Out!
Avoid the pronoun *you*, if possible. Instead of "You forgot to revise the schedule," try, "Next time, please remember to revise the schedule." This avoids the language of accusation and blame and puts the emphasis on avoiding a future mistake rather than on rehashing a mistake made in the past. No matter how recent, the past is gone; it can't be retrieved and changed.

Avoid blaming and name calling. These practices can only make the situation worse. Moreover, help the other person avoid blaming and name calling. Caught up in emotion, the other person may not realize he's lost his cool. Try something like this: "Ed, I can't think when I have to shout. Let's take it down a notch or two."

Listen and *hear*

Let the other person speak. Resist the temptation to interrupt or to shout him down. Use the active listening skills covered in Chapter 5. Very often, conflict can be resolved just by giving the other person an attentive hearing.

Everybody's a winner

If the techniques just discussed succeed in resolving the conflict, great. But even if they succeed only in cooling tempers and getting people to talk rather than shout, you've gone a long way toward resolution. Anger is a self-sustaining emotion. Something sets a person off, but it's the sound of raw voices, of bellowing, of the exchange of sharp words, that stokes the fires of rage. If everyone is acting angry, no one walks away feeling like a winner. If, on the other hand, angry emotions are resolved, everyone will feel that something has been accomplished. And once the shouting dies down, something may actually *be* accomplished.

Let's take conflict resolution another step forward by making all involved feel as if they have gained from the encounter.

A mutual solution is the Holy Grail

Let's face facts—not every conflict can be resolved with a perfect solution, one that makes all sides feel like winners. Nevertheless, that is your quest. Begin by recognizing that you and all the other people involved are on the same team, then abandon the idea of conflict resolution as a zero-sum game—that is, a process in which someone has to lose in order for someone else to win. Here are some steps to take toward resolving a conflict to everyone's satisfaction:

- After you've defined the conflict, begin to shift the focus from areas of disagreement to areas of agreement.

- Begin by working with the areas of agreement.

- Next, discover what is needed to bridge the areas of disagreement. What is working? What isn't? "We agree that the project is feasible, but, John, you need more data. Ellen, how much time do you need to provide the research?" Instead of tearing each other down, start putting together an action plan in which everyone has a doable function and a realistic objective.

Speak again specifically

As you formulate a solution, hang on to the facts. Just as it's important to describe the conflict or problems in specific rather than blanket terms, so it is critically important to formulate the solution in a specific way.

Agree on an action plan

Once a solution has been formulated, work out, together, an action plan. First, list the tasks that need to be done. Next, assign everyone involved a specific task. Then set objectives, goals, and measurable performance criteria.

Then execute the plan

Resolving a conflict is hard work; don't let all that effort slip away. Good office diplomacy has much in common with leadership in general, including the paramount need to follow through. Directives and plans are important, but they mean nothing without good execution. Remember to do the following:

- Follow the discussion with a memo outlining whatever action plan has been agreed to.

- Check up on the progress of the resolution. You may need to apply a gentle prod.

- Recognize that you may need to renegotiate various aspects of the resolution. Stay open. Avoid expressions of exasperation. Keep the tone collegial, cooperative, and upbeat.

Bright Idea
The follow-up memo should be distributed (by e-mail, perhaps) to all concerned. It should include all task assignments and relevant deadlines.

Thorns among the roses

Now here's some bad news. Workplace friction is not always issue-oriented. It does not always arise from this or that particular crisis or conflict. Some people are just . . . well, the polite word is "difficult." If you like, substitute your own less polite word.

Just as difficult bosses tend to fall into certain recognizable categories, as we discussed in Chapter 10, so difficult colleagues and subordinates may be readily classified, as we'll look at in this section.

Dealing with office bullies

One of the ugliest and, unfortunately, most common personality problems found in the workplace is the presence of the office bully. Bullies are usually easy to recognize. They bluster, bellow, and berate. Yet, perhaps surprisingly, some bullies employ subtler tactics. Instead of engaging in openly abusive language, they find ways of expressing themselves that nevertheless make you feel inferior.

Here's how that typically works. Let's say you propose a particular approach to a certain project. The subtle bully won't comment on the merits of your proposal, nor will she even criticize it. Instead, she'll say something like this: "You've *got* to be kidding. Who would even *think* of doing it that way?"

It can be difficult to remain poised and confident under such an attack. But, remember, these are only words, not facts. They're hollow, and they're quite without logic. You can puncture the bully's verbal bubble by replying—calmly, without annoyance or anger—with the facts: "This approach will accomplish such and such and will reduce costs by . . ." Facts blow right by the bully's verbal assault. They show it up as simply irrelevant.

A bully is never a solo act. She absolutely requires a victim. Without one, a bully is just a person screaming. So refuse to be a victim. If you find that difficult, examine your reasons for allowing yourself to be intimidated. What are you afraid of? Try listing these fears on a piece of paper, and then dealing with them one by one.

But avoiding victimization really doesn't require years of psychoanalysis. Try these simple tactics:

■ Avoid the bully whenever possible.

■ Substitute e-mail and memos for face-to-face contact when dealing with a bully.

■ When a bully explodes, just let it happen. Stand aside silently—while maintaining continuous

Bright Idea
Focus on facts
when dealing
with a bully's
explosion. Let
the bully rant,
wait for the
storm to die
down (even tem-
porarily), then
reply calmly with
the facts, what-
ever they may
be: "Three issues
remain outstand-
ing, that require
discussion
between you and
Smith. Let me
outline them for
you . . ."

eye contact—and let the bully vent, rant, and rave. Don't show fear or emotion. When things calm down, respond with the facts.

■ Stand your ground, without defiance. Don't argue, but be assertive. For example, you ask the bully for an expense report. His response is to holler about how he can't be bothered with things like that now. You let him holler, then you say: "I understand, but I still need the expense report." You may start sounding like a broken record, repeating whatever it is that you need. Fine, as long as you get the result you want. And you probably will—few bullies can survive a war of attrition.

Bullies are emotional vampires. They don't need to suck your blood in order to survive, but they do require your fear. Don't give them their nourishment.

Coping with passive-aggressive personalities

Passive-aggressive people come on as easygoing, even meek, but they have a knack for sabotage. They can be undependable. You ask for some critical task to be performed, the staffer agrees, and then, some-how, some way, it remains undone. You confront the passive-aggressive person. "Oh, I'll get to it," he assures you. "Don't worry."

And that is your signal to start worrying. Or, more accurately, it's your wake-up call to the fact that you are dealing with a passive-aggressive person. You must monitor such a person's work closely, or you will rarely get him to do what you need him to do. Use the following tips:

■ Monitor the person.

- Keep reminding him of the schedule. (Make certain that you establish a timetable for every assignment you give this type of person.)
- Monitor some more.
- Repeat instructions as necessary.
- Repeat objectives and goals.

Don't try to deal with the underlying sources of the passive-aggressive personality—you have neither the time nor the expertise to practice psychiatry. Just address the behavior and the results of behavior by the steady application of schedules, evaluation of progress, and repetition of instructions, goals, and objectives. Get what you need, then move on.

Handling the complainer

It is part of human nature to complain. If you work with a complainer who whines, but nevertheless gets the work done, count yourself at least semi-lucky. Listen to the complaints without much comment (you really don't want to draw them out), and press on with the tasks at hand. Some people use chronic complaining as a means of avoiding your assignments. Hardcore complainers tell you that such-and-such is impossible, won't work, or can't be done. Or they tell you they don't have the time, equipment, personnel, or even skill to do a given task.

If someone tries to pull this with you, you must act. Your first step must be to determine if the complaint has any basis in reality. It is a serious mistake to reject complaints out of hand, without considering the underlying reality. After all, our work environments are by no means perfect, and sometimes people are justified in claiming that certain tasks are impossible. Once you determine that you are dealing with a chronic complainer, however, be firm.

- Do not discuss the merits of the complaint.

- Do not sympathize with the complainer.

- Repeat how important the problem or task is to you.

- Repeat that it is necessary to solve it.

- Tell the complainer to try to tackle the problem, and assure him that you will evaluate the result and offer suggestions and help as necessary.

Resign yourself to having to remind the complainer, probably more than once, that he has agreed to tackle the assigned task. Repeat the steps just mentioned, as necessary.

Complainers are not just limited to subordinates, of course—their ranks include colleagues and bosses. And they don't just complain about assignments. Whiners are all-purpose gripers, cry-baby types who find no end of things to complain and protest about. You name it, they'll whine about it:

- Burdensome workloads

- The weather

- Broken rules

- A slow morning commute

- The behavior of others

Here are some tips for dealing with habitual whiners:

- If the whiner's issue can be feasibly addressed, do so. If you get complaints about the lousy coffee in the break room, it's easier and more efficient to assign the whiner the task of finding a better coffee than to try to persuade the

Watch Out!
Never automatically dismiss a complaint. Investigate the underlying reality before you assume that you are dealing with a chronic complainer or whiner. If something can be fixed, fix it.

whiner to stop complaining and act like a grown-up.

■ Whining may be a plea for attention. Your first impulse is probably to scold the whiner; your second just to avoid him. But instead of giving in to these natural impulses, make an effort to say something nice to the whiner. Offer a compliment. Look for something to praise. Do so as frequently as possible.

■ Gently confront the whiner with his whining. Suggest other ways of responding to the reality around us all.

■ If a whiner complains about another employee, don't get caught in the middle. Refuse to take sides, but do take steps to alleviate the tension. Arrange a meeting, in your presence, between the whiner and the object of his complaint. Talk through the issues.

Verbal abuse

Verbal abuse may take very obvious forms, such as name-calling, foul language, and "conversation" at the top of one's lungs. It should not be tolerated. Do not let the verbal abuser slide.

If you are the victim of verbal abuse, the most effective action you can take is to remain calm, but take control of the situation. The abuser wants to hurt and intimidate you. Don't let this happen. Instead, let the abuser know that her behavior will have an immediate consequence:

> Jill, this kind of language is inappropriate, and I won't listen to it. I'm going back to my office now. Why don't you come in to talk to me in half an hour—that is, if you can speak to me in a civil, professional manner by then.

Bright Idea
Not all forms of verbal abuse are directed at any particular person. Foul language and off-color humor directed at targeted groups of people are also dangerous ingredients in any office mix. For advice on coping with these, see Chapter 15.

Leave, but do so on your own terms. Respond to abusive language by simultaneously removing yourself from the situation *and* taking control of the situation as you do so.

If you find yourself in a situation where abusive language is directed at another person, prepare to intervene. Of course, it is possible that the combatants can settle the matter themselves, so don't rush in to referee. But if it's apparent that one worker is victimizing another, recognize that the probable cause is anger. It is your job, as a savvy office diplomat, to manage the anger:

- Place yourself between the combatants. This is often sufficient to interrupt the flow of nasty energy.

- Discuss the source of the anger. As usual, try to shift the focus from personalities to issues. If John is furious with Mary because she is repeatedly late with reports, focus on the steps that can be taken to expedite the reports, not on Mary's "laziness" or "incompetence" or "uncooperative attitude."

- If possible, remove the causes of anger. Through discussion, discover the trigger of anger. Address that trigger, especially if it's something that can be remedied.

- If the verbal abuser does not quickly calm down, make it your top priority to protect everyone else from him. Isolate the angry person. Take him outside, into your office, or into an empty office or conference room.

- With the verbal abuser isolated, let him vent. Don't scold. Don't censor. Don't issue admonitions to "calm down." You've got the person isolated. Now, let 'em rip.

- Don't insist that workers who are angry with one another "snap out of it" or "grow up and get back to work." You'll have to use more constructive approaches. Consider offering a time-out: "Joe, why don't you take the rest of the day off. Relax. Unwind."

Workplace violence: it's real

No one is quite certain who defined war as "a continuation of politics by every means," but the fact is that, just as among nations, so in the workplace politics and diplomacy sometimes degenerate into war.

We have all read and seen news stories about workers who go berserk and commit terrible acts of violence in the workplace. After what seemed a rash of such incidents among U.S. Postal Service employees, a new expression for workplace violence actually entered the language. Employees who exploded in anger were said to have "gone postal."

Fortunately, the incidence of mentally disturbed individuals perpetrating serious workplace mayhem is rare. However, given sufficient pressure, whether at the workplace, at home, or in combination, a perfectly "normal" individual can cross the line, escalating from angry talk to verbal abuse and finally to physical violence. Whatever form workplace violence takes, it must be considered completely unacceptable and dangerous.

If physical violence erupts, recruit the aid of others to separate the individuals involved, and *keep* them separated. If you have any doubt about your ability to handle the situation safely, put aside any John Wayne fantasies and summon your company's security officers or the police. After the violent episode, it's important that your company's Human Resources Department become involved. For the

Bright Idea
For advice on recognizing and coping with sexual harassment, see Chapter 16.

physical, emotional, and legal protection of everyone involved, the counsel of a specially trained individual is called for.

But remember: As with most workplace conflict situations, prevention is more effective than cure. You can help prevent workplace violence—and create a more congenial and productive work climate in general—if you lead by example. Practice projecting a calm, fair, anger-defusing attitude at all times. This will influence those who work for and with you to do the same. Think about your leadership style. Emphasize teamwork over an atmosphere of command. Often, violence is a desperate, primitive response to a feeling of being trapped. The savvy office diplomat manages workplace conflict so that people never feel trapped. At its best, office politics is about providing alternatives in which everyone gains something and walks away not angry, but feeling like winners.

Just the facts

- Conflict is an inevitable part of life and work; effective leaders use it productively rather than allow it to develop destructively.

- Conflict has many causes, but the typical root is the feeling of being trapped or cornered without choices. Avoid creating such situations.

- Remove emotion from conflict by focusing discussion on the issues involved in the dispute, not on people and personalities.

- Although it's not always possible to find a mutually agreeable resolution to conflict, make it a priority to work toward such a win-win solution.

- The most useful tools for dealing with difficult people are your ears; simply listening is a good first step to settling most conflicts.

- Prevention is the best cure for verbal and physical abuse in the workplace. Prevention is achieved by developing a nonabusive, nonviolent work environment.

GET THE SCOOP ON...
The business and career benefits of diversity ▪
Assessing your multicultural awareness ▪ The
value of "sensitivity training" ▪ Sexism in the
workplace ▪ Dealing with the disabled ▪ Seeing
people, not stereotypes

Old Boys and Glass Ceilings

Chapter 15

There was a time, not too long ago, when many American offices were racially, ethnically, culturally, sexually, and even politically homogeneous places. And as for people in wheelchairs, they were in hospitals, not offices. All this was especially true in higher levels of management.

Those days are past. Some people still resist diversity in the workplace, of course. Some do so consciously and purposely, while others just seem unable to help themselves. Most people, however, have realized that diversity is not only right (because it reflects the make-up of our society), it's also an essential asset to doing business, because it *does* reflect the make-up of our society. Still, not everyone is automatically comfortable with differences; there is diversity even in the way people deal with diversity. This chapter, on office politics in the diverse office, aims to increase that comfort level.

Bright Idea
Even today, it pays to fit in—but without sacrificing your uniqueness. (See Chapter 2 for what we mean by "fitting in.")

The power of diversity

The subject of diversity elicits a range of response, from "What's the big deal?" to outraged diatribes pitting "liberals" against "conservatives" and "big government" against "struggling free enterprise." In this book, we've talked a lot about the importance of feelings—giving people the "right feelings" and respecting other people's feelings. But in the case of diversity, feelings, whatever they may be, have to take a backseat to reality.

A favorite phrase of the 19th-century American writer-philosopher Margaret Fuller was "I accept the universe!" Hearing this, the notoriously crusty British writer-philosopher Thomas Carlyle is reported to have replied: "Gad, she'd better!"

This is one way of looking at workplace diversity. As with the reality of the universe, you'd *better* accept it—what choice do you have? But that's a sour, dyspeptic point of view. Why not accept the differences around you as the valuable gifts that they are?

Your multicultural assets

Multiculturalism has been fostered for primarily social and legal reasons, beginning, in the United States, with the Civil Rights Act of 1964. But multiculturalism is also critical to business. In the past, within the corporate world, as in nations, assimilation was the accepted norm. Companies and their managers insisted that people who were different must themselves bear the brunt of adjusting to the way everyone else looked and acted. "This is our corporate mold; squeeze in." Within a certain company or a given industry, you wore the "right" suits, you lived in the "right" neighborhoods, you drove the "right" car, and you spoke the "right" language.

Conformity seemed perfectly reasonable and sensible. What's more, it seemed natural: the way things were. And there was a good reason for this, for the culture of any company had evolved over the years in response to the realities of business. Employees were expected to conform. The realities of business reflected the realities of American culture, which was dominated by the idea of assimilation into the culture. People often dredge up the cliché about America as a "great melting pot," thinking it means that our nation has room for everyone of all backgrounds and heritages. But take a closer look at that metaphor. What, after all, is a "melting pot"? It is a crucible in which differences are blended and disappear. The melting pot metaphor is really all about making everyone conform.

And cultural conformity used to seem very important—*naturally*. It seemed to ensure unity and common purpose. It warded off chaos. Employers as well as employees bought into this idea. To conform meant to succeed. Cultural, racial, ethnic, and gender identity—even unique personality—all were checked at the office door.

That is history. Homogeneity is history. And as diverse as American society and the American workplace are today, they promise to be even more diverse in the days ahead. The trends toward more women, more partners in two-income families, more employees who are caring for children or elderly parents, more physically disadvantaged workers, and more older workers entering the workforce will continue and accelerate for the foreseeable future. Add to this the growing racial, ethnic, and cultural diversity in our communities and our

> **❝**
> I'm different, and proud of what makes me so. I can help your team, and I would like to join you, but only if I can do so without compromising my uniqueness.
> —Roosevelt Thomas, Jr., corporate diversity consultant, characterizing the attitudes of many employees today
> **❞**

places of business, and it's obvious that diversity is here to stay.

Demographic change that's this sweeping and profound brings changes to individual consciousness as well. People are less willing to be assimilated, even if it's only for the part of the day devoted to their jobs.

Still, some people think multiculturalism is a real problem, even a threat. The response to this point of view is simple: It's mistaken. For any business in a multicultural society, multiculturalism confers a great competitive advantage. America, always a nation of immigrants, continues to globalize internally even faster. And many American businesses also routinely reach beyond our borders, globalizing externally as well. The diverse workforce reflects and responds to the facts of the marketplace. More and more, corporate recruiters seek people who represent the markets to which they sell.

Know thyself

The first step toward working effectively in a diverse environment is to heed the admonition of the Oracle of Delphi: "Know thyself."

Starting from the twin assumptions—that multiculturalism is here to stay and that it's a positive benefit to your business (and, therefore, to your immediate present and future career)—ask yourself how you feel about diversity by taking this little quiz.

Yes No

☐ ☐ Can you readily look beyond gender? Color? Ethnicity? Disability? Sexual orientation? Can you look at the actual person instead of these things?

☐ ☐ Are you comfortable with people who are different from you?

☐ ☐ Does prejudice influence your treatment of others?

☐ ☐ Are you aware of your prejudices?

☐ ☐ Can you overcome or override your prejudices?

It's up to each of us to confront and answer these questions. The object of answering them is not—at least not for the moment—to create a better, more livable, more just society, though this is no doubt one goal. The immediate goal is simply to do better business, to work more effectively, and to enable ourselves to climb the corporate ladder faster and higher.

Make no mistake. If prejudice directed against you can make your corporate climb more difficult, the prejudices you direct against others, purposely or without thinking, are also weights that drag you down. Keep these points in mind:

■ You are likely to work for or under the supervision of people of all kinds.

■ Your clients and customers will increasingly come from all sorts of backgrounds.

■ The colleagues and subordinates on whom your career depends will increasingly differ in background.

It's easy to grasp and accept the value of understanding your customers' needs, desires, and attitudes. For that reason alone, diversity in the workplace is a valuable asset, as is accepting and working comfortably within a diverse environment.

But that is only one reason. Recall from Chapter 3 that we called bosses, subordinates, and colleagues—the people you work with— your organization's "internal" customers. "External" customers

> **"**
> No loss by flood and lightning, no destruction of cities and temples by the hostile forces of nature, has deprived man of so many noble lives and impulses as those which his intolerance has destroyed.
> —Helen Keller, 1903
> **"**

are the people you usually think of as your customers and clients. They're the people you're in business to serve. However, the people you work with—colleagues, subordinates, and bosses—are also your customers: your internal customers. Transacting business with them is an exchange of value for value, just as it is with external customers. Your advancement always depends on creating satisfaction among your customers, whether they're external or internal. To create satisfaction among internal customers from diverse backgrounds requires not only a mere *tolerance* of diversity, but a high valuation of diversity.

Acceptance of diversity in others decidedly does not require you to submerge your own identity. If you see yourself as a member of a minority—a minority, that is, relative to the others in the workplace—recognize that your unique perspective is an asset, not a liability, to you and your firm. Don't carry your ethnic, cultural, racial, or gender identity as a burden on your back or a chip on your shoulder. Recognize it for the gift it is, and offer it freely.

Sensitivity training

In recent years, many corporations—typically, the larger ones—have engaged consultants to offer "sensitivity training" to increase awareness of diversity and all that it implies in the workplace, and to increase the effectiveness with which people from various backgrounds work with one another.

Some employees and managers look on sensitivity programs with suspicion or cynicism. They see such programs as make-work for consultants or as a set of hoops to jump through in order to dodge the heavy hand of the federal government or a lawsuit from some disgruntled worker. The savvy office

Unofficially... "Minority" is an ambiguous term. "White guys in suits" are generally thought of as the majority in the business world, and everyone else as the minority. Yet, in many communities, white guys in suits would stand out as a small minority indeed. And women, classified by the federal government as a "minority" group, make up about 56 percent of the U.S. population. In 1996, women made up 46.2 percent of the workforce; by 2006, they are expected to make up 47.4 percent.

politician, however, always faces the truth—and let's face it, there is more than a grain of truth in this suspicion and cynicism. After all, federal legislation does protect the rights of minority workers. And lawsuits based on bias of various sorts are an industry in and of itself. These lawsuits can wreak havoc on a company's finances and reputation, and some companies sponsor sensitivity training only to avoid lawsuits, not because they believe in the value of the training.

A real downside to the suspicion and cynicism, however, is that these obscure the more positive reasons for sensitivity training:

- Increased efficiency, productivity, and harmony in the workplace
- Greater understanding of the internal and external customers
- Greater understanding of the marketplace
- Enhancement of career potential

Greater awareness of diversity is knowledge. Period. And more knowledge is always better than less knowledge. The bottom line: If your company offers sensitivity training, but does not require you to take it, take it anyway. And if your company does not offer such training, you might want to suggest that it make the investment. If this is not an option, make it your business to train yourself. The rest of the chapter will give you some ideas and direction.

The etiquette of inclusion

The most effective way to combat discrimination is to stop discriminating. Instead of looking for ways to exclude this or that person, find ways to include more people in more opportunities and more aspects of the job. Some specifics follow.

Male/female issues

Women continue to enter the workforce in increasing numbers. Adult single women, of course, often have to support themselves on their own income. Yet even among couples where the husband earns an income, many women work. In part, this is because couples aspire to a standard of living that is difficult to maintain on one income. But for many women, the choice to work outside the home has little to do with the necessity of bringing in a second income. A great many women derive essential human satisfaction from building a career. Whatever the motivation, by 2006 women will make up more than 47 percent of the workforce, and an ever-growing number of women have climbed to top management levels.

Whether you are a man or a woman, it is long past time to stop thinking of men as executives and women as secretaries, or as men in front offices and women in back.

One of the great obstacles that interferes with adapting thought to reality is language. Sexist language stereotypes people on the basis of gender. It assigns certain stereotyped qualities to men and to women. It reflects prejudicially narrow ways of thinking about the roles and the traits of men as well as women—although sexist language is most often used to the disadvantage of women.

What's so bad about sexist language?

- It is annoying, alienating, and offensive—to colleagues, to subordinates, to bosses, and to clients.

- It tends to limit expectations. Insofar as sexist language narrows the perception of a woman's skills and abilities, it lessens what is expected of her. Sexist language also perpetuates low aspirations.

- It tends to limit what women can do. By defining women's roles narrowly, sexist language excludes women from various jobs.

- Because it limits expectations, reduces aspirations, and sometimes sets limits on the assignments women are given, sexist language squanders valuable human resources and deprives a company of the benefits of diversity.

- Sexist language causes legal problems. The law recognizes the harmful effects of what is called a "hostile work environment." The use of sexist language can contribute to or even create a hostile work environment, and that is the foundation for lawsuits brought on the basis of sexual discrimination. (The important and potentially explosive subject of sexual harassment is dealt with in the next chapter.)

There is, then, every good reason to avoid sexist language. This can be easier said than done. The grossest forms of sexist language are the most easily recognized precisely because they are the most vulgar and most offensive. Any person even slightly advanced beyond the level of a Cro-Magnon will recognize the following language as unacceptable ways to address a woman in the workplace:

babe	fox
baby	gal
broad	honey
chick	sweetie
doll	toots

Unofficially...
According to *Working Woman* magazine, the compensation for top-level women executives increased by 166 percent from 1995 to 1998; however, women are still disproportionately represented in the lower-paying jobs, and they are still typically paid less than men in the same position. The gap between men's and women's salaries, though still significant, is steadily closing.

But much sexist language is so ingrained in English that it seems perfectly natural and takes some effort to become sensitive to. Historically, English uses the masculine pronoun *he* to refer to men as well as women. The effect, on a more-or-less unconscious level, is to render women culturally invisible, as if they were second-class beings.

It is not always easy to avoid the generic *he.* Such substitutes as *he/she, he or she,* or *s/he* often seem quite awkward. Look for inventive ways around the problem. For example, transform "The effective manager knows his employees" into "Effective managers know their employees." (In this book, we've tried to alternate between using *he* and *she* in an attempt to give them "equal time.")

Just as *he* is often made to do generic duty, so *man* is frequently used as a substitute for *human beings.* Make these transformations:

Bright Idea
When possible, use "humankind" or "humanity" in place of "mankind."

- "Man" to "people"
- "Manmade" to "artificial"
- "The man on the street" to "the average person" or "the person on the street"
- "Old wives' tale" to "superstition" or "superstitious belief"

In business, some more specific terms should also be transformed:

- "businessman" to something more specific, such as "advertising executive" or "stockbroker"
- "chairman" to "chair" ("chairwoman" is out, and the use of "chairperson," perceived as clumsy, is declining)
- "insurance man" to "insurance agent"
- "mailman" to "letter carrier"

- "male secretary" to "secretary"
- "men and ladies" to "men and women"
- "salesman/saleswoman" to "salesperson" or "sales representative"
- "spokesman" to "representative" (if possible, avoid the clumsier "spokesperson")
- "stewardess" to "flight attendant"

Unless a woman requests a different form of address, use *Ms.* rather than *Miss* or *Mrs.*

On the nonverbal front, observe the following:

- A man should shake hands as firmly with a woman as with a man. (Neither a man nor a woman should receive a knuckle-crushing grip—see Chapter 2 for handshake pointers.)
- It's okay for a man to open or hold a door open for a woman—or another man, for that matter. And it is fine for a woman to open and hold a door for a man. Practice common courtesy regardless of gender.
- In general, other than for a handshake, it is not appropriate for a man to touch a woman in a business context.

Enabling the disabled

Many of us feel nervous around persons with disabilities. We don't know how to act or what to say. This is unfortunate, although it often comes from a positive desire to avoid giving offense or making anyone feel bad. The biggest danger is that our own feelings of awkwardness may cause us to exclude disabled people from conversation or other activities.

The law—the Americans with Disabilities Act passed in 1992—makes it a crime to discriminate

I hate people who are intolerant.
—Laurence J. Peter, management guru (1919–1990) who originated the "Peter Principle"

against disabled persons in the workplace and other public places. But there are also compelling human and business reasons to avoid such discrimination. From a human point of view, any of us could become permanently or temporarily disabled at any time, and if this happened to us, we would want to be able to continue contributing to the working world. From the business standpoint, the disabled are a large minority, and their presence in the workplace is yet another valuable contribution to diversity.

The following are some suggestions for working with the disabled:

- Most important, focus on people, not their condition. This will help both of you get over most of the awkward patches.

- Don't ignore the person.

- Avoid referring to the disabled person in the third person. For example, if someone is pushing the person's wheelchair, don't direct questions to her: "Would he like to hang up his coat?" This is depersonalizing.

- When introduced, offer a normal greeting. Make allowances for the disability. If a hand or arm is disabled, be prepared to shake the left hand—or not to shake hands at all. If the person is blind, speak up: "Shall we shake hands?"

- Don't touch or handle the person's wheelchair. It is part of the person's "personal space" and should be treated as an extension of the body.

- If the person is visually impaired, alert him to your approach. A simple hello is often enough, but if the person doesn't return your greeting using your name, identify yourself.

- Unless explicitly invited to do so by the owner, do not pet or interact with a seeing-eye dog. The animal is not a house pet. It has a job to do.

- If the person is hearing impaired, make certain that you are clearly within sight before you make your greeting.

- If the person has an impairment of speech, exercise patience. Listen carefully, do not interrupt, and resist the temptation to complete the person's sentences.

Watch Out!
Just because a person is in a wheelchair does not mean that he or she is hearing impaired. Don't shout or exaggerate your words. Speak in a normal conversational tone and manner.

Should you help a disabled coworker? The answer is simple: ask. If the person is wheeling himself and encounters a steep ramp, don't automatically start pushing, and don't say "Let me help." Instead, ask: "May I help?" If a visually disabled coworker seems to be having trouble negotiating a hallway, offer your arm and ask: "May I direct you somewhere?"

The description of disabilities is a delicate matter for many people. The fact is that most people with disabilities don't object to being called blind, deaf, or disabled; but until you know that about a particular person, it's best to use the following terms, both when addressing the person directly and when referring to the person in his absence:

- For "blind" use "visually impaired"

- For "handicapped" use "physically challenged" or refer to a "person with a disability"

- For "deaf" use "hearing impaired"

- Never use "deaf and dumb"; refer to "hearing and speech impaired"

- For "diabetic" use "person with diabetes"

- For "obese" use "overweight"

- For "reformed alcoholic" use "recovering alcoholic"

Squash stereotyping

It is easy to abuse an abstraction, less easy to abuse a human being. Conversely, it is difficult to entertain fellow feelings with a stereotype, but quite natural to feel high regard for another person. In the workplace, do everything you can to avoid thinking, speaking, or acting in stereotypes:

- Hold on to the Golden Rule: Treat others as you would like to be treated.

- Be respectful and nonjudgmental about the differences you encounter.

- Be flexible. Rigid people create many unnecessary difficulties in dealing with people from different backgrounds.

- Listen—and learn.

When speaking or working with a person of an ethnic or racial origin different from your own, make no reference to it. Never put the other person in the position of speaking as a representative for her race or nation: "What do *you people* like to eat?" Feel free to follow the other person's lead, however. If she wants to share some aspect of cultural or ethnic heritage, by all means, listen and encourage the conversation.

Bright Idea
If a person wears something obviously cherished—a piece of traditional jewelry from her country of origin, for example—it's perfectly acceptable to compliment it and inquire about it. "What a beautiful ring! Is that from your country?" This is a wonderful way to start a friendly conversation.

Good manners or good risk management?

Good manners in the workplace are all about making others feel comfortable, so that creativity and productivity are encouraged and stress is minimized. Fortunately, the steps to ensure that you practice good manners in a diverse work environment are also the steps to good risk management.

What is risk management? These days, it often involves reducing the number of situations in which workers feel not merely offended, but discriminated against. Of course, both offense and bias should be avoided, but overt bias can land your company in court. Unfortunately, the line separating the merely impolite, crude, and offensive from the frankly biased and discriminatory is quite obscure. Even if a lawsuit against you or your company proves unsuccessful, defending such legal actions is expensive in terms of money, time, and emotional wear and tear. Good risk management seeks to keep everyone out of court.

A shade of blue

For many of us, salty language and a slightly off-color sense of humor are the spice of life. Others, however, may find these ways of speaking offensive. In the workplace, you have no viable choice but to respect how these people feel. You might consider them simply prudish and annoying. But it is also possible that their conception of right and wrong comes from religious belief or training, and your idea of language that is "colorful" may be emotionally painful and profoundly offensive—far more so than you realize.

The workplace is no place for off-color language or "blue" humor, including humor of an even mildly sexual nature. Of course, humor based on racial, sexual, ethnic, or other stereotypes is absolutely unacceptable.

If it gets ugly

Okay, so you know better than to make racist remarks or tell dirty stories. But what if you encounter these among your coworkers? Should you say something?

Watch Out!
If people whom you supervise speak or behave inappropriately, it is your responsibility to intervene. Emphasize that such talk or behavior is not acceptable. If the offense is sufficiently serious, begin progressive discipline procedures, as discussed in Chapter 12.

This is a judgment call only you can make in any given situation. If you do intervene, do so in collegial manner. Don't lecture. Don't scold. Use inclusive language, avoiding "you" as much as possible: "Sam, I couldn't help overhearing your conversation with Jack. We'd better be more careful about using that kind of language here, don't you think?"

If you are seriously offended by off-color talk or humor, speak frankly to those responsible. Again, don't scold. Present your concerns as a request for a favor: "Sam, I enjoy talking with you, but I have to tell you that jokes like the one you told yesterday, well, I find offensive. They hurt my feelings, and I think that a lot of our clients and plenty of the other people in the office feel that way. I don't want to cramp your style or anything, but I would appreciate it if you could keep that kind of humor out of our office."

If you feel that something even more serious has occurred—that you are the victim of some form of discrimination—you need to make a decision. Should you confront the person who is doing the discriminating? Or should you take the matter to management?

If you believe that the discrimination is unintentional, it is far preferable to communicate directly with the other person. Approach her in the spirit of education. You are about to give the person an opportunity to learn how to treat others positively and effectively. Be frank, but not provocative. Do not express rage. If you are truly angry, the incident or behavior is almost certainly serious enough to take directly to a supervisor or manager.

Pick a private time and place for the discussion: "Helen, may I speak to you a moment? Yesterday, you made a remark that has been disturbing me, and I care enough about our working relationship that I wanted to point it out to you and discuss it briefly."

In the case of more serious problems—out-and-out racial slurs, abusive language based on sex, or actions that demonstrate prejudice (for example, repeatedly being assigned menial jobs despite your excellent training and job performance)—you should speak with a manager, a representative from your firm's Human Resources Department, or, if appropriate, a union shop steward. Be certain that you can document all portions of your complaint.

Do not make threats of any kind. Do not warn of impending legal action. (If circumstance warrants, you can always resort to such action. But there is no advantage in discussing it beforehand.) Instead, present as many specific facts as possible. Before you make a complaint, decide just what your objectives are. Do you plan to look for another job? Are you preparing the way for legal action? Or do you want to figure out a way to make it possible to continue working in this place, productively and with all the dignity and opportunity that is due you?

Communication is the key. The days of the old-boy network and the glass ceiling may not be over, but they are numbered. Issues involving potential bias are best discussed in an open, frank manner. Resolution of such issues is not only legally and morally imperative, but important to your firm and to the continued advancement of your career.

Timesaver
When facing a hostile workplace, keep your overall goals in mind. If it's important to you to keep working where you are, you'll choose different responses than if you feel free to leave and take other work.

Just the facts

- Workplace diversity is inevitable, because it reflects the growing diversity of our larger society.

- It pays to embrace multiculturalism and diversity, not just because federal law mandates it or because it's the right thing to do, but because it's good business: Workplace diversity represents the marketplace.

- Sexism is difficult to overcome in large part because it is ingrained in and reinforced by our language.

- The key to overcoming prejudice and accepting diversity is to practice seeing the person behind the stereotype or condition.

- Accepting diversity and practicing the etiquette of inclusion in the workplace is crucial to "risk management": avoiding costly legal action based on accusations of bias.

GET THE SCOOP ON...
Office romance—its impact on productivity and
professionalism ▪ Coworkers' attitudes toward
office romance ▪ Identifying and avoiding sexual harassment situations ▪ The upside of
romance in the workplace ▪ Being discreet

Office Romance: The Most Dangerous Game?

Chapter 16

There is a short answer to the question of whether or not to have an office romance. And it is (may I have the envelope, please?)—*Don't.*

Now, let's get real. A week consists of seven days or 168 hours. Of this, 56 hours are devoted to sleep, leaving 110 hours. By law, you don't have to work more than 40 hours a week, but the work hours of most people approach something closer to 60 a week. Throw in an hour a day for the commute, and you have 65 hours, leaving you with 45 more-or-less free hours each week.

It doesn't take an Einstein to see that we spend most of our waking life at work. Who are the people we spend this time with? In these days of diversity (see Chapter 15), men *and* women are at work, often in nearly equal proportions. What are these men and women like? There is a good chance that, because they work together, they have a lot in common: same employer, similar career interests, and involvement in the same day-to-day issues.

So it's no wonder that, in some studies, 80 percent of employees report some sort of sociosexual experience with a coworker. In fact, these days, the workplace is the most likely place for Americans to meet a romantic partner.

Let's talk about it.

Is it love? Passion? Sexual harassment?

We all know that love can be grand. We also know that it can be catastrophic—or at least it can feel that way. Typically, whatever love is, it is rarely simple, and one of the factors that complicates it is work life. Assume you and your significant other do *not* work at the same place. You face some hurdles:

- Schedule conflicts during your 45 free hours each week.

- Possible extended periods of separation, for business trips and the like.

- Conflicting career demands. His work may be in Chicago, hers may suddenly take her to Paris. Her work may demand that she socialize with people he can't stand. His job with a big tobacco company may conflict with hers as an attorney for an anti-smoking activist organization.

As complicated as this situation is, romance with someone who does work in the same office as you is *potentially* (and this adverb is important) even more difficult. Let's start with the two problems many managers cite as associated with office romance: productivity loss and compromised professionalism. The office, these managers point out, is not the place for romance, but for work. If employees are focusing on the one, they say, the other suffers.

This is an employer's impression. Now, to be sure, love and romance can be quite distracting, to

> **66**
>
> No one is anti-romance. It's just that they want to keep the workplace as professional as possible and with as much competitive fairness as possible.
> —"Alice," during a University of Massachusetts panel discussion on gender issues in the workplace
>
> **99**

say the least. But this is true whether or not you happen to work in the same office as your love interest. Who doesn't spend a certain amount of time at work fantasizing and daydreaming? Who doesn't spend some work time making personal phone calls?

The fact is that some studies and "anecdotal data" (the experiences individuals relate to interviewers) suggest that office romance actually *increases* productivity. Industrial and organizational psychologist Charles A. Pierce, professor of psychology at Montana State University–Bozeman, points out that "employees often channel romantic energy to work tasks. They bring enthusiasm and energy to their work." Pierce criticizes companies that form "blanket policies" discouraging office romances, because such policies are "not based on research."

Workers often make comments similar to what a woman in a recent discussion group reported, that an office "relationship . . . benefited work performance. I found myself even more energized and enthusiastic than I had been before."

The conclusion is frustratingly nonconclusive: One's personal life can affect one's professional life for better or for worse. That's a given. There is evidence suggesting that bringing one's personal life into the workplace, in the form of an office romance, may, at least in some cases, enhance productivity. Surely, in other cases, it has a negative effect, and, in still others, an office romance has no effect on productivity at all.

Nature meets the corporation

The far thornier issue is the impact of an office romance on professionalism. Professionalism includes the following:

- Interacting with all employees—coworkers, subordinates, and bosses—fairly, attentively, and even-handedly

- Refraining from favoritism

- Avoiding the appearance of favoritism

Watch Out!
Office dynamics can be messy even in the best of circumstances; adding romance to the mix can make it messier, in unexpected ways. For example, you may have thought about what would happen if a romance ends. But what if the person you were involved with becomes involved with someone else in the office? The green-eyed monster does not wear pinstripes comfortably.

The first two points depend on the character of the two people involved in the romance. Only they can determine, with honesty, whether or not they will be able to maintain professional objectivity. And this is not at all easy to determine honestly. Think about it. The intensity of romantic feelings and their effects are difficult to gauge. And what will happen to objectivity if the romance ends badly?

Yet an even more serious concern is the third point, concerning the *appearance* of favoritism. Although some workers have reported a sort of "all the world loves lovers" effect in the workplace—that is, the presence of romance lifts the morale of the entire office—most comment on potential or actual negative reactions. As one woman put it in a recent panel discussion of the subject at the University of Massachusetts, "The bad news was the way other people reacted to us." She reported that she "started noticing that . . . coworkers weren't so open and sharing with me anymore. There were even some suggestions that my relationship . . . had more to do with career potential than sincere affection. Personally, I felt hurt. Professionally, I was frozen out of the information loop."

As if to prove the woman's point, a male participant on this panel responded that he was "not all that sympathetic to your situation":

> I've seen a few office romances, and from my point of view, they're just not fair. Romance within the company disrupts the level playing

field of professional competition. People who are a romantic couple are closer to each other than to other coworkers. I suspect that they share things with each other that they wouldn't share with the rest of us. If they are asked to evaluate their boyfriend/girlfriend's ideas or work output, are they going to be objective?

The point is less whether fairness and objectivity can be maintained than whether the *perception* of fairness and objectivity can be maintained. What's the answer to this? At best, maintaining the appearance of professionalism under such circumstances is very difficult. Other people assume, justly or not, that secrets will be shared and favoritism shown.

And while this perception is most critical and potentially damaging when the romance involves a boss and a subordinate, it is still important when peers are involved romantically. Members of the workplace team want to feel that they have equal access to one another. If they feel that the access of some is "more equal" than that of others, resentment and suspicion are naturally created.

Women tend to be less accepting of office romance than men. As one woman pointed out during the University of Massachusetts panel discussion, "Many of us have decided to keep our professional and romantic lives separate. For me, that makes having men and women working together easier to manage." Another woman made a more directly political statement: "Women have fought to be taken seriously in the workplace. I want to be accepted as a co-professional, not as a potential date. [Office romances] blur the sharp image of women as professionals I want to present."

Unofficially...
A survey in *Glamour* magazine, involving 1,002 men, reported that 42 percent said they had had an affair with a female coworker. An overwhelming 90 percent of those surveyed reported that the tensions created by such relationships could be "a hindrance to productivity."

Of course, it's one thing for those not involved in an office romance to declare how they feel and what they would or would not do, but it's quite another to act in accordance with such declarations when Cupid's arrow strikes. Plans made in the head often dissolve when the heart intervenes. If there is an unambiguous conclusion to be reached, it is that all office romances have the potential for creating a hostile response from fellow workers. Be aware of this, and do everything you can to maintain fairness, openness, and objectivity in dealing with everyone. Even more important, do what you can to *demonstrate* such fairness, openness, and objectivity.

Will this allay the suspicions and quell the hostility? The answer is a definite maybe. And then again, maybe not.

Bright Idea
Hardly anyone objects to romance between workers at the same company but in different departments. Consider looking beyond the four walls of Accounting, Sales, or wherever your cubicle is planted.

The H word

The prospect of an office romance interfering with productivity or office morale is serious enough. Of far greater consequence to one's firm and oneself is the issue of sexual harassment.

Sexual harassment is sociosexual behavior that has the purpose and effect of substantially interfering with an individual's work performance or creating an intimidating, hostile, or offensive working environment. The legal definition of sexual harassment, according to Title VII of the Civil Rights Act of 1964, follows:

> . . . [any] unwelcome sexual advances, requests for sexual favors, and other verbal and physical conduct of a sexual nature when submission to such conduct is made either explicitly or implicitly a term or condition of an individual's employment; submission to or rejection of such conduct by an individual is

used as the basis for employment decisions affecting such individual; such conduct has the purpose or effect of unreasonably interfering with an individual's work performance or creating an intimidating, hostile, or offensive working environment.

While the law is admirably clear in its definition, there is plenty of gray area in the interpretation. The following forms of behavior are examples of sexual harassment:

- Overt sexual advances

- Repeatedly asking for a date after being told "no"

- Suggestive comments

But just what constitutes a "suggestive comment"? Many such comments are obviously suggestive ("How about a little action tonight?"), but some are far less so ("You look gorgeous!"). Here are some of the prime ingredients of sexual harassment:

- **Physical contact and touching.** Anything other than a handshake is risky and should be avoided.

- **Sexual jokes, comments, suggestive language, and "locker-room talk."** Even if such jokes, comments, and language are not directed at a particular person, that person can reasonably lodge a complaint under Title VII of the Civil Rights Act of 1964, which protects individuals against being subject to "an intimidating, hostile, or offensive working environment."

- **Exhibiting pornographic material or sexual graffiti.** Okay, let's say you're a manager, and you have enough class to refrain from sharing the latest issue of *Hustler* with your administrative

Unofficially...
Sexual harassment is usually practiced by men against women; however, men can also be victims. Currently, no reliable data on same-sex harassment (men making unwelcome advances toward other men, women toward other women) is available.

assistant. But what about the dirty picture someone spray-painted on the wall of the loading dock? If you let that remain, you risk being accused of creating an "offensive working environment."

- **Discussing sexual matters.** This can include fantasies, sexual preferences, activities, and body parts.

- **Sexual innuendoes.** These include gestures, or facial expressions.

Let's get something straight. Sexual harassment is hardest on the *victim*. It is an intensely personal and profound violation that can be professionally and emotionally devastating. But it also has grave consequences for the offender, even if the offender was unconscious of his or her offense. Sexual harassment damages lives and destroys careers.

If you are a victim

If you believe that you are the victim of sexual harassment, recognize that you are the victim of a federal crime, and that you are entitled to the protection and remedies of the law. By the same token, when you accuse someone of sexual harassment, recognize that you are making a criminal accusation. You literally are "making a federal case out of it." The following steps are prudent:

- If the harassment is obvious or violent (whether verbally or physically), remove yourself from the situation immediately and seek help from company security and/or the police.

- If the harassment is less obvious or less immediately threatening, document the incident or incidents precisely. When you seek redress for the situation, you will eventually need names, dates, places, and details of what happened and what was said. But do *not* make notes concerning any aspect of sexual harassment on your office computer! And don't use corporate e-mail to discuss the matter. Your company can seize the material, use it against you, or even delete it. Keep notes on your personal computer or notebook you keep at home and purchase with your own funds.

- If you are uncertain about the nature or intention of the behavior, make some discreet inquiries to find out if anyone else has been subjected to similar treatment.

- If you are certain of the nature and intention of the behavior or if the behavior is repeated, contact your Human Resources Department to make a formal complaint.

- If Human Resources does not immediately resolve the problem, or if you feel that you've been intimidated or retaliated against because of your complaint, do not rely exclusively on the company's legal staff to help you. Retain your own attorney.

A question of rank

These days, it's not enough for managers and supervisors to behave like decent human beings; they have to take proactive steps to show that they are aware of sexual harassment and working to prevent it. Sexual harassment is a hot-button issue. Although the law is well defined, interpretation of actions and behavior is always subject to a great deal of ambiguity. Moreover, while most employees who complain about sexual harassment have legitimate reasons for doing so, some people do lie. Motives for lying range from profit (as in extortion) to mental illness.

Watch Out!
Don't let sexual harassment go on. First, you don't have to accept this illegal behavior. Second, bad behavior tends to get worse; you may be exposing yourself and others to danger. Third, by allowing the behavior to continue, your action may be interpreted by a Human Resources Department or by a judge and jury as condoning the behavior.

Managers should protect themselves by developing sexual harassment policies consistent with the law. Upper management and the company's legal counsel will need to get involved in formulating such policies. It's also a good idea to demonstrate an earnest desire to prevent sexual harassment by educating employees about it. Many firms institute sexual harassment education as part of a sensitivity training program.

Additionally, on a day-to-day basis, managers should avoid the following:

- Having intimate, overly familiar conversations with employees
- Touching employees
- Using offensive language
- Joking in a sexual manner
- Using sexist language (see Chapter 15)

If you feel uncomfortable with a certain employee, don't put yourself in a situation where you are alone with him or her. Bring in a third party to any one-on-one conference.

Finally, if you are a manager or supervisor, you'd better think *very* carefully before you become involved with a subordinate. The risks are high:

1. You are exposing yourself to accusations of sexual harassment.

2. You are exposing yourself—and the other person involved—to accusations of favoritism.

3. You are generally undermining your authority with your team.

Love, they say, will find a way. If a relationship between a boss and a subordinate is serious and enduring, it's probably best for all concerned if one of the parties involved looks for a different job—either with a different firm or, perhaps, in a different department within the same firm.

Consenting adults

Some genius once stated the secret of happiness this way: "Don't start no mess, won't be no mess." But as true romantics have long understood, love often has remarkably little to do with happiness. Love happens. And love can be . . . well . . . a mess.

When romance enters the workplace, you might decide to play it safe and run the other way. If you can't resist, however, perhaps you can still muster what it takes to at least look before you leap. Ask yourself whether the attraction is based on mutual affection or on perceived career gain. And if you are a boss or in any way senior to the other person, ask yourself whether he or she would say yes if you weren't in charge in the office. If the answer to this second question is no, then recognize that you are walking the fine line of sexual harassment, and in any case are setting yourself up for a relationship that is fed by power, not mutual respect and liking—let alone love.

Better than a singles bar

We've been dwelling on the downside of the office romance because the risks are real. But let's be honest: There can be an upside, too.

- As mentioned earlier, people who work together often have common interests, goals, and values. Not bad qualities for people in a relationship.

- Work and love can go together, allowing two people to share their lives in delightful and

Watch Out!
One decision regarding office romance is a no-brainer. If you make an overture or you ask someone for a date, and the other person says no, you must realize then and there that this means no. It doesn't mean "maybe," and it certainly doesn't "really mean yes." Take it as a no, act accordingly, back off, and stop asking.

fulfilling ways. Look at scientists Marie and Pierre Curie, actors Jessica Tandy and Hume Cronyn or Ruby Dee and Ossie Davis, or the owners of the mom-and-pop grocery store down the street. And what about Bonnie and Clyde? (Okay, bad example.)

■ Romances at work often develop over time. People can get to know one another before they make any commitments.

■ A person who meets his or her significant other at work tends to see that person as a whole person, not just as tonight's target on the next bar stool.

Is it romantic?

For the reasons just enumerated, office romances can be more romantic than relationships begun elsewhere. Some people who keep their relationship from the rest of their coworkers enjoy the secrecy of such a romance. On the other hand, some people like the idea of being "an item," letting everyone else know what's going on. And many people like the idea of being close to each other during the day. If a big part of love is sharing, what is better to share than a part of your working life?

Staying professional

Is it possible to be in love and remain professional? Well, anything's possible, but it isn't always easy. Psychoanalysts tell us that any romantic relationship involves at least six people—the two lovers and both sets of parents. Try romance at work, and you may have to toss in a few bosses, a handful of colleagues and subordinates, and maybe even a board member or two.

Company policy

Before you embark on an office romance, you'd better know your company's policy on the subject. Chances are, your company has none.

Although most larger corporations have policies forbidding sexual harassment, only about 6 percent of companies have written policies on "fraternization." Of this minority, very few attempt to completely forbid office romance between single, consenting adults. Of 500 companies surveyed in 1994 by the American Management Association for *Money Magazine*, only two barred employee dating. Even in the case of a married employee having an affair with a co-worker, just over 2 percent of companies have a stated policy prohibiting this. Overt, public demonstrations of affection elicit more regulation, however. According to *Personnel Administrator*, 27.6 percent of companies have policies banning such displays.

Companies fail to develop official policies on office romance not because they are lazy, but because such policies tread on constitutional and Bill of Rights issues. This does not mean that management *likes* office romances or ignores them. But as a rule they haven't wanted to try to forbid such behaviors with detailed and explicit rules.

Oh, behave!

Despite the dearth of official policy statements on office romance and employee dating, it's clear that discretion is called for. No one benefits from the display of dating behavior in the workplace. How open you are about a relationship is up to you, but the line should certainly be drawn at kissing, hugging, and other physical demonstrations of affection.

Unofficially... According to *Personnel Administrator*, only 2 percent of organizations reported that no official notice would be taken of in-office kissing by consenting adults.

Watch Out!
Avoid sending
love letters on
office e-mail—it
isn't private. The
contents of any
e-mail you send
using the com-
pany's computer
and the com-
pany's network is
the property of
the company.
You have no pri-
vacy rights in
this matter.

Kiss and tell?

Communication is important in any relationship, and one of the issues office daters should communicate most clearly about is how open you want to be about your relationship. Be assured of one thing: If you go out on more than a couple of dates, the entire office *will* discover your secret. The grapevine has many eyes, many ears, and a multitude of mouths. Nevertheless, the partners need to agree on whom they will tell and what they will say.

Communication, by the way, should not extend to romantic conversation in the office, and you certainly should not transmit love letters—or air your disagreements—via the office e-mail. This is unprofessional and a theft of the company's time and resources.

For all its pitfalls, office romance is appealing. For many people, the very hazards of the office dating game make it that much more appealing. Just remember that you have responsibilities toward your company, your clients or customers, your colleagues, the object of your affections, yourself, and your future. As an effective office politician, you don't have to be immune to relationships in the workplace, but you do need to keep in mind how they affect the way you are perceived and how they may add to the weight you have to carry up the corporate ladder.

Just the facts

- Although few employers have stated policies forbidding office romance, most believe that it has a negative influence on productivity, professionalism, and morale.

- Although office romance has real risks, there is also evidence that, in some cases, it actually enhances productivity.

- These days, most Americans meet their "significant other" in the workplace.

- The chief pitfalls of workplace romance are alienating other employees (who resent the appearance of favoritism) and being accused of sexual harassment.

- Sexual harassment is a federal crime, which poses dangers to the victim as well as to the person accused and to the company for which they both work.

- Although the safest personal policy on office romance may be abstinence, the more practical policy is simply to practice common sense and discretion in all aspects of behavior in the workplace.

PART V

The Savvy Schmoozer

GET THE SCOOP ON...
Getting into the business-social loop • Being on
time • Working a room • Remembering new
names • Dressing for the occasion • When you're
the host

An Out-of-Office Experience

Chapter 17

Office politics is not confined to the office. Effective managers see the people they work with as more than figures in cubicles. They see them as fully rounded human beings, and they want to become acquainted with them on a level that reveals styles of thought, abilities, and interests beyond what may be apparent in the confines of the office. Increasingly these days, too, managers are eager to reveal themselves to their staff as more than one-dimensional sources of assignments and directions. Finally, in a business era that puts the emphasis on teamwork and team building, out-of-office socializing is more important than ever.

Let's face it, a business social event is a command performance, but that doesn't mean it can't be fun—especially if you consider that a lot of the fun comes from knowing that by moving and shaking with the movers and shakers, you're moving and shaking yourself right up the corporate ladder.

Be there or be square

Let's say you work hard, long hours. Sixty hours a week is not unusual for you. From morning to evening, you see the same faces, deal with the same problems, hear the same gripes, listen to the same stories. Maybe the last thing you want now is to spend "social" time with this crowd. So, when the invitation to an after-work get-together comes, you decide to take a pass. Or perhaps you go right home after the sales conference and forgo the cocktail reception afterward. Just this once.

Who can blame you? Blame yourself. Think back to Chapter 3, where we talk about the two sets of customers you serve, your "external" customers—the clients and customers outside your company, whose business pays your salary—and your "internal" customers—the subordinates, peers, and bosses you work with every day. Any successful salesperson knows that customer contact is always valuable, an opportunity to be developed. The same is true of contact with your "internal" customers:

- Skilled people in sales know that getting a prospect to invest time in them is key to making a sale and converting a prospect into a customer.

- Savvy office politicians know that getting others in the office to invest time in them is key to building a future in the organization.

Open to all possibilities

Not only is it important to accept every invitation you get, you should angle for the invitations you *don't* presently get.

- Make it a habit to say "yes" to invitations.

- Accept all invitations with enthusiasm and expressions of pleasure.

- Don't be afraid to *push* from time to time.

Let's consider the last point for a moment. You can sit tight and wait for the invitations to come. And, if you present yourself as a cooperative, open, friendly presence in the workplace, the invitations probably *will* come. But you should also consider accelerating the process. If you are relatively new on the job, ask coworkers about social events. Then say something like: "That sounds like fun. How do I get invited?" Also, keep your eye out for events, then follow up. "George, do you know anything about the sales conference reception? How do you get invited to it? I'd really like to go."

Don't be shy. If business-related social events were strictly social get-togethers among friends, angling for an invitation could be considered obnoxious. But everybody knows that business-related social events are, well, *business-related.* No one will think you pushy if you ask about such events. More likely, they'll respect your ambition and commitment to the team.

Also consider thinking beyond the circle of the office. Chances are there are plenty of events outside of work that relate to your business or career interests. Seek out such events as charitable and political fundraisers, community get-togethers, cultural tours, concerts—you name it. Here are some suggestions for identifying career-building events:

- Figure out which events are likely to attract people you would like to get to know.

- Watch the local papers for such events.

- Read the free weeklies that are published in many communities. The *L.A. Weekly,* the *Chicago*

Watch Out!
Avoid accepting invitations in a half-hearted or grudging manner. Don't confuse a blasé response with sophistication, or the flow of invitations coming your way will soon dry up. In accepting an invitation, make it clear that you look forward to the event with great excitement and pleasure.

Bright Idea
Often, you can do well by doing good. Look around your community. Consider joining charitable organizations or doing volunteer work for organizations that are likely to attract other volunteers from the business world generally or from your industry in particular. Perhaps you can even interest others in your company in volunteering.

Reader, Atlanta's *Creative Loafing,* and the like regularly publish calendars of events.

- Read the journals relevant to your industry.

- Read city-based or regional business publications.

- Consult the local chamber of commerce.

- Surf the net. The Alta Vista search engine is great for searching for companies.

You should also make yourself aware of any professional or social clubs and organizations that attract folks in your industry. Check these out. Consider a membership.

Me? Keep a social calendar?

If you are committed to your career, it's time to start keeping a social calendar. This doesn't have to be separate from your current appointment book, but whatever method you use, you should take careful note of the following details:

- The event
- The place
- The date and time
- Directions to the place (if you require them)
- How to dress (formal? informal? in-between?)
- Special notes: why the event is important, who will be there, how to prepare ("Carol from Sales will be there. Review the new project for discussion.")

Of course, the principal purpose of a social calendar is to keep track of events so that you don't forget one or allow one to conflict with another. It's important to show others that your life after hours is as together as your life during the regular business day.

RSVP

Always respond promptly to any invitation you receive. If you're not sure whether you will be able to attend, respond to say that you would love to come, but you're not certain that you'll be free that evening. "Will it cause you inconvenience if I let you know by Thursday?"

Responding to an invitation is common courtesy. These days, it is also *uncommon* courtesy. Many, many people fail to respond, then either show up or don't—or they put the inviter in the position of having to make a phone call. Failure to respond is rude and will reflect very negatively on you. Conversely, a cheerful, grateful, and enthusiastic RSVP will make you look decent, charming, and caring.

Show up (on time)

Forget what you have been told about being "fashionably late":

- No one appreciates a latecomer.

- Many people actively resent a latecomer.

- Coming late suggests that you are irresponsible, impolite, or that you feel you have "something better to do." None of these reflects well on you.

Being on time is critically important in the case of a seated dinner, but less so for an open cocktail party. Often, invitations to such parties indicate the duration of the party rather than a specific starting time. Don't arrive at the last minute.

It is particularly important to be on time for any invitation involving a meal. Meals need to be served on time.

If there's anything worse than being late, it's failing to show up at all. If you promised to attend, be sure to attend.

> "
> Life is not so short but that there is always time enough for courtesy.
> —Ralph Waldo Emerson, 1876
> "

Bright Idea
Not only should you be certain to arrive on time— give some thought to arriving just a few minutes *early*. This gives you a chance to speak to the host or hosts of the party.

Accidents happen, of course. If it's clear to you that you're going to be late, or if an emergency prevents you from attending a function for which you have accepted an invitation, *call*. Briefly explain the problem and apologize. If you were very late, or if you could not attend, it's also a good idea to call the day after the event and express your regrets once again.

Networking lite

For many of us, few things in life are more awkward than the first few minutes of a party or a reception. You walk in. If the host is available, you say hello. If not, perhaps you sidle up to the bar or the buffet; then, drink and hors d'oeuvre in hand, you prop yourself up in a corner and watch with envy the people who walk in and enter into any number of conversations fearlessly and effortlessly.

What's their secret? They've mastered the schmoozer's art.

The schmoozer's art

Schmooze is a word borrowed from Yiddish. If you look it up in the dictionary, you'll find that it means "to chat." But that's a lot like defining, say, *singing* as "making noise with one's voice."

To schmooze is to chat *in a certain direction,* the direction of business and of furthering your career, but not too obviously and gracelessly. The adept schmoozer can:

- Enter a room, circulate, and identify precisely those people whom it's advantageous to talk to
- Create a conversation of interest to all involved
- Talk business without sounding like a salesperson
- Come away from a conversation with valuable knowledge

With practice, just about anyone can become a good schmoozer. If possible, prior to the party, find out the special interests of some of your main targets. This is what you should talk about. People love to talk about themselves and their interests. When you arrive at the party, begin by working the room. Look around. Be aware of the following issues:

- Are the people there people you know you should talk to? The boss? A valued colleague? Customers? Prospects? Zero in on them.

- If you're among strangers or relative strangers, identify the easy targets. These include people who are standing alone, perhaps looking a bit lost. Walk up, say hello, introduce yourself, and ask the standard question for any such gathering: "What brings you here?"

- The host or organizer of the get-together is also an easy schmooze target. It is this person's job to help guests mix and to make them feel comfortable. Ask the host for help: "I'm new here. Anybody I should talk to?"

- If there is a guest of honor, a featured speaker, or the like, single that person out for a schmooze. Be prepared with a relevant question or two.

After you've established yourself as an artful schmoozer by working some of these easier targets, you're ready to identify the guests who seem most important. How do you know who these are? Look for the people with a crowd around them. Enter the group, then bide your time. At a lull in the conversation, introduce yourself, then make an observation: "You certainly seem to know everybody here. I'm new to this group and would really like to meet

Timesaver
By planning in advance whom you hope to talk to at a social event, and what you hope to say to them, you'll be more efficient at meeting the right people and covering the topics most important to you. Don't leave this to chance.

some of the people here. What brings you here, and whom should I be getting to know?"

Many people mistake their own monologues for good conversation. It is said that Sir Arthur Conan Doyle, author of the Sherlock Holmes stories, once left a dinner party brimming with enthusiasm over the great conversational gifts of the playwright and novelist Oscar Wilde, a man famed for his wicked wit. "But you did all the talking," Conan Doyle's companion pointed out. "Exactly!" exclaimed the writer.

Meeting and greeting

In general, unless you have made a valuable contact and the conversation is going strong, it's best to keep circulating. Enlarge your circle of acquaintance beyond the usual crowd. Again, unless the conversation is of particular importance, limit yourself to no more than seven or eight minutes with any one person. Then move on to a stranger.

Play the name game

If you are naturally uncomfortable in social situations, your objective for the evening may be simply to *get through it.* But that's not enough. Remember, while this may look and feel like a social occasion, *it's still business.* You are still among "customers"— external and internal; your job is to gather information and to communicate information:

- Give your name to those you meet, as well as your title, function, and company.

- Get the names (plus title, function, and company affiliation) of everyone you meet.

- Try to establish acquaintances in common: "Oh, you're at Smith & Smith. Do you know Joe Blow?" This is important because it builds your professional network.

Bright Idea
Moving from person to person or conversational group to conversational group is easier if you leave the person or group after you have said something, rather than when somebody else stops talking. This makes for a smooth exit, and it avoids implying that you are bored with what another person has to say.

Many people have trouble remembering names. The solution to this deficiency is to *practice.* You'll improve. For the time being, try this: listen to the person introduce himself or herself, then repeat the name back:

> **Person**: Hi. I'm Sally Johnson, from Acme.
>
> **You**: Sally Johnson. Hi. I'm John Doe from Smith & Smith. Sally, do you work with Ed Sanders at Acme?

Psychologists who specialize in memory have long known the value of "rehearsing" material that you want to memorize. Repeating the relevant names—Sally Johnson, Sally, Acme—will help you rehearse in order to remember the names more effectively.

Practice the SOFTEN touch

Now is a good time to glance back over Chapter 5 for a quick review of small-talk tips. This will make social conversation easier. In particular, recall the "SOFTEN" formula:

- **Smile.** This is the single strongest signal you can send that you are open for conversation.

- **Open up.** Use open body language. Begin by facing the other person, and avoid folding your arms across your chest or putting your hands on your hips.

- **Forward, lean.** Lean forward from time to time to make a point or to listen more attentively. Don't touch the other person, and don't point.

- **Tone it down.** Keep the tone and volume of the conversation conversational. Avoid speaking at a high pitch.

- **Eye contact now.** Always make eye contact with your conversation partner.

Timesaver
You can memorize a name more quickly and surely if you repeat the person's name while making eye contact with him or her. The repetition and visual cue—the eye contact—work together to help cement the name in your memory. Besides, eye contact is always helpful in putting yourself across to a new acquaintance.

- **Nod—and nod some more.** Nodding periodically is a powerful body-language signal that communicates understanding and acceptance of what is being said. It also encourages the other person to continue talking.

The business card ceremony

When you engage in what seems like a fruitful conversation with a potentially valuable contact, ask for a business card and offer one of your own. Always ask for the other person's business card first.

Social savvy

If there is a single key to success in the social side of business, it is to appear comfortable around others, but never to feel too comfortable. Appearing comfortable will make others feel comfortable, and it's always a personal advantage in business to make others feel good. Retaining a bit of an edge, however, a consciousness that this is all ultimately about your career, will keep you from confusing social business with a purely social occasion. This is still business, and you are still being judged.

Social dressing

Dress appropriately for the occasion:

- For most events directly related to business—such as a cocktail hour associated with a sales meeting—regular business attire is appropriate.

- For dinner, you may want to dress a notch or two better than you dress every day—unless, of course, you already dress very well every day.

- "Black-tie" events call for formal wear.

- Sporting events, company picnics, and the like call for casual attire. Such attire, however, should be clean and in impeccable repair.

Bright Idea
If someone hands you a business card, whether solicited or not, always look at the card before putting it in your pocket, wallet, or handbag. Reading it is not only polite, it will also help you to remember the person's name and to connect the name with the face.

- Many corporations sponsor periodic retreats at various resorts. Typically, tasteful "resort wear" is called for.

Accentuate the positive, eliminate the negative

When you are at a business social occasion, do your utmost to project relaxed energy. You can accomplish this by doing the following:

- Keep conversation positive.

- Enjoy yourself, or at least act *as if* you are enjoying yourself.

- Don't sulk.

- Smile and use open body language—no slouching, no crossed arms.

The cocktail party

The cocktail party has long been an institution of social business. When you are invited to one, always RSVP promptly. Assume that your best business dress is most appropriate. Women can wear dresses rather than business suits.

- Arrive on time—or slightly earlier.

- If you are greeted by the host (or hostess), engage in conversation, but don't monopolize him. The host needs to attend to all the guests.

- Go easy on the alcohol. If you are uneasy or nervous, it's tempting to drink more than you should, just to "take the edge off." But the fact is that you are better off with that edge. This is a *business* social occasion. You want to appear sharp, and you certainly don't want to behave irresponsibly or recklessly. If you don't tolerate alcohol well, there is nothing wrong with drinking a soft drink, club soda, or seltzer.

Bright Idea
If you get your signals crossed and arrive at an event only to find that you are inappropriately dressed, acknowledge the error. "I didn't realize this event called for coat and tie." But don't beat yourself up. This will only make your host and the other guests feel bad. Acknowledging the gaffe is sufficient to show that you really do care.

- Go easy on the hors d'oeuvres. Gather a few on a small plate, if one is provided, or a napkin. Then resume circulating. Hovering over the hors d'oeuvre table is very bad form.

- Work the room. Circulate. If you're with your spouse or significant other, make sure to include him or her in the conversation.

- Carry your drink in your left hand, leaving the right hand free for handshakes.

- It's best to avoid smoking. If you must smoke, do so only if others are smoking.

- Avoid flirting. This is not a dating occasion.

- Watch the time, and watch what others do. When significant numbers of people begin to leave, leave. Don't be the last one out the door.

- The very next day, write a brief thank-you note to the host: "What a great time I had last night! Many thanks for the hospitality of your lovely home, and I enjoyed meeting so many of your associates."

The office party

Office parties range from tedious, cheerless annual exercises to wild affairs propelled by alcohol. Most office parties fall somewhere between these extremes. The first rule of the office party: Attend. This is a command performance. The second rule: Don't make a spectacle of yourself. Avoid offensive behavior of any kind.

Use the office party to engage in small talk with your usual crowd and to network with people you see less often. Do not ambush your colleagues, subordinates, or bosses with heavy business conversation. Even if the party turns out to be a dud, it's *supposed* to be fun. At the very least, maintain that fiction.

A favorite sport at office parties that somehow miss the mark is bashing the party. A knot of employees gather with no purpose, it seems, other than to complain about how bad the party is. Avoid these conversations. Approach the office party positively, and maintain a positive attitude and tone throughout.

If you know who organized the party, send a thank-you note the next day. An e-mail is fine. If the boss is nominally responsible for the festivities, send the note to her: "Another great party! I really enjoyed getting to know the folks from Accounting. Thanks."

The company picnic

Many companies these days encourage family get-togethers, including pool parties and picnics. The challenge here is to be attentive to your family, kids included, while also socializing with others. Meet the challenge by introducing your family to others in attendance. If your kids want to go off and play with the other kids, by all means let them. Otherwise, it's your responsibility to keep tabs on them and keep them under control. Prior to the get-together, explain gently that they should be on their best behavior.

If this is a good ol' fashioned cornball picnic, with potato-sack races, wheelbarrow races, three-legged races, and the like, join in—whether this is really what you want to do or not. You have everything to gain by showing yourself to be a good sport.

The boss's house

Treat a dinner or cocktail invitation to the boss's house as you would treat any other business invitation—but with an extra margin of care:

Watch Out!
The office party is not the place to lecture or reprimand a subordinate. Also avoid gossip and gripes.

Bright Idea
The house tour is a great opportunity to learn something about your boss's likes and dislikes. You may also discover his hobby or special interest: model railroads, gardening, reading, or whatever. Ask about the hobby. This is a wonderful topic for conversation.

- As with any other event, RSVP promptly, make sure you have directions to the house, and arrive on time.

- Bring a modest gift as a thoughtful expression of gratitude. It's best to avoid wine, since the host may feel obliged to serve it with the dinner, and it may not go with the menu. Instead, flowers or candy are appropriate.

- If this is your first time to the boss's house, be generous with your compliments. Ask for the "grand tour" of the house. Show special interest in artwork, mementos, and so on.

- Don't be the one to bring up business in conversation. Of course, follow your boss's lead on this.

- Include the boss's spouse—and your own—in the conversation.

- Compliment the dinner. Don't go overboard, but do be sincere, generous, and enthusiastic.

If the dinner is a formal one, it is *not* appropriate for you or your spouse to offer to help clean up. However, if dinner is informal, such a gesture is gracious and may well be welcome. Avoid overstaying your welcome. Generally, coffee or after-dinner drinks may be offered. After that, it's time to take your leave—unless your boss gives you strong conversational indications prompting you to stay. As always, write your thank-you note the very next day, and when you see your boss at work, be certain to comment on the wonderful time you and your spouse had. End by shifting the focus away from yourself: "I was really impressed by what you've done with your model railroad."

It's your call

At some point, it becomes your turn to take the initiative and invite colleagues, subordinates, or bosses to your house. Just when that point is reached, only you can judge:

- If you are a brand-new employee, refrain from inviting the boss over until the two of you are well-acquainted at work. You "owe" the boss an invitation, however, after she has invited you to dinner.

- A brand-new employee should hold off on inviting the whole office gang over until reasonably well-established; however, inviting a colleague (and spouse or significant other, if there is one) may be done after a few months.

- A key subordinate or subordinates may also be invited early in your employment or in theirs.

Dinner is a safe and welcome occasion for an invitation. For colleagues and subordinates, something less formal is also in order—perhaps a barbecue or an afternoon spent watching the "big game" (if you're certain that the invitees enjoy such things).

Invitation to your boss

A dinner invitation to the boss should be made in person. Be prepared to handle rejection with an unruffled "Oh, I'm sorry. Perhaps another time." If the invitation is accepted, offer directions to your house, reconfirm the time, and express pleasure: "Great. I'm really looking forward to it—and to meeting your wife."

- Allow time for cocktails before dinner. About an hour is plenty. Getting your guests drunk is *not* the object.

Watch Out!
These days more than ever, you must be careful not to give a colleague or (especially) a subordinate the wrong idea by inviting him or her to your house, especially if you are single and unattached. Use good judgment—and read over the material on sexual harassment in Chapter 16.

- Be a conscientious host. Make all necessary introductions.

- If your boss is not your only dinner guest, do not devote your attention solely to him; however, do treat the boss as the guest of honor.

Conversation should be guided by some of the same principles as if you were a guest at the boss's house. You should not bring up business; however, if the boss wants to discuss the job, follow his lead. And be certain to include the boss's spouse in all conversation.

Having the gang over

Ideally, you'll reach a point in your career with a particular firm and department when you'll feel comfortable enough to invite your immediate working group over for cocktails or a later-evening party. Here are a few pointers:

- Keep the group to a manageable number, but be careful not to leave anyone out who is a part of the group.

- Written or e-mailed invitations are a good idea.

- If you serve alcohol, be certain to have food available, as well as plenty of soft-drink alternatives to wine, beer, or hard liquor.

- Don't initiate a discussion of business. If a subordinate wants to discuss business (that promotion!), suggest gently but firmly that "we take this up in my office on Monday."

- Circulate among your guests. Include their spouses and significant others in conversation.

When you're ready for the crowd to leave, drop two strong hints: Stop replenishing food, and stop offering more drink. And if you have set up a bar, abandon it. If none of these actions clears the room, ask the hanger-on something to this effect: "May I offer you a cup of coffee to help with the long drive home?" And if that fails, just thank the guest for coming: "Well, it's been great having you over. Thanks so much."

Your family's role

When extending an invitation to the boss or others from work, consider your family—don't take them for granted, and don't neglect them.

- The decision to invite the boss or others from work should be jointly arrived at by employee and spouse.

- Explain to your children that the event is important to you and that you expect their cooperation. Describe how you would like them to behave. Be specific.

- At dinner or your party, don't neglect your spouse. Make frequent visits to him or her.

Your family should understand that the occasion is a business event and that it's important to the entire family that they make a favorable and positive impression. Emphasize to the children how proud you are of them, and how you want to show them off. Express to your spouse gratitude for helping you make the evening a memorable one.

Business entertaining is all about humanizing professional relationships. It's an opportunity to see others as fully dimensional human beings and allowing others to see you the same way. The object is not to create a "business family" to take the place of your real family, but to acknowledge life beyond the office and to share that life, sparingly and courteously, with coworkers.

Just the facts

- Accept as many business-related social invitations as you possibly can.

- Always reply promptly to invitations, and always show up on time—or even a few minutes early.

- It pays to become adept at the art of schmoozing, informal conversation directed at making contacts that can further your career.

- Behave at business-related social functions as you would at any social function—but without forgetting that it *is* business, after all.

GET THE SCOOP ON...
The business breakfast, lunch, and dinner ▪
About alcohol ▪ Ensuring a successful business
dinner ▪ Mealtime manners ▪ Productive table
talk ▪ Damage control

Please Don't Drink the Finger Bowl

I n one of his best stories, "The Man Who Studied Yoga," Norman Mailer observes that you can accuse a person of many terrible things, from lying and theft to murder, and the accused won't be nearly as angry or defensive as he or she would be if accused of ill manners or rudeness.

Okay. So maybe Mailer overstates the case. But the point is that anyone who thinks etiquette is dead these days is a dead duck. Etiquette is not about dabbing the corner of your mouth with the corner of your napkin or elevating your pinkie when you raise a glass. It's about demonstrating what is meant by *savoir-faire,* knowing how to do things—how to handle yourself with grace and efficiency.

In no human activity is etiquette more important, more open to display, and more subject to scrutiny than at mealtime. And in today's working environment, business meals may encompass breakfast and lunch as well as dinner. This chapter will

Chapter 18

331

help you emerge from a business meal covered in glory instead of marinara sauce.

The many meals of business

The business lunch is a time-honored tradition. And why not? It takes place smack dab in the middle of the business day, so it provides a social space for business without intruding on private time in the morning or evening. Business dinners are nothing new, either. Traditionally, they have been a means of entertaining special clients or even valued candidates a company is courting. More recently, the business breakfast has also become commonplace.

Power breakfast

Gordon Gecko, the greedy tycoon played by Michael Douglas in the movie *Wall Street,* quipped, "Lunch is for wimps." He was commenting on what was a recent phenomenon in the 1980s, the business breakfast. In the years since then, the "power breakfast" has emerged as an attractive alternative to the business lunch:

- It doesn't cut into the business day.

- Because it takes place at the start of the day, it can be used to plan things that can be acted upon in the course of the day.

- For most people, breakfast does not involve alcohol, so participants remain sharp after the meal.

- Breakfast isn't a multicourse meal. It generally takes less time than lunch, and certainly less than dinner.

- Psychologically, a power breakfast gives participants a feeling that they are the early bird catching the worm. They feel they are getting a head start on the day and a jump on the competition.

Bright Idea
The last thing you want is to show up for a breakfast or lunch meeting and find the other person missing. To avoid this, confirm such appointments the day before your meeting, especially if you arranged the meeting some time ago. If you can't reach the person, leave a voice-mail message.

Power lunch

Gordon Gecko's pronouncement to the contrary notwithstanding, lunch is still very much a time for doing business—although in a more relaxed way. Lunch meetings are still considered an excellent way to get to know colleagues and clients better and to get some real work done.

If you are the one arranging the lunch, choose or suggest a place that is not too dark. You want to be able to glance over papers and be able to take notes. Find a restaurant that's not too loud. Few things are more frustrating than having to shout during a business conversation, especially if you're interested in keeping certain details discreet or confidential.

The fabled "three-martini lunch" was once a macho institution of American business—in a day when business people were mostly business*men*. In part due to health consciousness and in part due to IRS reforms that restrict corporate deductions for business entertainment, the three-martini lunch is a thing of the past. Nevertheless, alcohol does accompany many business lunches.

If you are used to drinking at lunch time and have no trouble holding your liquor, fine. But if you're going to be conducting serious business and need 110 percent of your concentration, you're better off going easy on the booze or having none at all. You might be most comfortable following the others' leads. If no one else is drinking, you will probably want to abstain as well. Even if everyone else *is* drinking, no one will be offended if you order a soft drink.

Some business lunches are strictly for discussion. Others require the presence of paperwork, and this *can* be awkward. Fancier restaurants frown upon

Timesaver
Consider saving time by ordering food in. A "working lunch" still breaks up the workday, but does so with less interruption. Eating in also enhances collegiality and is ideal in situations where participants can't conveniently bring their work with them—for example, if you have a lot of paperwork or illustrative material to go over.

diners turning tables into desktops. If you know you'll be pulling out some papers, choose or suggest a more or less informal restaurant. And don't start in on work right away. Enjoy your meal. Engage in some pleasant small talk before getting to the business at hand. You can always get to the bottom line after the main course or during the dessert (if you have any). Power lunches are as much social occasions as they are business occasions.

A civilized dinner

Arranging a business dinner can be a formidable responsibility, but it is also one of the most gracious and effective ways of bonding with clients as well as members of your own team. The business dinner is more social than either the business breakfast or lunch. Typically, business is discussed in the broadest terms at dinner. This is not the time to get into the nitty-gritty, and it is certainly not the time or place to haul out the paperwork.

A successful business dinner begins with the selection of the appropriate restaurant:

- This is no time for experimentation. If you regularly take clients or associates to dinner, keep a file of favorite restaurants. If you are unfamiliar with the local restaurants, ask trusted associates for advice.

- Choose quality. If the restaurant serves a bad meal, it's not your fault, but it *is* your problem. The quality of the meal, the ambience, and the service all reflect on you and your firm.

- In general, avoid restaurants that are radically trendy or that offer exotic cuisine. These can be fun for strictly social occasions, but they are generally uncomfortable for business purposes.

- Choose restaurants that offer a large menu to accommodate people whose tastes are probably unfamiliar to you. For business meals, the options offered the better.

- While you may be tempted to choose a restaurant known for its fast service, be aware that fast service does not usually go with an atmosphere conducive to relaxed business conversation. Restaurants that serve quickly also move patrons along quickly. You will not be encouraged to linger and talk.

If you're hosting the dinner, it's your responsibility to issue invitations. Spouses should always be included in a dinner invitation. A written invitation is not necessary. Discuss dinner with clients or associates during the business day or make a phone call.

It is assumed, of course, that you (ultimately, your firm) will be picking up the tab, but you can communicate this unambiguously by beginning your invitation with something like, "Will you let me take you and your wife to dinner tomorrow evening?"

The time to make reservations is before you issue the invitations. This is especially important with popular restaurants and on traditionally busy evenings. Be sure to request any accommodations that will make the evening special: "I'd like seating in your Waterfront Room, please." If you are a regular customer, you may want to request your regular waiter.

Give extra thought to any of your guests' special needs. For example, if a guest uses a wheelchair, mention this when making the reservation and be certain to request a table rather than a booth, as well as seating that does not require climbing stairs and that is fully wheelchair accessible.

Bright Idea
Although you should choose a familiar (to you) or highly recommended restaurant, consider alternatives to your firm's customary business hangouts. You don't want to give clients the impression that you're treating them in any routine way. In addition, you don't want to subject yourself unduly to the scrutiny of colleagues or bosses who may be present at the restaurant.

Unless you are driving or accompanying your guests to the restaurant, be certain that you arrive before they do. Check in with the reservation desk, then wait for your guests in the lobby. Generally, you should wait until all members of the party have arrived before going to the table; however, if the majority is present, proceed to the table after waiting about 10 minutes, order drinks, and leave word up front, asking the maitre d' to direct the latecomers to your table.

In general, when you're in charge of planning the business dinner, the less left to chance, the better. If possible, check out the seating arrangements ahead of time. Ensure that the table is comfortably positioned, well away from the kitchen and not nestled under a booming stereo system loudspeaker. If you have a choice, select a round rather than rectangular table. Not only is a round table conducive to conversational flow, but it also neatly disposes of questions about priority of position (think of King Arthur and his knights). Round tables help create a more relaxed atmosphere.

Table manners refresher course

The basis of good manners is simply behaving in a way that makes everyone feel welcome and comfortable. Where dining is concerned, there are a few more specific details of etiquette to review as well.

Napkin first

Immediately on being seated, take your napkin, unfold it, and place it on your lap. Briefly inspect your place setting to make certain that nothing is missing and everything is clean. If anything's amiss, point it out politely when the waiter takes your order.

Watch Out!
At times you may need to make it clear that the invitation is a *business* invitation, not a social one. Keep your language and tone professional. If you have any concern that the other party may get the wrong idea, let him or her know that a third party will be joining you.

Some cramped table arrangements can make it difficult to decide what's yours and what's your neighbor's. Here are the rules:

- Your bread or roll plate is placed above and just to the left of your plate.

- All glassware—water, wine, and cocktail glasses—is placed above and to the right of your plate.

- If the coffee cup and saucer are present at the start of the meal, these are placed directly to the right of the dinner plate. (Often, however, they are brought out at the conclusion of the meal.)

Remembering these points will save you the embarrassment of drinking someone else's water or grabbing your neighbor's dinner roll. But, for many people, the array of glasses and flatware is what's most intimidating and confusing. Here's how to determine what's what:

- Don't worry about the fact that there are three glasses at your place setting. Your waiter knows which one to fill with what. For your information, however, the largest glass is for water (and will probably be filled before you are seated), the wine glass with the smaller bowl is for white wine, while the one with the larger, more "bowl-shaped" bowl is for red.

- Many restaurants use the outside-in place setting plan. In the course of the meal, you work your way through the utensils from the outside in on both sides, toward the plate. You'll need the soup spoon and salad fork first, then work in to the entrée knife and entrée fork.

- Some restaurants cloud the place-setting issue with a partial left-to-right arrangement. While the salad fork and entrée fork are positioned as in the outside-in plan, the soup spoon is placed closest to the plate, not farthest from it.

Bright Idea
Consider arriving at a restaurant a few minutes early to inspect the settings. Tell the manager that this is a very important night for you. Offer a little extra tip to everyone who can help make the meal a success.

▪ Still other restaurants retain the conventional placement of salad fork and entrée fork, but, to the right of the plate, place the entrée knife first, the teaspoon next, and the soup spoon outermost.

The potential for bewilderment is greatest with the super-formal dinner setting:

▪ The array of glassware may include a shallow champagne glass or tall champagne flute and a small, funnel-shaped sherry glass in addition to the red and white wine glasses and the water glass.

▪ You may find three forks to the left of your plate. A small fish fork is outermost, the entrée fork is next, and the salad fork is innermost.

▪ To the right of the plate, look for a small salad/cheese knife closest to the plate, with the entrée knife next, and a short, broad fish knife next to that. At the outermost position, you will find the soup spoon and, perhaps, a small seafood fork.

▪ As with the outside-in setting, you begin generally from the outside and work your way in. A sorbet spoon is brought with the sorbet, and a dessert spoon with dessert.

Ordering wisely

Usually, your waiter or waitress will take drink orders first. If you are the host, let your guests order, and follow their lead. If any of them orders a drink, do so as well. You do *not* have to order an alcoholic drink, regardless of what the guest orders, but you do not want to put your guest in the position of drinking alone. If you are the guest, order as you wish.

Remember: not everyone enjoys drinking—and some people *cannot* drink. Never urge liquor on any guest, even good-naturedly. Avoid such comments as "We *have* to have a drink," or "What's a meal without a fine wine?"

In a business context, it's best to limit yourself to a single drink, especially if wine will be served with the meal. If your guest orders a second drink, make yours nonalcoholic.

If you are the host, you will be presented with the wine list. If you know your wines, by all means do yourself and your guests the favor of making a selection. If you know little about wines, don't fake it.

- You might ask your guest if she would care to see the wine list. If she is knowledgeable or indicates a preference, ask the guest to indicate the wine, and you place the order.

- If the guest defers back to you, don't panic. Ask the waiter, waitress, or sommelier (wine steward) for a recommendation. "Have you a nice red?" Or, "Do you recommend the house white?"

- Order a bottle or carafe of wine rather than by the glass.

- Savor the ritual of the wine service. You will be shown the bottle. Check to see that it is, indeed, what you ordered, then nod to the server. He will uncork the bottle and hand you the cork. Some people sniff it. This is not necessary, but do squeeze it. The cork should be moist; if it is quite dry, the wine is probably not good. The

Watch Out!
It is relatively rare to run across a bottle of wine that has gone bad. Do *not* send the bottle back just because you decide you aren't wild about that particular type of wine. And, certainly, do not send the wine back in an effort to impress your guests.

server will now pour a bit of the wine into your glass. Sniff it. You don't have to be a connoisseur to know if the wine smells like vinegar. If it does, reject it. Assuming it passes the sniff text, take a sip. If all is well, ask the server to pour.

If your server is attentive, he will refill empty wine glasses during the course of the meal. If he fails to do so, feel free to pour for any guest you can conveniently reach. If you cannot reach a guest without getting up, ask: "Would you care for more wine?" If the answer is yes, summon the server. The guest should not have to pour her own wine. If you are a guest, don't take it upon yourself to refill your own glass or anyone else's.

When ordering the meal, feel free to make suggestions if you have a favorite dish or know that the restaurant is famous for a particular specialty. While everyone reviews the menu, you may offer a comment that this or that "sounds good." When the server comes to the table, you may ask what he recommends.

- If the server begins to take your order first, reply, "Please let my guest order first."

- If your guest orders a soup or salad course, do likewise. It's important that the guest not be put in the position of eating alone.

- As a guest, ask the host for recommendations.

- As a guest, and in the absence of a recommendation from your host, order something in the middle of the price range.

- If you are the guest, follow your host's recommendation—unless it happens to be a type of food you really dislike. "I'm sure the lamb is great, but I'm afraid I'm a committed steak person."

The golden mean

A business dinner is not the right time to experiment with exotic foods or with food you've never tried before. Also, if you know that certain foods don't always agree with you, avoid them.

■ Order what is familiar to you.

■ If you are a guest, order from the middle of the price range.

■ Avoid foods that are sloppy or difficult to eat. A business meal is no place to be caught wearing a lobster bib. Pasta served with messy sauces should be avoided, if possible (they end up on ties or on laps).

■ Don't over-order. You don't want to give the impression of gluttony, you certainly don't want to waste food, and you don't want to imply that the sky's the limit since someone else is picking up the tab. Moreover, the presence of too much food cuts into your conversation time.

As a host, encourage your guest to order dessert: "I'm told the desserts here are great!" If your guest orders dessert, follow suit. (If you are watching your weight, don't demur. Order a light dessert such as fruit.) If your guest declines, suggest a cup of coffee, and don't order dessert for yourself.

Settling up

It's appropriate to ask for the check when the coffee is served. Use a credit card to pay the bill: It's fast, efficient, and discreet.

■ As a guest, do not offer to pay the bill.

> 66
> My mother made me eat broccoli. I hate broccoli. I am the President of the United States. I will not eat any more broccoli.
> —President George Bush, March 1990
> 99

Bright Idea
If your meal included the services of a sommelier, add an additional $3 to $5 per bottle of wine served. You can indicate the amount of the tip to the sommelier credit card receipt.

- If a guest offers to pay, simply reply that "My company would like you to be our guest." This takes it out of the personal realm, so the guest doesn't feel she is being a burden on you.

- Do not laboriously add up the bill when it comes, but if you detect a problem, excuse yourself politely and go to the head waiter's station to clear it up. Do not discuss or dispute the bill at the table.

These days, tips tend toward 20 percent, with 15 percent as an absolute minimum, and 18 percent just fine. A quick way to calculate the tip amount is to take 10 percent of the total and double it. The tip may be left in cash or indicated on the credit card receipt.

In addition to tipping the server and sommelier (if there is one), remember to tip the coatroom attendant for any articles checked. A dollar per item is fine, and it should be given, in cash, directly to the attendant when the articles are retrieved. Valet parking attendants expect at least $2.

Table talk

A quick review of the "small talk" advice in Chapter 5 may help you with mealtime conversation. Just bear in mind the following distinctions:

- The conversation at "power breakfasts" is appropriately business-oriented and task-centered. You may even bring some paperwork.

- The business lunch is rather more social than the business breakfast, but you can still engage in some nitty-gritty, shirtsleeves business talk.

- The business dinner is more relaxed and more social. Go light on the business talk. This is not the place to push a deal through. (However, always follow the lead of your host or your guest in this area.)

Steering the conversation

The way to guide a conversation in the direction you wish it to go is to ask questions, listen to answers, then build another question based on the answer.

At breakfast and lunch, you should feel free to steer the talk to specific business issues: "John, how do you feel about financing the deal over 36 instead of 48 months? What's your take on that?" At dinner, try to focus on social subjects, such as family, hometowns, and hobbies.

You said a mouthful

Be a patient conversationalist. Chew and swallow your food before speaking. Speaking with a mouthful of food is disgusting and upsetting to most people. Take small bites, so you can keep the rhythm of the conversation going without interruption.

Keep it light

Mealtime meetings are not good places for arguments or heated debate. Even at breakfast and lunch meetings, steer the conversation away from any potentially explosive topics. Dinnertime conversation should be confined to relatively light topics. In addition to avoiding business nitty-gritty, steer clear of politics, religion, and sex. And don't get inappropriately personal. Avoid discussion of health problems and the like.

Surviving embarrassing moments

Need we say it? Accidents happen. Minor, food-related mishaps are not a big problem in and of themselves—you *will* be forgiven for them. More important is how you respond to such events. Keep your head, and keep your sense of humor. The

Watch Out!
Do not gesture with your utensils, especially if you've speared some article of food.

" Strange to see how a good dinner and feasting reconciles everybody. —Samuel Pepys, diary entry for November 9, 1665 "

accident will be far less upsetting to your guests than an unpleasant response from you. And the more unpleasant the response, the more closely the other diners will focus on you and your mishap.

Self-inflicted spills

If you spill something on the table, *handle* the situation—now. Use your napkin to control the spread of a spill. And if your host does not immediately summon a server, you should do so.

If you spill food or drink on yourself, there is no need to call the attention of others to it. Use your napkin to wipe yourself off, and summon the waiter. Ask for club soda, and dab a little on the stain. This is a time-honored method of coping with minor spills. Often, it actually does remove or minimize the stain, but even if it doesn't, it at least demonstrates that you know what to do in a crisis.

Spills by others

If another diner spills something on you, you have two urgent tasks: Act to minimize the damage (napkin, server, club soda), and make the other person feel okay about the incident. The person who did the spilling feels terribly stupid just now. Help her feel better. Make light of the incident: "Sarah, think nothing of it. I can have the tie put in a doggie bag and eat it when I get home."

Do not express anger or irritation. Do not point out that this was "my favorite blouse" or "I just had this suit cleaned." By totally forgiving your neighbor and taking the accident in good humor, you will gain much more professional capital than you lose in the cost of a dry cleaning.

Spills on others

Chances are that the person you spill on will be gracious. But he won't be happy and, let's face it, you *will* look and feel foolish. However, you must recover from this incident, and you must behave in a way that does not magnify it:

- Apologize immediately.

- Ask what you can do to help. Do *not* start wiping down the victim.

- Suggest a remedy: "Let me call the waiter and get you some club soda for that."

Once the immediate crisis has been taken care of, offer your apology again: "I am *really* sorry about this." Do not, however, offer to pay for dry cleaning or replacement of the article of clothing. This puts the other diner in an embarrassing position. He is likely to feel pressured to decline the offer.

This said, get on with the meal. Nothing—not a minor catastrophe, not an unpleasant conversation topic, not fretting over a mistake in the bill—should be allowed to interfere with the pleasurable momentum of a successful business meal. You've invested emotional and intellectual energy in this business-social event. Don't squander any of your investment.

Just the facts

- These days, breakfast, lunch, and dinner are appropriate business mealtimes; choose the one that best suits the purpose of your meeting.

- Reviewing the rules of mealtime etiquette will make you more self-confident and comfortable. This will make everyone else more confident and comfortable as well—and that's the true purpose of good manners.

- At breakfast and lunch, the nitty-gritty of business presents acceptable and appropriate table conversation; at dinner, focus on the social, and keep the conversation light and lively.

- Mealtime mishaps—spills and the like—present an opportunity to show how well you handle a crisis situation.

Promoting Yourself

GET THE SCOOP ON...
Advancement within your current organization ▪
Hearing about opportunities ▪ Becoming identi-
fied with "portable skills" ▪ Finding a mentor ▪
Enlisting your boss's help in your climb ▪
Creating versus *finding* opportunities

Movin' On Up

Chapter 19

T he goal of office politics is not to hang on to your job, but to move onward and upward, build a career, attain more power, accept more responsibility, and reap more rewards.

Old-timers in sales are addicted to inspirational acronyms, and one of the oldest is as simple as ABC—in fact, it *is* ABC. It stands for **A**lways **B**e **C**losing. It's intended to keep the salesperson focused on the end purpose of her profession: to close the sale. You can borrow and modify this formula to remind you of the end purpose of the whole 9-to-5 (or 8-to-7) routine: **A**lways **B**e **C**limbing. In this chapter, we'll discuss how.

Your best prospects

Let's take another leaf from the book of the sales professional. Good salespeople make sales. Great salespeople create customers. They don't just take the money and run, but work at developing cus-tomer satisfaction and customer loyalty. The reason is simple. They understand that the best customers are the customers you already have, your current customers. These are the customers you know about—ones who know about you. They are the customers you have had the opportunity of satisfying. Positive experience is the best advertisement.

Much the same is true about your prospects for career advancement. Much of the time, your best opportunities lie within your current company and among the people who are, after all, your current "internal" customers. Where your performance is concerned, positive experience is the best advertisement.

Timesaver
If your company has an in-house Web site, you may be able to put yourself on a "mailing list" to automatically receive announcements of new positions or position upgrades. Check it out.

Finger on the pulse

Unfortunately, this doesn't mean you can afford to sit on your hands and wait in the hope and expectation that, someday, your boss will throw an arm around your shoulder, give your scalp a good-natured "noogie," and tell you "We're kickin' ya upstairs, kid." That is the way of the movies—*old* movies—not the real world. Typically, you don't rise in an organization. You climb. And to climb, it is necessary first to find the rungs on the ladder.

The good news is that, most of the time, the rungs aren't hidden. Just as savvy employees realize that their first, best chance for growth is within their current firm, so savvy organizations understand that their most promising "management material" is to be found among the ranks of current employees. Accordingly, many companies go out of their way to announce new positions and new opportunities internally. They may even offer programs to promote employee development.

Make it your business to become thoroughly familiar with how, where, and when new positions are posted. Some companies use a bulletin board in the break room. Some publish weekly or monthly memos. Some post positions on an internal Web site. However jobs get announced at your organization, monitor these sources daily. And respond to anything that interests you immediately. Good jobs don't stay open for long.

Ear to the ground

The company bulletin board, whatever form it takes, is an obvious place to look for new opportunities. Never overlook the obvious, but don't pass up the less obvious, either. Through every office a grapevine grows, which is an *unofficial* source of company news. Listen to that grapevine:

- Be alert to word of opportunities within the company, in your department and in others.

- Pursue any leads that interest you. Ask questions. If you hear that Department X is looking for an assistant manager, speak to the manager of Department X. Tell her what you've heard. Pursue the lead.

- Use the grapevine interactively. Put out the word that you are interested in moving up. It's best to be as specific as possible: "I really want to get into a sales supervisor position."

Eye on the stars

The most realistic view of your corporate climb is to advance one rung at a time, moving up incrementally in position and salary.

Don't get tied down to what you—or others—perceive as reality. Keep the top jobs in view, even as you inch your way up. Don't be afraid to let the scope of your ambition be known. If a job several jumps up from where you are becomes available, don't deny yourself a shot at it. Out of habit, most people set their sights too low.

Bright Idea
When you put out the word that you want to move up, it's important that you express your wishes only in positive terms: "With the success I've had selling this line, I'm ready to direct a department." Do not express your wishes negatively, as frustration with your current position, boss, or coworkers.

Niche versus pigeonhole

One of the most effective climbing strategies is to carve out a niche for yourself. Expert career consultants talk in terms of *job-specific* skills versus *portable* skills. Job-specific skills belong to a given job: For example, you're a whiz selling vacuum cleaners; you know a lot about how they work and how to impress people about the value of one brand (yours) over another. In contrast, portable skills belong to you: You're a vacuum cleaner salesperson, but you promote yourself as someone with excellent communications skills and a personality that others find highly persuasive.

When you carve your niche, concentrate on portable skills. This is the difference between creating a niche and sticking yourself in a pigeonhole. These days, those in senior management are less interested in finding people who can do a specific job—anyone can be trained in specifics—than they are in finding people who are great at solving problems or who learn quickly.

Let's say you're the person everyone calls on to get the copy machine unjammed. Does this make you a skilled copy-machine repair person? Or a problem solver? It's better to become famous in your office as a problem solver *in general* than as the person who can fix the copy machine or the person who knows whether to fill out Requisition Form A or B. So when you solve a problem, point it out. Not: "I've always been good with office copiers," but "I've always been a problem solver."

Do everything you can to become identified with portable skills. Remember that a portable skill is always expressed in terms of function—doing something with people or data or things. For example, the statement "I am persuasive" describes a trait (persuasiveness), while "I am a salesperson" is nothing more than a pigeonholing job description.

To transform trait and job description into a presentation of a portable skill, begin by combining the two: "I am a persuasive salesperson." Now take another step by changing the adjective describing the trait into a verb describing a portable skill: "I am persuasive" becomes "I persuade." Next, expand the job description by deciding whether "salesperson" *primarily* involves a function with people, data, or things. The answer is people, and the description of a transferable skill now becomes "I persuade people."

A word from our sponsor

As you become identified with the right set of skills, think about ways to become identified with the right people—or, more precisely, the right person.

Mentoring is an organizational and corporate buzzword these days. It describes the practice and process whereby a senior staffer takes a junior under her wing and provides both sponsorship and training. What a deal! How do you get in on that?

Find the power, follow the power

The first step is to target a prospective mentor. The prospect should be:

- Someone to whom you have access

- Someone in a field or area that interests you and that is appropriate to your skills and training

- Someone with the power to promote you or who is in a position to recommend promotion

In addition, a good mentor will help you generally to move your career along, and will introduce you to the right people—the people you need to expand your professional network.

Watch Out!
Be sure to choose a mentor who is willing to work with you. Being connected to someone powerful in a field of your interest is pointless if he or she isn't interested in helping you move ahead.

One way to approach a prospective mentor is to ask a likely person for business-related advice. Make the approach in an ego-stroking way: "Mr. Rawls, you're the expert on widgets in this office. What would you do . . . ?" If the person is repeatedly interested in your questions and receptive to them, you have the makings of a mentor.

Should you use HR?

Another prime candidate for mentorhood is the person with the power to promote you—*now*. If you are interested in a junior management position in Department X, seek out and talk to the senior manager of Department X. This means *by-passing* the Human Resources Department.

"But," you say, "we're *supposed* to go through HR when we want to change jobs. It's the rule!" Right. And maybe you *will* have to go through HR. But, in the end, it isn't HR that's going to get you the position you want. It's the person with the power to promote you. It's whoever is running a particular program, or operation, or department.

By definition, there are always more also-rans than winners. The route of the also-rans is always through Human Resources. You have a better chance at winning if you appeal directly to the person in charge.

What do you ask the person in charge for? Well, you ask for nothing. Instead, you start making some offers:

- "For the past three years, I've been in the trenches in Customer Service. I've learned a lot about what our customers value most, and now I'd like to apply what I've learned to managing accounts in your department."

Timesaver
Among the chief functions of Human Resources is *screening* candidates for jobs and promotions. Why waste your time and compromise your chances by submitting yourself to a screening? Proceed directly to the person whose job it is to hire, not to filter out or exclude.

- "I'm ready to bring what I've learned to you."
- "May I share some ideas with you?"

Offer value to the person with the power to promote you. Don't come *asking* for it. The idea is to put that person in a position either to promote you now or to mentor you, thereby putting you in line for promotion and career growth.

When you want to make your move

Just as your best prospects for career growth may be with your present firm, so your best mentor may be your current boss. In any case, it's often easier to move up within a department than to move out and up. Not that you should limit yourself to your current boss and department. Stand out and shine to anyone who will take notice, in your present department or outside of it—and, for that matter, in your present company or outside of it.

Focus on the firm, the department, and the boss

Assuming you have performed well in your job, you come to the negotiating table armed with something the outsider lacks: a track record with *this* department and *this* boss. When you approach the boss to discuss a promotion (or a raise), avoid focusing on your needs. These, doubtless, are uppermost in your mind ("I need a new car, I need a new house, I need to straighten my kid's teeth"), but they are not of much interest to your boss.

- Focus on what you can do for the firm.
- Focus on what you can do for the department.
- Focus on what you can do for the boss. How can you make this person's life easier and more successful? How can your climb up the corporate ladder buoy up the boss as well?

Watch Out!
Take care not to target the *wrong* mentor—someone at the end of the line or on the way out. You want to hitch your wagon to a rising star, not a falling star. Otherwise, you may well get pulled down.

Build your case

You cannot depend on your boss's being intimately familiar with your record. When you discuss career growth or a promotion, come into the conversation amply stocked with a list of solid accomplishments. Don't be vague: Avoid self-puffery supported by empty adjectives. And show, don't tell. Use words and numbers to *show* results, not to talk about them. Whenever possible, express these results in dollars: dollars made and dollars saved.

Glad you thought of it!

If a particular promotion is at stake—perhaps a new vacancy has been announced—of course you should target this in your discussion. However, sometimes a less direct approach is more effective. People are most readily persuaded by their own ideas. Do what you can, therefore, to coax the boss into "originating" the idea of promoting you:

- Approach him in the spirit of seeking advice on career growth.

- Present the evidence of your current growth— the facts and figures relating to your performance.

- Pose the question: "Where do I go from here?"

This process may evolve over a series of discussions. That's fine. Let your boss come gradually to the conclusion that you are an employee worth developing—and rewarding.

Do-it-yourself kit

The savvy career builder puts the emphasis on building. Sometimes opportunities are not waiting to be found. They must be created. The most feasible way of creating a new position is to work within your current department, in which, after all, you have firsthand experience and in which you have created credibility in the form of a quantifiable track record.

Why you should build a new position

But why should you have to *build* a new position in the first place?

- You may perceive a real, pressing need for such a position in your firm or department.

- The opportunities currently available do not meet your needs and aspirations.

- There is nothing wrong with creating or pursuing your dream.

What you need

Creating a new position is a formidable challenge, but it's also among the most exciting and fulfilling career moves you can make. Your first step is to make it your business to learn just exactly how your department or organization works and, equally important, how it works with other departments. Now imagine that you are a consultant hired by your department or organization:

- Report to yourself on how your department might be improved by the addition of such-and-such a position or the replacement of one position by another.

- Work out your recommendations in detail.

- Decide what facts and figures you need to support your recommendations, and do all that you can to secure this data.

- Create scenarios demonstrating the benefits of the new position.

- Combine these scenarios with your facts and figures and with data relating to your own

Bright Idea
Don't overlook creating your own position. If you create it, you own it. The risks may be substantial, but you have an opportunity for great creativity within your organization. You can put your stamp on it. You can become a driving force within it.

performance in your current position. Your objective is to demonstrate how you are the ideal candidate for the position.

Selling it

Once you have worked out a set of scenarios and matched yourself seamlessly to the job, take the whole show to your boss.

Don't present your proposal as something to remedy a deficiency your boss has somehow created or failed to address. Instead, put the emphasis on yourself in relation to the department: "I'd like to talk to you about how I might make more of a contribution to this department. I want to get your take on a few ideas I've been working out."

Put the emphasis on yourself as an asset to the department, and don't begin by stating the need for creating a brand-new position. Instead, as you explain to your boss how you see your new role, she—not you—should be the one to point out that you're really talking about redefining your present position or creating a new one. Let the concept of a redefined or new position come from the boss, not you. Let it be her idea, so that she will feel an ownership stake in it, which will greatly multiply its chances for becoming reality.

Lateral moves and strategic steps down

The common metaphor of "climbing" the corporate ladder can blind us to the fact that *up* is not the only direction in which a successful career might be taken. Or, put another way, perhaps we define *up* too narrowly in terms of increased salary. Sometimes *up* is a lateral move, to a position that offers about the same pay but more intellectual or spiritual satisfaction.

Watch Out!
Here is the *wrong* way to approach your boss: "I've got a great idea that will get this department into shape." New ideas can be threatening, an indictment of the status quo, implying that the boss is doing a poor job; therefore, present your proposal as something that will make the department "even better than it is now."

Besides greater job satisfaction, there is another reason to consider a lateral move—or perhaps even a downward one. Sometimes such maneuvering is necessary to position yourself for greater growth in the long run. Sometimes such moves are necessary to avoid getting locked into a career track that, ultimately, offers less money or fulfillment down the road. For example, you may have good reason to believe that a certain position offers more room for advancement than your current one. Making a lateral move *now* will position you for greater advancement later.

Lateral moves are both easier and harder to make than moves up the salary ladder. They are easier because you are on solid ground. Your boss understands that you are not motivated by salary, but by a sincere desire for the position. This suggests commitment, or, better yet, passion.

Yet the lateral move is also more difficult than the conventional upward climb—if you choose to move laterally out of your current unit or department. Your boss may find it easier to accept an outward move made for salary reasons than one motivated by a desire for some intangible this particular boss cannot offer.

Of course, there is another difficulty with the lateral move. What if your grand strategy falls apart? The potential of the new position or new department may fail to materialize, and the lateral move may retard rather than promote your growth. So unless you have a strong *personal* motive for making a lateral move, be certain that you have a sound *strategic* reason for it. Weigh future strategic gains against current risks.

The final frontier is the strategic move down. Is this ever a viable option? The short answer is *almost*

Timesaver
Don't waste your time making serial lateral moves; they are career killers. By making a habit of moving from one same-salary position to another, you convey the impression of low ambition and perhaps even unreliability. Who will invest time and energy in a subordinate who is likely to leave for no readily understood reason?

never. The risks of a purposeful downward move are great. There are a few good reasons for contemplating it:

- You have a very pressing personal reason.

- A hot new department in your company is offering an opportunity you feel you *must* take.

- You have reason to believe that your current position is in imminent peril.

Although a step down may pay off in the long run, you must confront a serious perception problem. That ladder-of-success idea is so deeply ingrained in business culture that anyone reviewing a resume or salary history that includes a decline will have a difficult time believing that your downward climb was voluntary. And, remember, the savvy career-builder always takes appearances—the record of fact—into account with every move she makes.

Just the facts

- Generally, your best opportunities for career growth are within your current firm and often your current group or department.

- Career advancement requires proactive steps, including skillful self-promotion and even creating positions, rather than a passive approach of hopeful waiting.

- Work to identify yourself with a valued set of portable skills rather than exclusively with job-related skills.

- Sometimes a strategic lateral move or (rarely) a strategic downward move will position you for long-term career growth.

GET THE SCOOP ON...
Obligations to yourself and to your employer ▪
Looking for a new job—on company time ▪
Where loyalty ends ▪ Creating and using your
personal employment network ▪ The politics
of the employment interview ▪ Transforming
rejection into a positive event

Movin' On Out

Chapter 20

The savvy office politician looking to build a career has a significant advantage over a politician seeking government office. The office politician, if dissatisfied, unsuccessful, or mindful of greater opportunity elsewhere, can always change companies. Few politicians in government service can pack up and change countries.

Think hard about Chapter 19 before you start packing your attaché case, however. All things being equal, some of your best opportunities for advancement are typically found within your current company. Unfortunately, quite often, all things are decidedly *not* equal. In fact, according to the U.S. Department of Labor, the average American worker changes employers seven times during his or her career. The days when a career-building executive started on the ground floor with a firm, then served out his or her professional life with it, are over. Don't be in a hurry to change employers, but expect to do so—more than a few times.

This chapter gives you some highly political guidelines on how to make those changes in a consistently positive direction.

What you owe yourself

You owe yourself the best working life you can create. This means, among other things:

- Doing the best job you can
- Impressing your colleagues, subordinates, and bosses with your work and style of work
- Enlarging your network of useful professional contacts
- Growing your career within your present firm
- Growing your career outside your present firm

You may feel a sense of loyalty to your present employer or your current boss. This is laudable and probably represents a healthy attitude; however, barring rare contractual restrictions, you have the right to look elsewhere for opportunity, and you have the right to quit working with your current employer at any time.

What you owe your employer

You may have a formal contract with your current employer, or you may, as a condition of employment, have agreed to certain specific terms. Beyond these, what do you owe your employer? You owe the products, services, and commitment of time you have agreed, verbally or in writing, to deliver.

The unwritten contract

Beyond this basic covenant, you are justified in feeling that you have an additional unwritten contract with your employer. You owe the highest-quality work you can do. This is a fortunate obligation,

Watch Out!
I'm not advising you simply to walk off your job. In addition to eroding or destroying your reputation, leaving without notice may result in your forfeiting some salary due you, as well as some insurance benefits. There is never a good business reason to burn your bridges.

because it is something you also owe yourself. You also owe your employer a certain degree of loyalty.

Let's explore this second point a bit further. Remember, you have the right to look for opportunities elsewhere, and you have the right to quit whenever you want. While it is common business practice to give the employer reasonable notice before you leave—and we will discuss this in a moment—no law obligates you to do so. Nevertheless, you owe your employer a *certain degree* of loyalty. You have an ethical obligation to protect his good name. This means that, in conducting a job search elsewhere, you should not bad-mouth your current employer. You also have an ethical obligation to give your current employer adequate notice before you quit.

Loyalty and adequate notice are ethical, not legal or (in most cases) contractual obligations. Failing to meet these ethical obligations typically comes back to haunt you. If you malign your current employer to a prospective employer, you will appear disloyal, and she will wonder—understandably—if you'll end up being disloyal to her as well. Moreover, if you quit on the spur of the moment, you risk acquiring a reputation within your industry as undependable.

In short, while you do not owe your employer your professional life, you do have an obligation to treat the firm honorably. If behaving well to people in your office creates good "corporate karma" for you, treating your current employer well creates positive karma industry-wide. Shabby acts have a way of returning to the doorstep of the shabby actor.

Time thief

Doing serious research into job possibilities takes time and work. The fact that you have to do that

> 66
> Anyone who says he isn't going to resign, four times, definitely will.
> —John Kenneth Galbraith, 1979
> 99

work without drawing attention to yourself in your own company makes it that much more demanding.

Remember that as long as you are in the workplace, you are on your employer's time. Ideally, you should restrict your job searching to lunch hours. You can also do some work after hours, but telephone inquiries, of course, will have to be handled during work hours. Keep this to a minimum, and don't let it interfere unduly with your daily work.

Don't stab yourself in the back

Here's your worry. You've spoken to a prospective new employer, and now you're afraid that he will call your present employer with the news. Are you just being paranoid?

Not necessarily. While it's true that even in small, close-knit industries, where everyone knows everyone else, most prospective employers keep applications in confidence; however, it's also possible that a loose lip will sink your ship. To reduce the chances of this, emphasize to any prospective employer that your inquiry or application is strictly privileged information. Be certain to use the phrase *privileged information,* and do not explain it further. Do not express a fear that "My boss will fire me if she finds out I'm looking around." Remember, you are trying to persuade your listener to be your *new* boss. Don't tell him that you're skulking around behind your current boss's back.

Plan how you want any potential employers you contact to communicate with you:

- Ask that all communication be sent to your home address. Even if your office mail comes directly to you, it's possible for a letter to go astray or be opened accidentally by someone else.

- Do *not* communicate with a prospective employer via office e-mail! E-mail sent and received on a company's e-mail account or via the company's network or on a company computer is the property of the company. You have no right to privacy where such documents are concerned. If you wish to communicate with a prospective employer via e-mail, use your own individual account and download the e-mail on your own computer, purchased with your own funds and kept at home.

- The prospective employer will probably have to contact you by telephone at your office. Given the nature of normal business hours, this is inevitable. Ask the employer to leave no sensitive messages. As with e-mail, your voice mail is not ultimately private. Your employer owns it and owns the messages left on it.

- Do not give the prospective employer a company fax number. Most fax machines are positioned in fairly public parts of an office.

Bright Idea
Don't tell others at work that you are looking for a new job. You risk being seen as a grumbler or disloyal, or even being fired. In addition, swearing them to secrecy is as effective as posting a notice on the bulletin board in the coffee room.

Keeping it positive

The moment many job changers dread most is breaking the news to the boss. It's helpful to remember that this is not a divorce. You have not pledged fidelity till death do you part, and chances are, your boss has long ago learned to accept employee turnover as par for the course.

Nevertheless, it is possible that your news will be greeted with something less than grace and maybe even viewed as a defection and a betrayal. Remember that any attempt to make you feel guilty is not your problem. It's your boss's. Also, try reminding her that your move is a matter of business and conveys no personal message of any kind.

Keep the conversation with your boss as positive as possible. This means avoiding statements to the effect of, "Look, we never really saw eye to eye, so I decided it was time for a change," or "We never really got along," or "This just wasn't right for me." Any and all of these statements may be quite true, but now is the time to draw the focus away from the company and the boss you are leaving and to concentrate the spotlight solely on yourself: "The time is right for me to make the move."

If your boss presses you for a fuller account of your motives, try to maintain the focus on the opportunities the new company offers rather on why you are leaving your current company.

Weaving your net

In Chapter 19, we discussed establishing a network within your office. Your network is *your* network. It need not be bounded by the confines of your current company.

If you're serious about finding a position outside your current company, make certain that you locate and monitor all the relevant published sources of information about your industry, including newsletters and journals, Web sites, and professional recruiting agencies. And be sure to build a personal network.

Your network starts with yourself and colleagues in other firms with whom you are acquainted. You may see your peers and colleagues at social gatherings, conventions, and professional meetings and seminars. You may also work cooperatively with colleagues in other firms. Take full advantage of any collegial contact to get to know names and faces at other companies. Become an avid collector of business cards. Start a contact file.

66

A servile loyalty [is] demeaning both to master and servant. —B. H. Liddell Hart, in *Why Don't We Learn from History?* (1944)

99

The purpose of a personal network is twofold: to obtain information, including news of jobs, and to obtain referrals and recommendations.

Casting your net

Review your list of contacts carefully before calling on anyone for a referral or recommendation. You want a person who will say good things about you and who is not motivated by any hidden agenda.

Telephone manners

How do you pop the question and ask for the recommendation?

- Frame your phone call as a request for advice.

- Summarize your current situation. Always keep the tone positive: "I've had a great year at XYZ, Inc., so, while I'm riding high, it seemed to me the perfect time for a career move."

- Ask for the referral or reference.

If your contact is not immediately 100 percent enthusiastic about providing a reference, politely thank him, then move to the next name on your list. Do *not* try to persuade the contact to make a referral or furnish a reference. This job requires total, unrestrained enthusiasm and support.

Correspondence course

So the voice on the other end of the phone replies, "Sure! Happy to do it!" You're relieved. At least *that's* over with!

Not really. Don't depend on your contact's knowing what to say about you in a verbal recommendation or a written letter of recommendation. Help out by offering an "update" on what you've been doing most recently:

Bright Idea
Keep contacts current with an occasional friendly phone call or, if appropriate, a breakfast or lunch. This will help transform your contact file into a genuine network.

- Spend a few moments enumerating some key accomplishments. Be specific, placing emphasis, if possible, on projects you and your contact worked on together.

- List for your reference your half-dozen most important duties and responsibilities.

- Mention at least three of your greatest strengths.

- Offer to fax or e-mail the points you've just made in conversation. (Remember: Don't use your current company's e-mail or fax machine to send this information! It's not private.)

Acing the interview

Most good books on the art of job-hunting include some pointers on effective interview techniques. Mark Dorio's *The Complete Idiot's Guide to the Perfect Interview* (see Appendix C) gives specialized advice on the topic. The following are some main points for the savvy career builder to bear in mind.

A matter of time

Job interviews don't have to be as intimidating as most folks find them to be. The scary thing about a job interview is that you aren't in control and that you are expected to think fast and on your feet.

At least that's what most people believe. The fact is that you don't have to relinquish control of the interview—at least not totally—and you don't have to rely completely on your capacity for ad-libbing.

Typically, you have a fair amount of time between an employment query and a call for an interview. Most people spend this time in a mixture of excited anticipation and idle worry. Instead of *spending* the time, *invest* it:

- Learn as much as you can about the organization to which you are applying.

- Learn about the role of your target position within the organization.

- Anticipate the organization's special needs, goals, and problems, then figure out how you can fulfill the needs, help achieve the goals, and solve the problems.

- Assemble a list of your *relevant* and *specific* accomplishments.

- Formulate your salary needs.

Sources of information abound, if you take the time to look for them. Check out the following:

- The company's Web site (These are often chock-full of information and may be all you need to consult.)

- The company's annual report

- Catalogs, brochures, ads, and other material issued by the firm

- Journals and newsletter articles devoted to the company

Timesaver
The ideal situation is to walk into the interview with all the answers, immediately and without question demonstrating that you are the perfect fit for the open position. The more you know about the company and its needs before you go into the interview, the nearer you will approach this ideal.

Pressing the flesh

When you walk into the interview, do so as something more than an upright, ambulatory, but otherwise lifeless version of your resume. Review Chapter 2 for pointers on body language, especially the nonverbal communication that accompanies making an entrance. Smile, make and maintain eye contact, and use a warm, firm (but not crushing) handshake.

Taking names

When dealing with the names of people you've just met, review the techniques outlined in Chapter 17.

Bright Idea
Holding a hand-shake until just after you've finished your greeting not only helps you remember the other person's name, it's also a way of making the handshake (and, therefore, you) more memorable for that person. It makes a routine gesture powerful.

When introduced to a person, repeat the name back: "Mr. Johnson, good to meet you." And repeat the name back as you continue to shake hands. The combination of the physical contact and the repetition of the name will help fix the name in your memory.

Helping out

The best-kept secret of the employment interview is that it is almost as great an ordeal for the interviewer(s) as it is for the interviewee. How so?

- Most interviewers are unaccustomed to interviewing job candidates.

- Most interviewers are more or less unprepared for the interview.

- Most interviewers see the interview as an interruption in their day. They'd rather be doing their "real business."

Remember, the ideal job candidate appears at the interview as the answer to the company's needs—a problem solver. If you've done your homework, you should have some idea of what kinds of problems the company faces. There is one problem, however, you can be absolutely certain the interviewer faces: the problem of how to get through the interview with you.

Here is a terrific opportunity to present yourself as a problem solver. Walk into the interview armed with questions and topics of conversation. Bring up the issues your research has raised. In short, solve the interviewer's immediate problem by helping him *get through the interview.*

Aim for closure

At the conclusion of the interview, push toward closure. Some interviews conclude with a job offer.

Now *that's* closure. A minority of interviews conclude with the interviewer telling you that you're not the person he had in mind. This is rare—bad news generally comes in the form of a follow-up letter. But at least it, too, represents closure. Most interviews, however, conclude with a "you'll hear from us." This is not sufficient closure.

To provoke closure, you can thank the interviewer(s) for his time, interest, and conversation, then try to prompt the interviewer into giving you a positive next step: "When should I expect to hear from you?" And: "Will it be a letter or a phone call?" This forces the issue without backing the interviewer into an uncomfortable corner.

And I thank you

As soon as you get back home—or back to your office—write a thank-you note to the interviewer(s):

- Express the pleasure you took in the conversation (even if you didn't really enjoy it).

- Say something nice about the company.

- Reiterate anything said about further contact: "I look forward to hearing from you sometime next week."

- Add any brief points you may have neglected in the interview.

- Close with thanks.

Next to the interview itself, the thank-you note is the most important element in the interview process—yet it is *usually* omitted! Your thank-you note *will* be noticed, and it *will* set you apart from the crowd.

Easy on the spurs

A post-interview silence can be deafening. In the aftermath of some events, no news is good news, but

Watch Out!
Don't issue ultimatums warning that your "availability is limited" or you've "really got to get an answer now." If you push too hard for a quick answer, you risk provoking the quickest answer of all: *No*. If you really do have another offer on the table, explain this as a fact, without implying any threat.

following an interview, no news is, well, no news. It's important to end the interview by agreeing on a specific date by which you will hear from the interviewer. When this date has come and gone without word, you have a good reason to call. Ask about the status of the decision. And, as always, offer help: "Is there any additional information I can supply that will help you reach a decision?"

If the follow-up call produces no definitive result, conclude by attempting to establish a new decision date.

Don't slam that door

If the answer, when it finally comes, is no, don't let the door slam behind you. In business, *no* doesn't have to be forever. Experienced salespeople don't like losing sales any more than novice salespeople do, but they take some satisfaction in knowing that they *have* gained something from their investment of time and effort. They have gained valuable contact with a customer. Even an interview that fails to yield an offer is an opportunity for contact with powerful people—that is, people powerful enough to hire you. There may well be another time and another position, and, at the very least, you have expanded your network of contacts by one or more individuals.

Reply positively to a no, repeating your thanks for the time invested, for the opportunity of meeting the interviewer(s), and for the interest shown in you. Emphasize the latter. Remind these people that they thought highly enough of you to be interested in you. That is, end on a note of acceptance—or, at least, of consideration, rather than rejection.

Just the facts

- You owe yourself the determination and means to create the best career possible; you owe your current employer a fair return in value on the value she has invested in you.

- Looking for a new job on your current company's time is usually unavoidable, but must be done discreetly and with the least possible impact on the service you owe your current employer.

- Invest time and effort in continually developing and expanding your network, transforming business contacts into career resources.

- The key to performing well in a job interview is to know enough about the target company to be able to present yourself as the ideal answer to the prospective employer's needs and the solution to her problems.

Glossary

General terms

Body language The nonverbal cues, usually unconscious, including gestures, postures, and facial expressions, by which we often communicate our "real" feelings.

Downward move Any job move involving a decrease in salary.

Dynamic listening Listening with the mind and imagination. Dynamic listening requires the listener to identify the interest he or she has in common with the speaker.

E-mail Short for "electronic mail," e-mail consists of messages sent electronically, via telecommunication links (phone lines and/or installed network lines), from one computer to one or more other computers.

Fired Dismissed from a position because of failure to perform or failure to perform satisfactorily. See also **fired for cause.**

Fired for cause Dismissed from a position because of wrongdoing (such as theft, sexual harassment,

375

and drug use). This is the most pejorative form of termination.

Hardball negotiation   Negotiation—usually over salary—of a take-it-or-leave-it variety. Except in very special circumstances, hardball negotiation rarely gets either side everything it wants.

Human resources department   The department in larger corporations that handles routine personnel matters and that screens employment applications and, often, requests for promotion or transfers from one department to another.

Informational interview   An interview a job hunter requests in order to gather information about a particular company or even an entire industry. The purpose of the informational interview, besides gaining information, is to develop one's network of career contacts.

Internet   The name for a group of worldwide information resources linked together in a complex of electronic networks and accessible by anyone with a computer, modem, telephone line, and an account with an Internet service provider. A large number of employment-related services, as well as information relevant to all aspects of business and to many professions, is available on the Internet.

Lateral move   Leaving one position to move to another offering the same salary or, at most, a compensation increase of 3 percent or less.

Networking   The systematic acquisition of contacts for the purpose of learning about job opportunities, developing one's career, and growing within one's current company.

Office politics   The ways in which people interact with one another in the workplace; also, the strategies savvy employees use to achieve and maintain a competitive advantage in the workplace.

Portable skills   Skills specific to a person rather than to a particular job. They always describe a function, that is, how one *works* with people, data, or things. See also **specific skills.**

Proactive   Acting in advance to deal with an anticipated problem or issue rather than waiting for the problem or issue to happen, forcing you simply *to react* to it. To be proactive is to *anticipate* problems as well as opportunities rather than to react to them *after* they emerge.

Sexual harassment   Socio-sexual behavior that has the purpose and effect of substantially interfering with an individual's work performance or creating an intimidating, hostile, or offensive working environment. Sexual harassment violates Title VII of the Civil Rights Act of 1964.

Small talk   Casual conversation not directly related to business, but important in establishing a feeling of productive community and teamwork in the office.

Specific skills   In contrast to **portable skills**—general skills one can take from one job (or life experience) to another—specific skills are more or less associated with a particular job. Carpentry is a specific skill, whereas an ability to work with materials is a transferable skill.

Fifty power words

The following words are essential building blocks of effective business communication. They tend to build positive business relationships. Try to introduce them, as appropriate, into your workday speech.

Action   This word expresses what most of the people you deal with want from you. They are suspicious of words, but trust action. Promising action creates a strong positive bond and is a powerful motivator.

Analysis, analyze   Promising an analysis of an issue or problem is of far greater value than pledging to "think about" it. A formal analysis is a more or less definable product, something of value, whereas mere thought is less tangible. Always offer the greatest value you can.

Brainstorm   This word is good because it makes the prospect of group discussion sound as exciting as it can, indeed, be. It also suggests a special process and is, therefore, like *analysis*, a high-value word.

Collaborate   Use this word as an invitation to joint effort—a way of recruiting people for your project.

Collaborative   Apply this adjective to any project you want to sell to the organization as a whole. The word is powerfully inclusive.

Confer   The strength of this inclusive word is that it puts you and whomever you confer with on an equal footing, yet it also pays homage to the other person by acknowledging your belief that he or she offers worthy counsel.

Control   Used judiciously, this is a most reassuring word. Control is a valuable commodity in business, and you should interject this concept into any discussion of projects you are promoting.

Cooperate   Cooperation is a less powerful concept than collaboration, but it is useful when you are describing a project or action that requires others to be passively compliant rather than actively collaborative.

Cooperative   A reassuring adjective that is best applied to a third party. "Bill, don't worry about Shipping. They're very cooperative about these matters."

Good listener One of the things your colleagues and subordinates most fear is that they will not be heard. Assure them that they will be. This phrase invites comment, input, ideas, and feedback—all good things.

Guide The concept behind this word is of great value, because it marks a middle ground between creative freedom and strict instruction.

Hear From time to time, let others know that you *hear* what they are saying: "I hear you."

Helpful A simple and vital adjective that everyone wants to hear.

Huddle It is usually best to avoid sports metaphors, which are not only overused, but tend to be exclusive, putting off men and women who don't happen to care about sports. *Huddle,* however, is such a general term that this warning doesn't apply. It is a warm, informal invitation to group brainstorming, team-building, or discussion.

Idea A label to apply not only to your thoughts and opinions, but to those of others. The term is especially valuable for the dignity it confers on what others say.

Learn A word that conveys a sense of positive progress in the course of any process.

Listen Conveys openness; an invitation to creativity.

Manage Like **control,** this is a word people in organizations like to hear. It implies direction.

Offer Used correctly, *offer* creates a climate of fair exchange in which both sides benefit.

Open mind Used sincerely, this phrase invites creativity by disavowing prejudgment.

Productive Always a strong word in business, which is, by definition, product-oriented.

Solve A word that conveys relief and a satisfying sense of closure. *Solve* conveys a powerful promise.

Synergy Something of a buzzword, *synergy* is easily overused; however, it conveys an important concept, on which all effective organizations rest—namely, that the sum is greater than its parts.

Team Use this frequently to develop and reinforce an attitude of ongoing collaboration and interdependence.

Team player This is best used to describe oneself—as committed to others and the welfare of the organization.

Team up An informal invitation to collaborate, this injunction implies creative strength.

Thanks A word that should be used as often as possible. Acknowledging the contributions of others is not merely polite, but confers a sense of ownership, prompting people to buy into your ideas and projects.

Together Another powerful word that should be injected into dialogue at every opportunity.

Work together Remind those around you that you are all in the enterprise together.

Exchange words

The words we've just discussed emphasize inclusion and collaboration. The following do this as well, but they put the accent on the exchange of value. This makes them even more specifically relevant to business situations.

Accountability A straightforward pledge that the bucks stops here.

Cost-effective Typically, business comes down to numbers. This phrase embodies a very compelling concept.

Creative   Use this as an alternative to *resourceful*. It is a more positive, active term.

Develop   The value of this word is that it promotes creativity while buying the time for that creativity. The implication is that development takes time. Use this word to reinforce the sense of long-term commitment among members of the organization or with clients and vendors.

Effective   A word that certifies progress and/or the value of an investment of resources.

Evaluate   A stronger, more active alternative to *consider*.

Expedite   This is a great advocacy word. A promise to expedite is not only a pledge to speed something up, but also implies that you'll make it easier and, perhaps, more secure. Use of this word conveys your willingness to take charge.

Experience   Time-dependent qualities are of great value because, as a rule, there is no substitute for them. Use this word sparingly, but do not fail to use it when it is warranted.

Feasible   Conveys sound judgment and caution without negativity or timidity.

Improve   The mechanic's hoary adage—*if it ain't broke, don't fix it*—has no place in a successful enterprise. Use words that convey a certain restless need to make everything better.

Increase   A most inviting word in many business contexts.

Ownership   Used in the sense of taking responsibility for something, for seeing a project through, this conveys an uncompromising acceptance of accountability.

Profitable   A word of old-fashioned, back-to-basics power.

Reduce   This is one of the few negative words that, in a business context, is not pejorative. Use this in preference to the more panicky *cut back.*

Smart   A much cannier word than *intelligent,* smart suggests intelligence in action, the pragmatic application of wisdom.

Successful   Always look for an opportunity to use this word.

Valuable   Be generous with this word as a description of others' points of view and ideas.

Value   Avoid such words as *price* or *cost* (except in the context of *cost-effective*), and embrace the far more meaningful concept of *value.* This word can elevate a mere transaction to the status of a business relationship.

Vigorous   Suggests an active, but not hyperactive, approach to a problem, situation, or opportunity.

Vital   The root of this word is Latin for life and all that relates to life. In English, it retains this very basic connotation.

Resource Guide

National offices

For authoritative, up-to-date information on all legal aspects of employment issues, consult any of the following U.S. Department of Labor resources:

U.S. Department of Labor
Main Office
Office of Public Affairs
200 Constitution Ave., NW
Room S-1032
Washington, DC 20210
(202) 693-4650

U.S. Department of Labor Agency Offices:
Bureau of International Labor Affairs (ILAB)
U.S. Department of Labor
ILAB Office of Public Affairs
200 Constitution Ave., NW
Room S-5006
Washington, DC 20210
(202) 219-6373 Ext. 4

Bureau of Labor Statistics (BLS)
U.S. Department of Labor
BLS Office of Public Affairs
Postal Square Building
2 Massachusetts Ave., NE
Room 4110
Washington, DC 20212
(202) 606-5900

Employment Standards Administration (ESA)
U.S. Department of Labor
ESA Office of Public Affairs
200 Constitution Ave., NW
Room S-3325
Washington, DC 20210
(202) 693-0023

Employment and Training Administration (ETA)
U.S. Department of Labor
ETA Office of Public Affairs
200 Constitution Ave., NW
Room N-4700
Washington, DC 20210
(202) 219-6871

Mine Safety and Health Administration (MSHA)
U.S. Department of Labor
MSHA Office of Public Affairs
Ballston Towers #3
4015 Wilson Blvd.
Room 601
Arlington, Virginia 22203
(703) 235-1452

Occupational Safety and Health Administration
(OSHA)
U.S. Department of Labor
OSHA Office of Public Affairs
200 Constitution Ave., NW
Room N-3649
Washington, DC 20210
(202) 693-1999

Pension and Welfare Benefits Administration
(PWBA)
U.S. Department of Labor
PWBA Office of Public Affairs
200 Constitution Ave., NW
Room N-5656
(202) 219-8921

Veterans' Employment and Training Service
(VETS)
U.S. Department of Labor
VETS Office of Public Affairs
200 Constitution Ave., NW
Room S-1310A
Washington, DC 20210
(202) 219-5573

Women's Bureau (WB)
U.S. Department of Labor
WB Office of Public Affairs
200 Constitution Ave., NW
Room S-3311
Washington, DC 20210
(202) 219-6652

Regional offices

Region I—Connecticut, Maine, Massachusetts, New Hampshire, Rhode Island, Vermont

U.S. Department of Labor
Office of Public Affairs
1 Congress St.
11th Floor
Boston, Massachusetts 02114
(617) 565-2072

Region II—New York, New Jersey, Puerto Rico, Virgin Islands

U.S. Department of Labor
Office of Public Affairs
201 Varick St.
Room 605
New York, New York 10014
(212) 337-2319

Region III—Delaware, District of Columbia, Maryland, Pennsylvania, Virginia, West Virginia

U.S. Department of Labor
Office of Public Affairs
3535 Market St.
Room 14120
Philadelphia, Pennsylvania 19104
(215) 596-1139

Region IV—Alabama, Florida, Georgia, Kentucky, Mississippi, North Carolina, South Carolina, Tennessee

U.S. Department of Labor
Office of Public Affairs
1371 Peachtree St., NE
Room 317
Atlanta, Georgia 30367
(404) 562-2080

Region V—Illinois, Indiana, Michigan, Minnesota, Ohio, Wisconsin

U.S. Department of Labor
Office of Public Affairs
230 South Dearborn St.
Room 3192
Chicago, Illinois 60604
(312) 353-4807

Region VI—Arkansas, Louisiana, New Mexico, Oklahoma, Texas

U.S. Department of Labor
Office of Public Affairs
525 Griffin St.
Room 724
Dallas, Texas 75202
(214) 767-4777

Region VII—Iowa, Kansas, Missouri, Nebraska

U.S. Department of Labor
Office of Public Affairs
City Center Square
1100 Main, Suite 1220
Kansas City, Missouri 64105
(816) 426-5481

Region VIII—Colorado, Montana, North Dakota, South Dakota, Utah, Wyoming

U.S. Department of Labor
Office of Public Affairs
1801 California St.
Suite 950
Denver, Colorado 80202-2614
(303) 844-1300

Region IX—Arizona, California, Guam, Hawaii, Nevada

U.S. Department of Labor
Office of Public Affairs
71 Stevenson St.
Suite 1035
San Francisco, California 94105
(415)975-4740

Region X—Alaska, Idaho, Oregon, Washington

U.S. Department of Labor
Office of Public Affairs
1111 Third Ave.
Room 805
Seattle, Washington 98101
(206) 553-7620

Other information

For local information on employment-related issues, go to the World Wide Web at http://www.loc.gov, which contains indexes for state and local government information, especially relating to employment issues.

If you have a specific job-related issue or problem, check out the National Labor Relations Board Help Desk at http://www.nlrb.gov.

If you have an issue or problem related to discrimination or sexual harassment, visit the Web site of the U.S. Equal Employment Opportunity Commission at http://www.eeoc.gov.

For more broadly based career issues, the two best online starting-place resources are:

- America Online (AOL): The "Career Center" (AOL keyword "careers").

- Compuserve (Csi): Check out the E-Span Online Job Listing. Also type "go" words related to your field. The Professions Forum (GO PROFESSIONS) is a good source for networking.

Recommended Reading

General

Axelrod, Alan, and Jim Holtje. *201 Ways to Deal with Difficult People.* McGraw-Hill, 1997.

———. *201 Ways to Manage Your Time Better.* McGraw-Hill, 1997.

———. *201 Ways to Say No Gracefully and Effectively.* McGraw-Hill, 1997.

Axtell, Roger E., ed. *Do's and Taboos Around the World,* third edition. John Wiley, 1993.

Benton, D. A. *Lions Don't Need to Roar: Using the Leadership Power of Professional Presence to Stand Out.* Warner Books, 1992.

Carr, Clay. *The New Manager's Survival Manual,* second edition. John Wiley, 1995.

Clifton, Donald O., and Paula Nelson. *Soar with Your Strengths.* Dell, 1992.

Covey, Stephen R. *The Seven Habits of Highly Effective People.* Simon & Schuster/Fireside Books, 1989.

Dorio, Marc. *The Complete Idiot's Guide to the Perfect Interview.* Alpha Books, 1997.

Appendix C

———. *The Complete Idiot's Guide to Getting the Job You Want*. Revised Edition. Alpha Books, 1998.

Dubrin, Andrew J. *10 Minute Guide to Leadership*. Macmillan Spectrum/Alpha Books, 1997.

Ellis, Arthur, and Arthur Lange. *How to Keep People from Pushing Your Buttons*. Carol Publishing Group, 1994.

Fast, Julius. *Body Language*. Pocket Books, 1970.

———. *Body Language in the Work Place*. Viking Penguin, 1994.

Griffin, Jack. *Lifetime Guide to Business Writing and Speaking*. Prentice Hall, 1996.

———. *How to Say It at Work*. Prentice Hall, 1998.

Hemphill, Barbara. *Taming the Office Tiger: The Complete Guide to Getting Organized at Work*. Kiplinger Books, 1996.

Kleiman, Carol. *The 100 Best Jobs for the 1990s and Beyond*. Dearborn Financial Publishing, 1992.

Mandell, Terri. *Power Schmoozing: The New Etiquette for Social and Business Success*. McGraw-Hill, 1996.

McCormack, Mark H. *What They Don't Teach You at Harvard Business School*. Bantam Books, 1984.

———. *What They Still Don't Teach You at Harvard Business School*. Bantam Books, 1990.

Osborn, Susan M. *The System Made Me Do It! A Life-changing Approach to Office Politics*. Lifethread, 1997.

Pachter, Barbara, and Marjorie Brody. *Complete Business Etiquette Handbook*. Prentice Hall, 1995.

Roberts, Wess. *Straight A's Never Made Anybody Rich: Lessons in Personal Achievement*. Harper Perennial, 1991.

Rozakis, Laurie, and Bob Rozakis. *The Complete Idiot's Guide to Office Politics.* Alpha Books, 1998.

Sinetar, Marsha. *Do What You Love, the Money Will Follow: Discovering Your Right Livelihood.* Paulist Press, 1987.

Snelling, Robert O., Sr. *The Right Job: How to Get the Job That's Right for You.* Penguin Books, 1993.

Solomon, Muriel. *Working with Difficult People.* Prentice Hall, 1990.

Sutcliffe, Andrea J. *First-Job Survival Guide.* Henry Holt, 1997.

Tannen, Deborah. *Talking from 9 to 5: How Women's and Men's Conversational Styles Affect Who Gets Heard, Who Gets Credit, and What Gets Done at Work.* William Morrow, 1994.

Toropov, Brandon. *The Complete Idiot's Guide to Getting Along with Difficult People.* Alpha Books, 1997.

Van Fleet, James K. *Conversational Power: The Key to Success with People.* Prentice Hall, 1984.

On leadership

Axelrod, Alan. *Patton on Leadership: Strategic Lessons for Corporate Warfare.* Prentice Hall Press, 1999.

Bennis, Warren. *On Becoming a Leader.* Addison-Wesley, 1997.

Cleary, Thomas, tr. *The Book of Leadership and Strategy: Lessons of the Chinese Masters.* Shambhala Publications, 1996.

Cohen, William A. *The Art of the Leader.* Prentice Hall, 1991.

Conger, Jay Alden. *Charismatic Leader: Behind the Mystique of Exceptional Leadership.* Jossey-Bass, 1989.

Harvard Business Review on Leadership. Harvard Business School Press, 1998.

Hayward, Steven F. *Churchill on Leadership: Executive Success in the Face of Adversity.* Prima Publications, 1998.

Kaltman, Al. *Cigars, Whiskey, and Winning: Leadership Lessons from Ulysses S. Grant.* Prentice Hall, 1998.

Krass, Peter, ed. *The Book of Leadership Wisdom: Classic Writings by Legendary Business Leaders.* John Wiley, 1998.

Krause, Donald G. *The Art of War for Executives.* Berkley Publishing Group, 1995.

McFarland, Lynne Joy, et al. *21st Century Leadership: Dialogues with 100 Top Leaders.* Leadership Press, 1998.

Phillips, Donald T. *Lincoln on Leadership: Executive Strategies for Tough Times.* Warner Books, 1992.

Rosenbach, William E., et al., eds. *Contemporary Issues in Leadership.* Westview, 1998.

Sun Tzu. *Art of War.* Oxford University Press, 1984.

Wills, Garry. *Certain Trumpets: The Call of Leaders.* Touchstone, 1995.

Important Documents

On sexual harassment

The following material is excerpted from the "Policy Guidance on Current Issues of Sexual Harassment," from the Equal Employment Opportunity Commission (EEOC). Footnotes have been deleted.

1. **SUBJECT:** Policy Guidance on Current Issues of Sexual Harassment.

2. **EFFECTIVE DATE:** Upon receipt.

3. **EXPIRATION DATE:** As an exception to EEOC Order 295.001, Appendix B, Attachment 4, § a(5), this notice will remain in effect until rescinded or superseded.

4. **SUBJECT MATTER:** This document provides guidance on defining sexual harassment and establishing employer liability in light of recent cases.

Section 703(a)(1) of Title VII, 42 U.S.C. § 2000e-2(a) provides:

It shall be an unlawful employment practice for an employer...to fail or refuse to hire or to discharge any individual, or otherwise to discriminate against any individual with respect to his compensation, terms conditions or privileges of employment, because of such individual's race, color, religion, sex, or national origin.

In 1980 the Commission issued guidelines declaring sexual harassment a violation of Section 703 of Title VII, establishing criteria for determining when unwelcome conduct of a sexual nature constitutes sexual harassment, defining the circumstances under which an employer may be held liable, and suggesting affirmative steps an employer should take to prevent sexual harassment. *See* Section 1604.11 of the Guidelines on Discrimination Because of Sex, 29 C.F.R. § 1604.11 ("Guidelines"). The Commission has applied the Guidelines in its enforcement litigation, and many lower courts have relied on the Guidelines.

The issue of whether sexual harassment violates Title VII reached the Supreme Court in 1986 in *Meritor Savings Bank v. Vinson*, 106 S. Ct. 2399, 40 EPD ¶ 36,159 (1986). The Court affirmed the basic premises of the Guidelines as well as the Commission's definition. The purpose of this document is to provide guidance on the following issues in light of the developing law after *Vinson*:

- determining whether sexual conduct is "unwelcome";

- evaluating evidence of harassment;

- determining whether a work environment is sexually "hostile";

- holding employers liable for sexual harassment by supervisors; and

- evaluating preventive and remedial action taken in response to claims of sexual harassment.

(b) Background

A. Definition

Title VII does not proscribe all conduct of a sexual nature in the workplace. Thus it is crucial to clearly define sexual harassment: only unwelcome sexual conduct that is a term or condition of employment constitutes a violation. 29 C.F.R. § 1604.11(a). The EEOC's Guidelines define two types of sexual harassment: "quid pro quo" and "hostile environment." The Guidelines provide that "unwelcome" sexual conduct constitutes sexual harassment when "submission to such conduct is made either explicitly or implicitly a term or condition of an individual's employment," 29 C.F.R § 1604.11 (a) (1). "Quid pro quo harassment" occurs when "submission to or rejection of such conduct by an individual is used as the basis for employment decisions affecting such individual," 29 C.F.R § 1604.11(a)(2). 29 C.F.R. § 1604.11(a)(3). The Supreme Court's decision in *Vinson* established that both types of sexual harassment are actionable under section 703 of Title VII of the Civil Rights Act of 1964, 42 U.S.C. § 2000e-2(a), as forms of sex discrimination.

Although "quid pro quo" and "hostile environment" harassment are theoretically distinct claims, the line between the two is not always clear and the two forms of harassment often occur together. For example, an employee's tangible job conditions are affected when a sexually hostile work environment results in her constructive discharge. Similarly, a supervisor who makes sexual advances toward a subordinate employee may communicate an implicit threat to adversely affect her job status if she does not comply. "Hostile environment" harassment may acquire characteristics of "quid pro quo" harassment if the offending supervisor abuses his authority over employment decisions to force the victim to endure or participate in the sexual conduct. Sexual harassment may culminate in a retaliatory discharge if a victim tells the harasser or her employer she will no longer submit to the harassment, and is then fired in retaliation for this protest. Under these circumstances it would be appropriate to conclude that both harassment and retaliation in violation of section 704(a) of Title VII have occurred.

Distinguishing between the two types of harassment is necessary when determining the employer's liability (*see infra* Section D). But while categorizing sexual harassment as "quid pro quo," "hostile environment," or both is useful analytically these distinctions should not limit the Commission's investigations, which generally should consider all available evidence and testimony under all possibly applicable theories.

B. Supreme Court's Decision in Vinson

Meritor Savings Bank v. Vinson posed three questions for the Supreme Court:

1.   Does unwelcome sexual behavior that creates a hostile working environment constitute employment discrimination on the basis of sex;

2.   Can a Title VII violation be shown when the district court found that any sexual relationship that existed between the plaintiff and her supervisor was a "voluntary one"; and

3.   Is an employer strictly liable for an offensive working environment created by a supervisor's sexual advances when the employer does not know of,

and could not reasonably have known of, the supervisor's misconduct.

1) **Facts**—The plaintiff had alleged that her supervisor constantly subjected her to sexual harassment both during and after business hours, on and off the employer's premises; she alleged that he forced her to have sexual intercourse with him on numerous occasions, fondled her in front of other employees, followed her into the women's restroom and exposed himself to her, and even raped her on several occasions. She alleged that she submitted for fear of jeopardizing her employment. She testified, however, that this conduct had ceased almost a year before she first complained in any way, by filing a Title VII suit, her EEOC charge was filed later (*see infra* at n.34). The supervisor and the employer denied all of her allegations and claimed they were fabricated in response to a work dispute.

2) **Lower Courts' Decisions**—After trial, the district court found the plaintiff was not the victim of sexual harassment and was not required to grant sexual favors as a condition of employment or promotion. *Vinson v. Taylor*, 22 EPD ¶ 30,708 (D.D.C. 1980). Without resolving the conflicting testimony, the district court found that if a sexual relationship had existed between plaintiff and her supervisor, it was "a voluntary one...having nothing to do with her continued employment." The district court nonetheless went on to hold that the employer was not liable for its supervisor's actions because it had no notice of the alleged sexual harassment; although the employer had a policy against discrimination and an internal grievance procedure, the plaintiff had never lodged a complaint.

The court of appeals reversed and remanded, holding the lower court should have considered whether the evidence established a violation under the "hostile environment" theory. *Vinson v. Taylor*, 753 F.2d 141, 36 EPD ¶ 34,949, *denial of rehearing en banc*, 760 F.2d 1330, 37 EPD ¶ 35,232 (D.C. Cir. 1985). The court ruled that a victim's "voluntary" submission to sexual advances has "no materiality whatsover" to the proper inquiry: whether "toleration of sexual harassment [was] a condition of her employment." The court further held that an employer is absolutely liable for sexual harassment committed by a supervisory employee, regardless of whether the employer actually knew or reasonably could have known of the misconduct, or would have disapproved of and stopped the misconduct if aware of it.

3) Supreme Court's Opinion—The Supreme Court agreed that the case should be remanded for consideration under the "hostile environment" theory and held that the proper inquiry focuses on the "unwelcomeness" of the conduct rather than the "voluntariness" of the victim's participation. But the Court held that the court of appeals erred in concluding that employers are always automatically liable for sexual harassment by their supervisory employees.

a) "Hostile Environment" Violates Title VII—The Court rejected the employer's contention that Title VII prohibits only discrimination that causes "economic" or "tangible" injury: "Title VII affords employees the right to work in an environment free from discriminatory intimidation, ridicule, and insult whether based on sex, race, religion, or national origin. 106 S. Ct. at 2405. Relying on the

EEOC's Guidelines definition of harassment, the court held that a plaintiff may establish a violation of Title VII "by proving that discrimination based on sex has created a hostile or abusive work environment." *Id.* The Court quoted the Eleventh Circuit's decision in *Henson v. City of Dundee*, 682 F.2d 897, 902, 29 EPD ¶ 32,993 (11th Cir. 1982):

Sexual harassment which creates a hostile or offensive environment for members of one sex is every bit the arbitrary barrier to sexual equality at the workplace that racial harassment is to racial equality. Surely, a requirement that a man or woman run a gauntlet of sexual abuse in return for the privilege of being allowed to work and made a living can be as demeaning and disconcerting as the harshest of racial epithets.

106 S. Ct. at 2406. The Court further held that for harassment to violates Title VII, it must be "sufficiently severe or pervasive 'to alter the conditions of [the victim's] employment and create an abusive working environment.'" *Id.* (quoting *Henson*, 682 F.2d at 904).

b) Conduct Must Be "Unwelcome"—Citing the EEOC's Guidelines, the Court said the gravamen of a sexual harassment claim is that the alleged sexual advances were "unwelcome." 106 S. Ct. at 2406. Therefore, "the fact that sex-related conduct was 'voluntary,' in the sense that the complainant was not forced to participate against her will, is not a defense to a sexual harassment suit brought under Title VII...The correct inquiry is whether [the victim] by her conduct indicated that the alleged sexual advances were unwelcome, not whether her actual participation in sexual intercourse was voluntary." *Id.* Evidence of a complainant's sexually

provocative speech or dress may be relevant in
determining whether she found particular advances
unwelcome, but should be admitted with caution in
light of the potential for unfair prejudice, the Court
held.

**c) Employer Liability Established Under Agency
Principles**—On the questions of employer liability
in "hostile environment" cases, the Court agreed
with EEOC's position that agency principles should
be used for guidance. While declining to issue a
"definitive rule on employer liability," the Court did
reject both the court of appeals' rule of automatic
liability for the actions of supervisors and the
employer's position that notice is always required.
106 S. Ct. at 2408-09.

The following sections of this document provide
guidance on the issues addressed in *Vinson* and subsequent cases.

(b)Guidance

**A. Determining Whether Sexual Conduct Is
Unwelcome**

Sexual harassment is "unwelcome...verbal or physical conduct of a sexual nature..." 29 C.F.R. §
1604.11(a). Because sexual attraction may often play
a role in the day-to-day social exchange between
employees, "the distinction between invited, unin-
vited-but-welcome, offensive-but-tolerated, and flatly
rejected" sexual advances may well be difficult to dis-
cern. *Barnes v. Costle*, 561 F.2d 983, 999, 14 EPD ¶
7755 (D.C. Cir. 1977) (MacKinnon J., concurring).
But this distinction is essential because sexual conduct becomes unlawful only when it is unwelcome.
The Eleventh Circuit provided a general definition
of "unwelcome conduct" in *Henson v. City of Dundee*,
682 F.2d at 903: the challenged conduct must be

unwelcome "in the sense that the employee did not solicit or incite it, and in the sense that the employee regarded the conduct as undesirable or offensive."

When confronted with conflicting evidence as to welcomeness, the Commission looks "at the record as a whole and at the totality of circumstances..." 29 C.F.R. § 1604.11(b), evaluating each situation on a case-by-case basis. When there is some indication of welcomeness or when the credibility of the parties is at issue, the charging party's claim will be considerably strengthened if she made a contemporaneous complaint or protest. Particularly when the alleged harasser may have some reason (e.g., prior consensual relationship) to believe that the advances will be welcomed, it is important for the victim to communicate that the conduct is unwelcome. Generally, victims are well-advised to assert their right to a workplace free from sexual harassment. This may stop the harassment before it becomes more serious. A contemporaneous complaint or protest may also provide persuasive evidence that the sexual harassment in fact occurred as alleged (*see infra* Section B). Thus, in investigating sexual harassment charges, it is important to develop detailed evidence of the circumstances and nature of any such complaints or protests, whether to the alleged harasser, higher management, co-workers or others.

While a complaint or protest is helpful to charging party's case, it is not a necessary element of the claim. Indeed, the Commission recognizes that victims may fear repercussions from complaining about the harassment and that such fear may explain a delay in opposing the conduct. If the victim failed to complain or delayed in complaining, the investigation must ascertain why. The relevance of whether the victim has complained varies depending upon "the nature of the sexual advances and the context in which the alleged incidents occurred." 29 C.F.R. § 1604.11(b).

Example—Charging Party (CP) alleges that her supervisor subjected her to unwelcome sexual advances that created a hostile work environment. The investigation into her charge discloses that her supervisor began making intermittent sexual advances to her in June, 1987, but she did not complain to management about the harassment. After the harassment continued and worsened, she filed a charge with EEOC in June, 1988. There is no evidence CP welcomed the advances. CP states that she feared that complaining about the harassment would cause her to lose her job. She also states that she initially believed she could resolve the situation herself, but as the harassment became more frequent and severe, she said she realized that intervention by EEOC was necessary. The investigator determines CP is credible and concludes that the delay in complaining does not undercut CP's claim.

When welcomeness is at issue, the investigation should determine whether the victim's conduct is consistent, or inconsistent, with her assertion that the sexual conduct is unwelcome.

In *Vinson*, the Supreme Court made clear that voluntary submission to sexual conduct will not necessarily defeat a claim of sexual harassment. The correct inquiry "is whether [the employee] by her conduct indicated that the alleged sexual advances were unwelcome, not whether her actual participation in sexual intercourse was voluntary." 106 S. Ct. at 2406 (emphasis added). *See also* Commission Decision No. 84-1 ("acquiescence in sexual conduct at the workplace may not mean that the conduct is welcome to the individual").

In some cases the courts and the Commission have considered whether the complainant welcomed the sexual conduct by acting in a sexually aggressive manner, using sexually oriented language, or soliciting the sexual conduct. Thus, in *Gan v. Kepro Circuit Systems*, 27 EPD ¶ 32,379 (E.D. Mo. 1982), the plaintiff regularly used vulgar language, initiated sexually oriented conversations with her co-workers, asked male employees about their marital sex lives and whether they engaged in extramarital affairs, and discussed her own sexual encounters. In rejecting the plaintiff's claim of "hostile environment" harassment, the court found that any propositions or sexual remarks by co-workers were "prompted by her own sexual aggressiveness and her own sexually explicit conversations" *Id.* At 23,648. And in *Vinson*, the Supreme Court held that testimony about the plaintiff's provocative dress and publicly expressed sexual fantasies is not *per se* inadmissible but the trial court should carefully weigh its relevance against the potential for unfair prejudice. 106 S. Ct. at 2407.

Conversely, occasional use of sexually explicit language does not necessarily negate a claim that sexual conduct was unwelcome. Although a charging party's use of sexual terms or off-color jokes may suggest that sexual comments by others in that situation were not unwelcome, more extreme and abusive or persistent comments or a physical assault will not be excused, nor would "quid pro quo" harassment be allowed.

Any past conduct of the charging party that is offered to show "welcomeness" must relate to the alleged harasser. In *Swentek v. US AIR, Inc.*, 830 F.2d 552, 557, 44 EPD ¶ 37,457 (4th Cir. 1987), the Fourth Circuit held the district court wrongly concluded that the plaintiff's own past conduct and use of foul language showed that "she was the kind of person who could not be offended by such comments and therefore welcomed them generally, " even though she had told the harasser to leave her alone. Emphasizing that the proper inquiry is "whether plaintiff welcomed the particular conduct in question from the alleged harasser," the court of appeals held that "Plaintiff's use of foul language or sexual innuendo in a consensual setting does not waive 'her legal protections against unwelcome harassment.'" 830 F.2d at 557 (quoting *Katz v. Dole*, 709 F.2d 251, 254 n.3, 32 EPD ¶ 33,639 (4th Cir. 1983)). Thus, evidence concerning a charging party's general character and past behavior toward others has limited, if any, probative value and does not substitute for a careful examination of her behavior toward the alleged harasser.

A more difficult situation occurs when an employee first willingly participates in conduct of a sexual nature but then ceases to participate and claims that any continued sexual conduct has created a hostile work environment. Here the employee has the burden of showing that any further sexual conduct is unwelcome, work-related harassment. The employee must clearly notify the alleged harasser that his conduct is no longer welcome. If the conduct still continues, her failure to bring the matter to the attention of higher management or the EEOC is evidence, though not dispositive, that any continued conduct is, in fact, welcome or unrelated to work. In any case, however, her refusal to submit to the sexual conduct cannot be the basis for denying her an employment benefit or opportunity; that would constituted a "quid pro quo" violation.

B. Evaluating Evidence of Harassment

The Commission recognizes that sexual conduct may be private and unacknowledged, with no eyewitnesses. Even sexual conduct that occurs openly in the workplace may appear to be consensual. Thus the resolution of a sexual harassment claim often depends on the credibility of the parties. The investigator should question the charging party and the alleged harasser in detail. The Commission's investigation also should search thoroughly for corroborative evidence of any nature. Supervisory and managerial employees, as well as co-workers, should be asked about their knowledge of the alleged harassment.

In appropriate cases, the Commission may make a finding of harassment based solely on the credibility of the victim's allegation. As with any other charge of discrimination, a victim's account must be sufficiently detailed and internally consistent so as to be plausible, and lack of corroborative evidence where such evidence logically should exist would undermine the allegation. By the same token, a general denial by the alleged harasser will carry little weight when it is contradicted by other evidence.

Of course, the Commission recognizes that a charging party may not be able to identify witnesses to the alleged conduct itself. But testimony may be obtained from persons who observed the charging party's demeanor immediately after an alleged incident of harassment. Persons with whom she discussed the incident—such as co-workers, a doctor or a counselor—should be interviewed. Other employees should be asked if they noticed changes in charging party's behavior at work or in the alleged harasser's treatment of charging party. As stated earlier, a contemporaneous complaint by the victim would be persuasive evidence both that the conduct occurred and that it was unwelcome (*see supra* Section A). So too is evidence that other employees were sexually harassed by the same person.

The investigator should determine whether the employer was aware of any other instances of harassment and if so what was the response. Where appropriate the Commission will expand the case to include class claims.

Example—Charging Party (CP) alleges that her supervisor made unwelcome sexual advances toward her on frequent occasions while they were alone in his office. The supervisor denies this allegation. No one witnessed the alleged advances. CP's inability to produce eyewitnesses to the harassment does not defeat her claim. The resolution will depend on the credibility of her allegations versus that of her supervisor's. Corroborating, credible evidence will establish her claim. For example, three co-workers state that CP looked distraught on several occasions after leaving the supervisor's office, and that she informed them on those occasions that he had sexually propositioned and touched her. In addition, the evidence shows that CP had complained to the general manager of the office about the incidents soon after they occurred. The corroborating witness testimony and her complaint to higher management would be sufficient to establish her claim. Her allegations would be further buttressed if other employees testified that the supervisor propositioned them as well.

If the investigation exhausts all possibilities for obtaining corroborative evidence, but finds none, the Commission may make a cause finding based solely on a reasoned decision to credit the charging party's testimony.

In a "quid pro quo" case, a finding that the employer's asserted reasons for its adverse action against the charging party are pretextual will usually establish a violation. The investigation should determine the validity of the employer's reasons for the charging party's termination. If they are pretextual and if the sexual harassment occurred, then it should be inferred that the charging party was terminated for rejecting the employer's sexual advances, as she claims. Moreover, if the termination occurred because the victim complained, it would be appropriate to find, in addition, a violation of section 704(a).

C. Determining Whether a Work Environment Is "Hostile"

The Supreme Court said in *Vinson* that for sexual harassment to violate Title VII, it must be "sufficiently severe or pervasive 'to alter the conditions of [the victim's] employment and create an abusive working environment.'" 106 S. Ct. at 2406 (quoting *Henson v. City of Dundee*, 682 F.2d at 904. Since "hostile environment' harassment takes a variety of forms, many factors may affect this determination, including: (1) whether the conduct was verbal or physical, or both; (2) how frequently it was repeated; (3) whether the conduct was hostile and patently offensive; (4) whether the alleged harasser was a co-worker or a supervisor; (5) whether the others joined in perpetrating the harassment; and

(6) whether the harassment was directed at more than one individual.

In determining whether unwelcome sexual conduct rises to the level of a "hostile environment" in violation of Title VII, the central inquiry is whether the conduct "unreasonably interfer[es] with an individual's work performance" or creates "an intimidating, hostile, or offensive working environment." 29 C.F.R. § 1604.11(a)(3). Thus, sexual flirtation or innuendo, even vulgar language that is trivial or merely annoying, would probably not establish a hostile environment.

1) Standard for Evaluating Harassment—In determining whether harassment is sufficiently severe or pervasive to create a hostile environment, the harasser's conduct should be evaluated from the objective standpoint of a "reasonable person." Title VII does not serve "as a vehicle for vindicating the petty slights suffered by the hypersensitive." *Zabkowicz v. West Bend* Co., 589 F. Supp. 780, 784, 35 EPD ¶ 34, 766 (E.D. Wis. 1984). *See also Ross v. Comsat*, 34 FEP cases 260, 265 (D. Md. 1984), *rev'd on other grounds*, 759 F.2d 355 (4th Cir. 1985). Thus, if the challenged conduct would not substantially affect the work environment of a reasonable person, no violation should be found.

Example—Charging Party alleges that her coworker made repeated unwelcome sexual advances toward her. An investigation discloses that the alleged "advances" consisted of invitations to join a group of employees who regularly socialized at dinner after work. The co-worker's invitations, viewed in that context and from the perspective of a reasonable person, would not have created a hostile environment and therefore did not constitute sexual harassment.

A "reasonable person" standard also should be applied to be more basic determination of whether challenged conduct is of a sexual nature. Thus, in the above example, a reasonable person would not consider the co-worker's invitations sexual in nature, and on that basis as well no violation would be found.

This objective standard should not be applied in a vacuum, however. Consideration should be given to the context in which the alleged harassment took place. As the Sixth Circuit has stated, the trier of fact must "adopt the perspective of a reasonable person's reaction to a similar environment under similar or like circumstances." *Highlander v. K.F.C. National Management Co.*, 805 F.2d 644, 650, 41 EPD ¶ 36,675 (6th Cir. 1986). The reasonable person standard should consider the victim's perspective and not stereotyped notions of acceptable behavior. For example, the Commission believes that a workplace in which sexual slurs, displays of "girlie" pictures, and other offensive conduct abound can constitute a hostile work environment even if many people deem it to be harmless or insignificant. *Cf. Rabidue v. Osceola Refining Co.*, 805 F.2d 611, 626, 41 EPD ¶ 36,643 (6th Cir. 1986) (Keith, C.J., dissenting), cert. denied, 107 S. Ct. 1983, 42 EPD 36,984 (1987). *Lipsett v. University of Puerto Rico*, 864 F.2d 881, 898 48 EPD ¶ 38,393 (1st Cir. 1988).

2) Isolated Instances of Harassment—Unless the conduct is quite severe, a single incident or isolated incidents of offensive sexual conduct or remarks generally do not create an abusive environment. As the Court noted in *Vinson*, "mere utterance of an ethnic or racial epithet which engenders offensive feelings in an employee would not affect the conditions of employment to a sufficiently significant degree to violate Title VII." 106 S.Ct. at 2406 (quoting *Rogers v. EEOC*, 454 F.2d 234, 4 EPD ¶ 7597 (5th Cir. 1971), cert. denied, 406 U.S. 957, 4 EPD ¶ 7838 (1972)). A "hostile environment" claim generally requires a showing of a pattern of offensive conduct. In contrast, in "quid pro quo" cases a single sexual advance may constitute harassment if it is linked to the granting or denial of employment benefits.

But a single, unusually severe incident of harassment may be sufficient to constitute a Title VII violation; the more severed the harassment, the less need to show a repetitive series of incidents. This is particularly true when the harassment is physical. Thus, in *Barrett v. Omaha National Bank*, 584 F. Supp, 22, 35 FEP Cases 585 (D. Neb. 1983), *aff'd*, 726 F.2d 424, 33 EPD ¶ 34,132 (8th Cir. 1984), one incident constituted actionable sexual harassment. The harasser talked to the plaintiff about sexual activities and touched her in an offensive manner while they were inside a vehicle from which she could not escape.

The Commission will presume that the unwelcome, intentional touching of a charging party's intimate body areas is sufficiently offensive to alter the condition of her working environment and constitute a violation of Title VII. More so than in the case of verbal advances or remarks, a single unwelcome physical advance can seriously poison the victim's working environment. If an employee's supervisor sexually touches that employee, the Commission normally would find a violation. In such situations, it is the employer's burden to demonstrate that the unwelcome conduct was not sufficiently severe to create a hostile work environment.

When the victim is the target of both verbal and non-intimate physical conduct, the hostility of the environment is exacerbated and a violation is more likely to be found. Similarly, incidents of sexual harassment directed at other employees in addition to the charging party are relevant to a showing of hostile work environment. *Hall v. Gus Construction Co.*, 842 F.2d 1010, 46 EPD ¶ 37,905 (8th Cir. 1988); *Hicks v. Gates Rubber Co.*, 833 F.2d 1406, 44 EPD ¶ 37,542 (10th Cir. 1987); *Jones v. Flagship International*, 793 F.2d 714, 721 n.7, 40 EPD ¶ 36,392 (5th Cir. 1986), *cert. denied*, 107 S. Ct. 952, 41 EPD ¶ 36,708 (1987).

3) Non-Physical Harassment—When the alleged harassment consists of verbal conduct, the investigation should ascertain the nature, frequency, context, and intended target of the remarks. Questions to be explored might include:

- Did the alleged harasser single out the charging party?
- Did the charging party participate?
- What was the relationship between the charging party and the alleged harasser(s)?
- Were the remarks hostile and derogatory?

No one factor alone determines whether particular conduct violates Title VII. As the Guidelines emphasize, the Commission will evaluate the totality of the circumstances. In general, a woman does not forfeit her right to be free from sexual harassment by choosing to work in an atmosphere that has traditionally included vulgar, anti-female language. However, in *Rabidue v. Osceola Refining Co.*, 805 F.2d 611, 41 EPD ¶ 36,643 (6th Cir. 1986), *cert. denied,*

107 S. Ct. 1983, 42 EPD ¶ 36,984 (1987), the Sixth
Circuit rejected the plaintiff's claim of harassment
in such a situation.

One of the factors the court found relevant was
"the lexicon of obscenity that pervaded the environment of the workplace both before and after the
plaintiff's introduction into its environs, coupled
with the reasonable expectations of the plaintiff
upon voluntarily entering that environment." 805
F.2d at 620. Quoting the district court, the majority
noted that in some work environments, "'humor
and language are rough hewn and vulgar. Sexual
jokes, sexual conversations, and girlie magazines
may abound. Title VII was not meant to—or can—
change this.'" *Id.* At 620-21. The court also considered the sexual remarks and poster at issue to have
a "de minimus effect on the plaintiff's work environment when considered in the context of a society that condones and publicly features and com-
mercially exploits open displays of written and pic-
torial erotica at the newsstands, on prime-time television, at the cinema, and in other public places." *Id.*
at 622.

The Commission believes these factors rarely will
be relevant and agrees with the dissent in *Rabidue*
that a woman does not assume the risk of harassment by voluntarily entering an abusive, anti-female
environment. "Title VII's precise purpose is to prevent such behavior and attitudes from poisoning the
work environment of classes protected under the
Act." 805 F.2d at 626 (Keith, J., dissenting in part
and concurring in part). Thus, in a decision disagreeing with *Rabidue,* a district court found that a
hostile environment was established by the presence
of pornographic magazines in the workplace and

vulgar employee comments concerning them; offensive sexual comments made to and about plaintiff and other female employees by her supervisor; sexually oriented pictures in a company-sponsored movie and slide presentation; sexually oriented pictures and calendars in the workplace; and offensive touching of plaintiff by a co-worker. *Barbetta v. Chemlawn Services Corp.*, 669 F. Supp. 569, 45 EPD ¶ 37,568 (W.D.N.Y. 1987). The court held that the proliferation of pornography and demeaning comments, if sufficiently continuous and pervasive "may be found to create an atmosphere in which women are viewed as men's sexual playthings rather than as their equal co-workers." *Barbetta*, 669 F. Supp. At 573. The Commission agrees that, depending on the totality of circumstances, such an atmosphere may violate Title VII. *See also Waltman v. International Paper Co.*, 875 F.2d 468, 50 EPD ¶ 39,106 (5th Cir. 1989), in which the 5th Circuit endorsed the Commission's position in its amicus brief that evidence of ongoing sexual graffiti in the workplace, not all of which was directed at the plaintiff, was relevant to her claim of harassment. *Bennett v. Coroon & Black Corp.*, 845 F.2d 104, 46 EPD ¶ 37,955 (5th Cir. 1988) (the posting of obscene cartoons in an office men's room bearing the plaintiff's name and depicting her engaged in crude and deviant sexual activities could create a hostile work environment).

4) Sex-based Harassment—Although the Guidelines specifically address conduct that is sexual in nature, the Commission notes that sex-based harassment—that is, harassment not involving sexual activity or language—may also give rise to Title VII liability (just as in the case of harassment based on race, national origin or religion) if it is "sufficiently patterned or pervasive" and directed at employees because of their sex. *Hicks v. Gates Rubber Co.*, 833 F.2d at 1416; *McKinney v. Dole*, 765 F.2d 1129, 1138, 37 EPD ¶ 35,339 (D.C. Cir. 1985).

Acts of physical aggression, intimidation, hostility or unequal treatment based on sex may be combined with incidents of sexual harassment to establish the existence of discriminatory terms and conditions of employment. *Hall v. Gus Construction Co.*, 842 F.2d 1014; *Hicks v. Gates Rubber Co.*, 833 F. 2d at 1416.

5) Constructive Discharge—Claims of "hostile environment" sexual harassment often are coupled with claims of constructive discharge. If constructive discharge due to a hostile environment is proven, the claim will also become one of "quid pro quo" harassment. It is the position of the Commission and a majority of courts that an employer is liable for constructive discharge when it imposes intolerable working conditions in violation of Title VII when those conditions foreseeably would compel a reasonable employee to quit, whether or not the employer specifically intended to force the victim's resignation. *See Derr v. Gulf Oil Corp.*, 796 F.2d 340, 343-44, 41 EPD ¶ 36,468 (10th Cir. 1986); *Goss v. Exxon Office Systems Co.*, 747 F.2d 885, 888, 35 EPD ¶ 34, 768 (3d Cir. 1984); *Nolan v. Cleland*, 686 F.2d 806, 812-15, 30 EPD ¶ 33,029 (9th Cir. 1982); *Held v. Gulf Oil Co.*, 684 F.2d 427, 432, 29 EPD ¶ 32,968 (6th Cir. 1982); *Clark v. Marsh*, 655 F.2d 1168, 1175 n.8, 26 EPD ¶ 32,082 (D.C. Cir. 1981); *Bourque v. Powell Electrical Manufacturing Co.*, 617 F.2d 61, 65, 23 EPD ¶ 30,891 (5th cir. 1980); Commission Decision 84-1, CCH EEOC Decision ¶ 6839. However, the Fourth Circuit requires proof that the employer imposed the intolerable conditions with the intent of forcing the victim to leave. *See EEOC v. Federal Reserve Bank of Richmond*, 698 F.2d 633, 672, 30 EPD ¶ 33,269 (4th Cir. 1983). But this case is not a sexual harassment case and the Commission believes it is distinguishable because specific intent is not likely to be present in "hostile environment" cases.

An important factor to consider is whether the employer had an effective internal grievance procedure. (*See* Section E, *Preventive and Remedial Action*). The Commission argued in its *Vinson* brief that if an employee knows that effective avenues of complaint and redress are available, then the availability of such avenues itself becomes a part of the work environment and overcomes, to the degree it is effective, the hostility of the work environment. As Justice Marshall noted in his opinion in *Vinson*, "Where a complainant without good reason bypassed an internal complaint procedure she knew to be effective, a court may be reluctant to find constructive termination ..." 106 S.Ct. at 2411 (Marshall, J., concurring in part and dissenting in part). Similarly, the court of appeals in *Dornhecker v. Malibu Grand Prix Corp.*, 828 F.2d 307, 44 EPD ¶ 37,557 (5TH Cir. 1987), held the plaintiff was not constructively discharged after an incident of harassment by a co-worker because she quit immediately, even though the employer told her she would not have to work with him again, and she did not give the employer a fair opportunity to demonstrate it could curb the harasser's conduct.

[D. Deleted 6/1999]

E. Preventive and Remedial Action

1) Preventive Action—The EEOC'S Guidelines encourage employers to: take all steps necessary to prevent sexual harassment from occurring, such as affirmatively raising the subject, expressing strong disapproval, developing appropriate sanctions, informing employees of their right to raise and how to raise the issue of harassment under Title VII, and developing methods to sensitize all concerned.

29 C.F.R. § 1604.11(f). An effective preventive program should include an explicit policy against sexual harassment that is clearly and regularly communicated to employees and effectively implemented. The employer should affirmatively raise the subject with all supervisory and non-supervisory employees, express strong disapproval, and explain the sanctions for harassment. The employer should also have a procedure for resolving sexual harassment complaints. The procedure should be designed to "encourage victims of harassment to come forward" and should not require a victim to complain first to the offending supervisor. *See Vinson*, 106 S. Ct. at 2408. It should ensure confidentiality as much as possible and provide effective remedies, including protection of victims and witnesses against retaliation.

2) Remedial Action—Since Title VII "affords employees the right to work in an environment free from discriminatory intimidation, ridicule, and insult" (*Vinson*), 106 S. Ct. at 2405), an employer is liable for failing to remedy known hostile or offensive work environments. *See, e.g., Garziano v. E.I. Dupont de Nemours & Co.*, 818 F.2d 380, 388, 43 EPD ¶ 37,171 (5th Cir. 1987) (*Vinson* holds employers have an "affirmative duty to eradicate 'hostile or offensive' work environments"); *Bundy v. Jackson*, 641 F.2d 934, 947, 24 EPD ¶ 31,439 (D.C. Cir. 1981) (employer violated Title VII by failing to investigate and correct sexual harassment despite notice);

Tompkins v. Public Service Electric & Gas Co., 568 F.2d 1044, 1049, 15 EPD 7954 (3d Cir. 1977) (same); *Henson v. City of Dundee*, 682 F.2d 897, 905, 15 EPD ¶ 32,993 (11th Cir. 1982) (same); *Munford v. James T. Barnes & Co.*, 441 F. Supp. 459, 466 16 EPD ¶ 8233 (E.D. Mich. 1977) (employer has an affirmative duty to investigate complaints of sexual harassment and to deal appropriately with the offending personnel; "failure to investigate gives tactic support to the discrimination because the absence of sanctions encourages abusive behavior").

When an employer receives a complaint or otherwise learns of alleged sexual harassment in the workplace, the employer should investigate promptly and thoroughly. The employer should take immediate and appropriate corrective action by doing whatever is necessary to end the harassment, make the victim whole by restoring lost employment benefits or opportunities, and prevent the misconduct from recurring. Disciplinary action against the offending supervisor or employee, ranging from reprimand to discharge, may be necessary. Generally, the corrective action should reflect the severity of the conduct. *See Waltman v. International Paper Co.*, 875 F.2d at 479 (appropriateness of remedial action will depend on the severity and persistence of the harassment and the effectiveness of any initial remedial steps). *Dornhecker v. Malibu Grand Prix Corp.*, 828 F.2d 307, 309-10, 44 EPD ¶ 37,557 (5th Cir. 1987) (the employer's remedy may be "assessed proportionately to the seriousness of the offense"). The employer should make follow-up inquiries to ensure the harassment has not resumed and the victim has not suffered retaliation.

Recent Court decisions illustrate appropriate and inappropriate responses by employers. In

Barrett v. Omaha National Bank, 726 F.2d 424, 33 EPD ¶ 34,132 (8th Cir. 1984), the victim informed her employer that her co-worker had talked to her about sexual activities and touched her in an offensive manner. Within four days of receiving this information, the employer investigated the charges, reprimanded the guilty employee placed him on probation, and warned him that further misconduct would result in discharge. A second co-worker who had witnessed the harassment was also reprimanded for not intervening on the victim's behalf or reporting the conduct. The court ruled that the employer's response constituted immediate and appropriate corrective action, and on this basis found the employer not liable.

In contrast, in *Yates v. Avco Corp.*, 819 F.2d 630, 43 EPD ¶ 37,086 (6th Cir. 1987), the court found the employer's policy against sexual harassment failed to function effectively. The victim's first-level supervisor had responsibility for reporting and correcting harassment at the company, yet he was the harasser. The employer told the victims not to go to the EEOC. While giving the accused harasser administrative leave pending investigation, the employer made the plaintiffs take sick leave, which was never credited back to them and was recorded in their personnel files as excessive absenteeism without indicating they were absent because of sexual harassment. Similarly, in *Zabkowicz v. West Bend Co.*, 589 F. Supp. 780, 35 EPD ¶ 34,766 (E.D. Wis. 1984), co-workers harassed the plaintiff over a period of nearly four years in a manner the court described as "malevolent" and "outrageous." Despite the plaintiff's numerous complaints, her supervisor took no remedial action other than to hold occasional meetings at which he reminded employees of the company's policy against offensive conduct. The supervisor never conducted an investigation or disciplined any employees until the plaintiff filed an EEOC charge, at which time one of the offending co-workers was discharged and three others were suspended. The court held the employer liable because it failed to take immediate and appropriate corrective action.

When an employer asserts it has taken remedial action, the Commission will investigate to determine whether the action was appropriate and, more important, effective. The EEOC investigator should, of course, conduct an independent investigation of the harassment claim, and the Commission will reach its own conclusion as to whether the law has been violated. If the Commission finds that the harassment has been eliminated, all victims made whole, and preventive measures instituted, the Commission normally will administratively close the charge because of the employer's prompt remedial action.

Important Statistics

Employment projections, adapted from the Bureau of Labor Statistics

Civilian labor force by sex, age, race, and Hispanic origin: 1986, 1996, and projected 2006

Total labor force, 16 years and over:
1986: 117,834,000 (100%)
1996: 133,943,000 (100%)
2006: 148,847,000 (100%)

Age 55 to 64:
1986: 11,894,000 (10.1%)
1996: 12,146,000 (9.1%)
2006: 18,753,000 (12.6%)

Age 65 and over:
1986: 3,010,000 (2.6%)
1996: 3,828,000 (2.9%)
2006: 4,221,000 (2.8%)

Men, 16 years and over:
1986: 65,422,000 (55.5%)
1996: 72,087,000 (53.8%)
2006: 78,226,000 (52.6%)

Women, 16 years and over:
1986: 52,413,000 (44.5%)
1996: 61,857,000 (46.2%)
2006: 70,620,000 (47.4%)

White, 16 years and over:
1986: 101,801,000 (86.4%)
1996: 113,108,000 (84.4%)
2006: 123,581,000 (83.0%)

Black, 16 years and over:
1986: 12,654,000 (10.7%)
1996: 15,134,000 (11.3%)
2006: 17,225,000 (11.6%)

Asians, Pacific Islanders, American Indians, Alaska
Natives, 16 years and over:
1986: 3,371,000 (2.9%)
1996: 5,703,000 (4.3%)
2006: 8,041,000 (5.4%)

Hispanic origin, 16 years and over:
1986: 8,076,000 (6.9%)
1996: 12,774,000 (9.5%)
2006: 17,401,000 (11.7%)

Other than Hispanic origin, 16 years and over:
1986: 109,758,000 (93.1%)
1996: 121,169,000 (90.5%)
2006: 131,446,000 (88.3%)

White non-Hispanic, 16 years and over:
1986: 94,026,000 (79.8%)
1996: 100,915,000 (75.3%)
2006: 108,166,000 (72.7%)

Employee tenure in 1998: how long does a worker stay with the same employer?

(Adapted from the Bureau of Labor Statistics)

The median number of years that wage and salary workers had been with their current employer (referred to as employee tenure) was 3.6 years in February 1998, edging down from 3.8 years in February 1996.

Among men, median employee tenure decreased for most age groups, as it did in 1996. Among women, overall tenure changed little from 1996 to 1998.

- The proportion of men who had worked for their current employer for 10 years or more fell over the 1983-to-1998 period, while the proportion of women rose.

- The median years of tenure for older workers ages 45 to 54 was more than double that for workers ages 25 to 34.

- About a quarter of all workers age 16 and over had been with their current employer for 12 months or less.

- Workers in government had the highest median tenure of the major industries.

- Managers and professionals had the highest median tenure among the major occupational groups, while workers in service occupations had the lowest median tenure.

- The proportion of men age 25 and over who had worked for their current employer for 10 years or more fell by 5 percentage points over the 1983-to-1998 period, to 32.7 percent.

- Declines occurred in every age group over the 1983-to-1998 period.

- For men ages 40 to 64, the proportion who had worked for their employer at least 10 years fell by about 10 percentage points, in each five-year age group.

- The percent of women age 25 and over with 10 years or more of tenure with their current employer was 28.4 in February 1998, up by 3.5 percentage points from January 1983. The trend toward rising proportions of women with long tenure occurred mainly among 35- to 54-year-olds.

A

Acheson, Dean, 160
Achievements, commemoration of, 51–52
Action memos, 136–37
Acton, Lord, 184
Admiration, 204
Admirative listening, 86
Advancement (climbing), 350–51
  building your case for, 356
  creating opportunities for, 356–58
  focusing on the firm, the department, and the boss, 355
  Human Resources Department and, 354–55
  lateral moves and strategic steps down, 358–60
  mentors and, 353–54
  niche versus pigeonhole approaches to, 352–53
  opportunities for, 351
  setting your sights high and, 351
Agendas, for meetings, 93–95
AIDA (Attention Interest Desire Action) formula, 68
  for memos, 134
Alcoholic drinks, 323
Allies, making, 242
Americans with Disabilities Act, 287–88
Analogies, motivational speech and, 222
Anecdotes, 222
Anger, 47–50
  conflict management and, 264
  telephone calls from irate callers, 120–23
  verbal abuse and, 272–73
Anniversaries, 51–52
Answering machine. See also Voice mail
Anxiety, breathing and, 22
Apology(-ies), 48–50
  to bosses, 196–97
  letters of, 148–50

Appearance. See
    Clothes (dress-
    ing); Physical
    appearance
Archimedes, 240
Arms, crossing, 25
Arts and entertain-
    ment, as topic of
    small talk, 80
Attention, small talk
    and, 85, 86

B
Back-stabbing, 246–50
Bandwagon strategy,
    240
Benefits, selling,
    240–41
Bereavement, 52–53
Birthdays, 50–51
Births, 51
"Blamer" bosses,
    189–90
Block style, 145–46
    modified, 146
Blouses, 30
Body language, 15
    blunders in, 24–25
    criticism and, 47
    open, at social
        events, 321, 323
    small talk and, 83
    talking to your boss
        and, 180
    Body Language
        (Fast), 22
Bonding, with power-
    ful and influential
    people, 241–42
Books, as topic of
    small talk, 80

Borrowing equipment,
    40
Boss(es), 177–201. See
    also Employer
    apologizing to,
        196–97
    "blamer," 189–90
    bonding with,
        194–97
    compliments from,
        195–96
    emotional volcano,
        193–94
    extending a dead-
        line and, 200–201
    fear of, 179–80
    giving good feelings
        to your, 178–79
    guiltmonger, 187–89
    impractical, 190–92
    incompetent,
        192–93
    invitation to your,
        for dinner at your
        house, 327–28
    needs and wants of,
        182–83
    promoting an idea
        and, 199–200
    salary reviews and,
        197–98
    social events at
        house of, 325–26
    talking to your,
        179–81
    tyrannical (dictatori-
        al), 184–87
Brainstorming, 98
Breakfasts, business,
    332
    conversation at, 342

Breathing, 21–22, 180

Brody, Marjorie, 83

Brower, Charles, 105

Bullies, 19–20, 266–68

Business cards, ceremony of exchanging, 322

Business letters. See Letters

Business meals. See Meals, business

Business meetings. See Meetings

C

Caffeine, 121

Calls to action, at meetings, 106–8

Carlyle, Thomas, 278

Carr, Clay, 260

Carroll, Lewis, 132

Celebrations and special occasions, 50–53. See also Social events (socializing), business-related (out-of-office)

Chairs, 41. See also Sitting

Chapman, George, 18

Chesterfield, Lord, 34

Chin, lowered, 24

Civil Rights Act of 1964, 300–301

Clausewitz, Karl von, 261

Climbing. See Advancement

Closure, job interviews and, 370–72

Clothes (dressing), 27–29, 38
"a notch above" your customer, 31
height and, 16–17
less is more, 31–32
politically effective, 29–32
for social events, 322–23

Cocktail parties, 323–24

Coffee, 121

Colors, of clothes, 29

Comfort, dressing for, 29

Commentators, at meetings, 103–4

Communication, 58–70. See also Conversation(s); E-mail; Fax messages; Small talk
leadership and, 205–7
list of objectives and issues and, 59–61
openers and closers, 67–70
with potential employers, 364–65

Community, 33, 34

Commuting, as topic of small talk, 80

Company picnics, 325

Complainers, 269–71

Complaint, letters of, 150–51

Complete Business
    Etiquette Handbook
    (Pachter and
    Brody), 82–83
Complete Handbook of
    Model Business
    Letters, The
    (Griffin), 145
Complete Idiot's Guide to
    the Perfect Interview,
    The (Dorio), 368
Compliments
    from bosses, 195–96
    unsolicited, 28
Conan Doyle, Sir
    Arthur, 320
Conflict, 255–74
    causes of, 257–58
    inevitability of,
        256–57
    at meetings, 106
    of objectives, goals,
        or needs, 258
    of personalities,
        257–58
Conflict management,
    258–66
    action plan for, 266
    addressing issues,
        not people,
        263–64
    bullies and, 266–68
    complainers and,
        269–71
    focusing on a single
        issue, 263
    labeling the conflict
        and, 261–62
    listening and hear-
        ing, 264
    mutual solutions,
        265

passive-aggressive
    personalities and,
    268–69
picking a time and a
    place for fights,
    262–63
picking your fights,
    262
specifics and, 263,
    265
steps toward,
    261–64
verbal abuse and,
    271–73
violence and,
    273–74
win-win approach,
    264–66
Conformity, cultural,
    279
Constructive criticism,
    44–47
Conversation builders,
    86–87
Conversation killers,
    73–75
Conversation(s). See
    also Small talk
    at business meals,
        342–43
    eavesdropping on
        neighboring, 86
    when to end a,
        77–78
    with your boss,
        179–83
Correspondence. See
    E-mail; Letters;
    Memos
Cost of personal items,
    as topic of small
    talk, 81

Cover pages, fax, 172–73
Credit, giving, 196, 243, 247–48
Crisis situations, conflict caused by, 257
Critical feedback, leadership and, 212–15
Criticism, 45–47
  small talk and, 75
  without the crush, 225–27
Crossing arms, 25
Cubicles, 39–40
  decoration of, 41–42
Cultural diversity. See Diversity
Current events, 76
  as topic of small talk, 80

D

Daydreaming, at meetings, 90–91
Deadline, extending a, 200–201
Death, of a colleague, 52–53
Decoration of offices or cubicles, 41–42
Defensiveness, 205
Delegating, 209
  leadership and, 206
Diary, 76
Dictatorial bosses, 184–87
Dinners
  at the boss's house, 325–26

business, 334–36. See also Meals, business
  conversation at, 342–43
  at your house, 327–29
Dirty stories, 291–93
Disabled persons, 287–90
Discipline, progressive, 227–29
Discrimination, 292
Disenfranchised attitude, at meetings, 91
Diversity, 277–90. See also Inclusion
  personal feelings about, 280–81
  power of, 278–83
  sensitivity training and, 282–83
Dominators, at meetings, 103
Dorio, Mark, 368
Downcast look, 24
Dress codes, 27–29
Dressing. See Clothes

E

Ears, rubbing, 25
Eat-or-be-eaten world, 10
Edison, Thomas, 223
E-mail, 155–74
  as avoidance of meaningful communication, 161
  backup copies of, 168, 170

with bells and whistles, 166
confirming receipt by phone, 168
critical, nasty, or intimidating, 161
deleting, 170–71
emoticons in, 165–67
etiquette, 157–63
greetings and felicitations, 162–63
overuse and abuse of, 159–61
precautions, 168–69
security and privacy concerns, 166, 168, 169–70
sending "cc" copies to additional recipients, 160
style of, 164–65
telegraphic versus conversational, 163–64
as time saver, 156–57
to/from prospective employers, 365
undeliverable, 168
Embarrassing moments, at business meals, 343–45
Emerson, Ralph Waldo, 45, 317
Emoticons, 165–67
Emotional manipulation, 249
Emotional support, 227. See also Praise

Emotional volcano bosses, 193–94
Empathy, 34–35
apologies and, 49
Employer. See also Boss(es)
unwritten contract with, 362–63
Empowerment, leadership and, 208–9
Enemies (opponents), 242
Energy
eye contact and, 18–19
relaxed, 22–23
Entertaining. See also Meals, business; Social events
at your house, 329
Enthusiasm, leadership and, 212
Entrance (entering a room), 25–27
tentative, 24
Envelopes, 146–47
Equal Employment Opportunity Commission (EEOC), on sexual harassment, 395–421
Ethical manipulation, 238–43
Exclusion, language of, 37
Eyebrows, raised, 25
Eye contact, 18–20, 24, 180, 321
conveying relaxed energy with, 22–23

during handshake, 21

small talk and, 84

Eyeglasses, peering over the top of, 25

Eyes
narrowing of, 25
rubbing, 25

Eye-to-eyebrow contact, 19

F

Fabrics, 30

Facilitating the discussion at meetings, 100–101

Falls, Cyril, 204

Family, dinner or party at your house and, 329

Fast, Julius, 22

Fatigue, telephone calls from irate callers and, 120

Favors, letters asking for, 151–53

Fax messages, 171–74
confidentiality statement for, 173–74
cover page for, 172–73
"junk mail," 172
from prospective employers, 365

Fear, voice of, 179

Feedback. See also Criticism
leadership and, 212–15
motivation and, 225

Fidgeting, 24

Fitting in, 15

Flattery, 178

Focus, on you rather than on your clothes, 28

Fonts, for letters, 146

Ford, Henry, 57, 58

Friction, 256. See also Conflict

Friendships. See also Office romances
with powerful and influential people, 241–42

Fuller, Margaret, 278

Furniture, 41

G

Gelman, Eric, 238

Geneen, Harold, 210

Goals, leadership and, 206

Goldwyn, Sam, 131

Good manners, 290–93

Gossip, 38, 75, 243–46

Graffiti, sexual, 301–2

Grapevine, as source of company news, 351

Greetings
failure to greet, 38
morning, 39
when entering a room, 26

Grief, 52–53

Griffin, Jack, 145

Grooming, 29

Guiltmonger bosses, 187–89

H

Hand gestures, 23–24,
180
small talk and, 83
Hands, talking to your
boss and, 180–81
Handshaking, 20–21
dead-fish, 24
death-grip, 24
women and, 287
Head, rubbing the
back of, 24
Head scratching, 24
Health, as topic of
small talk, 80–81
Height, physical, 16–17
Help, 42–43
accepting, 43–44
asking for, 43
Helping words, 36–37
Herbert, George, 182
Hold
putting a caller on,
118–20
resisting being put
on, 127–28
Human Resources
Department,
advancement and,
354–55
Humor, off-color or
offensive, 291
as topic of small
talk, 82

I

Ideas, promoting,
199–200
Impractical bosses,
190–92

Inclusion, 283–90
of disabled persons,
287–90
male/female issues,
284–87
stereotyping and,
290
Income, as topic of
small talk, 81
Incompetent bosses,
192–93
Indented style of
letters, 146
Indispensability, 13
Influence, 239
associating with peo-
ple who have,
240–42
Inspiration, 222
Interests or hobbies,
as topic of small
talk, 80
Interrupting, as con-
versation killer,
74, 86
Interviews, job,
368–72
Intimate relationships.
See Office
romances
Intimate revelations,
as topic of small
talk, 82
Invitations
to meetings,
96–97
to social events, 314,
317
Irritability, telephone
calls from irate
callers and, 120

J

Jealousy, 38
Job hunting, 363–72
Journal, 76

K

Kanti, Michael J., 178
King, Martin Luther,
    Jr., 207
Korda, Michael, 244
Kroll, Alex, 98

L

Language
    inappropriate, 37
    sexist, 284–87
Latecomers, to social
    events, 317–18
Lateness, 37
Lateral moves, 358–60
Leaders (leadership),
    203–15. See also
    Motivation
    choice of followers
        and, 208
    communication
        and, 205–7
    critical feedback
        and, 212–15
    defensiveness and,
        205
    empowerment and,
        208–9
    enthusiasm and, 212
    general attitude and
        demeanor and,
        211–15
    giving the right feel-
        ings and, 209–11
    listening and, 205

    personality and,
        209–11
    praise and, 215
    as role models,
        232–33
    self-confidence and,
        204–5
    team talk and,
        215–17
Leaning forward, 321
    small talk and, 83
Letters, 131
    of apology, 148–50
    asking for a favor,
        151–53
    beginning of, 147
    closing of, 147–48
    of complaint,
        150–51
    envelopes for,
        146–47
    forms and formats
        of, 145–46
    of recommendation,
        367
    style of, 142–44
    thank-you, 153–54
    themes of, 148
    when to write,
        144–45
Liddell, B. H., 366
Lincoln, Abraham,
    214–15
Lip biting, 24
Listening, 38
    admirative, 86
    criticism and, 226
    leadership and, 205
    not, as conversation
        killer, 73–74
    overly critical, 86

saying "no" and,
    229–30
small talk and,
    84–87
to telephone calls
    from irate callers,
    121
Looks. See Physical
    appearance
Loyalty, to employer,
    363
Lunch, business, 332,
    333–34
conversation at,
    342

M

Machiavelli, Niccolò,
    238
Mailer, Norman, 331
Manipulation
    emotional, 249
    ethical, 238–43
Manners, good,
    290–93
Meals, business,
    331–45
embarrassing
    moments at,
    343–45
table manners at,
    336–42
Meetings, 89–108
agendas for, 93–95
    flexibility of,
    97–99
attendance at, 95
brainstorming at, 98
breaking up into
    small discussion
    groups, 99

calls to action at,
    106–8
clear objectives for,
    99
conflict at, 106
individual problems
    and, 90–91
invitations to, 96–97
manners at, 104–6
organizational prob-
    lems at, 91–92
power and, 101–4
problem polling at,
    97–98
reflecting and facili-
    tating the discus-
    sion at, 100–101
seating arrange-
    ments at, 92,
    101–2
size of, 95–96
steps in holding suc-
    cessful meetings,
    93
time management,
    99–100
Mehrabian, Albert, 16,
    114
Memos, 131, 132–42
action, 136–37
format of, 133–34
for keeping every-
    one on the same
    page, 137
as official junk mail,
    132
problem-solving,
    139–40
"SUBJECT" line, 133
suggestion,
    140–42

in urgent or crisis
situations, 137–38
voice of, 134–36
Mentoring, 353–54
Metaphors, motivational speech
and, 222
Misfortune, as topic of
small talk, 81
Modified block style,
146
Moscow, Alvin, 210
Motivation (motivational speech),
219–27
as high-maintenance
endeavor, 225
information and,
222
praise and, 223–24
Mueller, Robert K., 96
Multiculturalism,
278–80. See also
Diversity

N

Names, people's
free and frequent
use of, 27
job interviews and,
369–70
at social events, 320
use of,
Napkins, 336
Naysayers, at meetings, 104
Neck, rubbing the
back of, 24
Negative words and
phrases, 37,
65–67

substituting positive
terms for, 221–22
Negativity (negative
attitudes), 38
as conversation
killer, 75
at meetings, 104
Negotiating
a promotion, 198,
199
for a raise, 198
Nervousness, breathing and, 22
Networking (networks), 251–53,
318–22
personal, 366–68
New Manager's Survival
Manual, The
(Carr), 260
"Nice guys," 33–37
Niche approach to
advancement,
352–53
Nizer, Louis, 59
Nodding, 23, 322
small talk and, 84
Nonverbal communication, 15
"No," saying, 229–32
Nose, rubbing side of,
25

O

Objectives, leadership
and, 206
Off-color stories, 82
Office diplomacy, 255,
258. See also
Conflict management

Office parties, 324–25
Office politics
  back-stabbing and,
    246–50
  essential truths
    about, 4
  ethical manipula-
    tion and, 238–43
  influence and, 239
  networking and,
    251–53
  quiz on, 4–9
  rumors and, 243–46
  victims of, 237–38
Office romances,
    296–308
  company policy and,
    307
  between consenting
    adults, 305–6
  discretion and, 307
  openness of, 308
  professionalism and,
    306–8
Open body language,
    321, 323
  small talk and, 83
Openers, for small
    talk, 78–79
Open-handedness, 23
Opponents (enemies),
    242
Optimism, 38, 220,
    221, 233
Overstreet, Harry, 103

P
Pachter, Barbara, 83
Paraphrasing, as con-
    versation builder,
    86–87

Parker, Dorothy, 159
Parks, Rosa, 207
Parties. See also Social
    events
  cocktail, 323–24
  office, 324–25
Passive-aggressive per-
    sonalities, 268–69
Patronizing, as conver-
    sation killer, 75
Peer pressure, 38–42
People business, 12,
    14
Pepys, Samuel, 344
Personal grooming.
    See Grooming
Personality, of leaders,
    209–11
Personality(-ies)
  conflict of, 257–58
  passive-aggressive,
    268–69
Personal problems, as
    topic of small talk,
    81
Personal space, small
    talk and, 83
Persuasion, 242–43
Physical appearance,
    height, 16–17
Physical contact and
    touching, 301
Picnics, company, 325
Pierce, Charles A., 297
Place settings, 337
Politics, as topic of
    small talk, 82
Pornographic materi-
    als, 301–2
Portable skills,
    352–53

Positive attitude,
     221–22. See also
     Optimism
  at social events, 323
Positive telephone atti-
     tude (PTA), 111
Posture
  conveying relaxed
     energy with, 23
  height and, 17
Power
  following people
     with, 240–42
  meetings and, 101
Powerless words and
     phrases, 65–67
Praise, 44–47
  leadership and, 215
  as motivational tool,
     223–24
Precision Nirvana
     (Shapiro), 260
Prejudice, 281. See
     also Diversity
Presentations, 95
Privacy
  cubicles and, 40
  e-mail and, 169–70
  failure to respect, 38
Problem polling,
     97–98
Problems, in letters of
     complaint, 150–51
Problem-solving
     memos, 139–40
Progressive discipline,
     227–29
Promoting
  an idea, 199–200
  yourself. See Self-
     promotion

Promotion. See also
     Advancement
  negotiating a, 198,
     199
  turning down a
     request for,
     231–32
Pronunciation, tele-
     phone calls and,
     114
Punctuality, at social
     events, 317–18

Q
Questions, small talk
     and, 74, 87

R
Racist remarks,
     291–93
Raise
  asking and negotiat-
     ing for a,
     198–99
  refusing a request
     for a, 230
Ramundo, Michael,
     115
Rapport
  increasing, 35–36
  wreckers of, 37
Real rules of the
     game, 11
Recommendation(s)
  asking for, 367
  letters of, 367–68
Reflecting the discus-
     sion at meetings,
     100
Relaxed energy, 22–23

Religion, as topic of small talk, 82

Religious items, decorating with, 41

Restaurants, for business meals, 333–35, 337–342. See also Meals, business

Retreats, 323

Ridicule, 75

Risk, avoidance of, 10–11

Role models, leaders as, 232

Romantic relationships. See Office romances

Ross, Joel E., 178

Rules of the game, real, 11

Rumors, 75, 243–46

Ruthlessness, 239

S

Salaries, as topic of small talk, 81

Salary reviews, bosses and, 197–98

Sarcasm, 75

Scarves, 31

Schmoozing, 318–20

Scoffers, 104

Scrapbook, 76

Script(ing), 64–65
creating a, 61

Seating (seating arrangements), at meetings, 92, 101–2

Self-confidence, of leaders, 204–5

Self-fulfilling prophecy, meetings and, 90

Self-interest, communication and, 62–64, 68, 70

Self-promotion, 12–13. See also Advancement (climbing)
bosses and, 198–99

Sensitivity training, 282–83

Sexist language, 284–87

Sexual graffiti, 301–2

Sexual harassment, 300–305
Equal Employment Opportunity Commission (EEOC) policy paper on, 395–421
rank and, 303–5

Sexual jokes. See also Humor, off-color or offensive
sexual harassment and, 301

Shapiro, Dean H., Jr., 260

Sharing, 38

Shaw, George Bernard, 64

Shirts, 30

Shoes, for short men, 17

Short people, 16–17

Sighing, 24

Sincerity, eye contact and, 18

Sitting
    conveying relaxed
        energy, 23
    where to sit, 26
Small talk, 71–88
    benefits of, 72–73
    conversation killers
        and, 73–75
    in e-mail, 164
    eye contact and, 84
    keeping it light, 79
    leaning forward
        and, 83
    listening and, 84
    making the time for,
        72
    at meals, 342
    nodding and, 84
    open body language
        and, 83
    openers for, 78–79
    opportunities for,
        77–78
    positive ingredients
        of, 76–82
    smiling and, 83
    at social events,
        321
    SOFTEN formula
        for, 82–84
    speaking voice and,
        84
    taking it to the next
        level, 87–88
    safe topics, 79–80
        weighty or risky
            topics, 80–82
Smiling, 17–18, 321
    small talk and, 83
Smoking, 324
Snooping, 40
Social calendar, 316

Social events (socializ-
    ing). See also
    Office romances
    business-related
        (out-of-office),
        313–18. See also
        Parties
    at the boss's
        house, 325–26
    business card
        ceremony, 322
    cocktail parties,
        323–24
    company picnics,
        325
    dressing appro-
        priately,
        322–23
    invitations, 314,
        317
    keeping a social
        calendar, 316
    meeting and
        greeting peo-
        ple, 320
    name game,
        320–21
    networking,
        318–22
    office parties,
        324–25
    openness to,
        314–16
    "SOFTEN" for-
        mula at,
        321–22
    at your house,
        327–29
SOFTEN formula for
    small talk, 82,
    321–22
Space proxemics, 40

Speaking. See also
    Motivational
    speech
  fear of, 91
  to your boss, 179
Specifics, conflict
    management and,
    263, 265
Spills, at business
    meals, 344–45
Spontaneity, small talk
    and, 76–77
Steepling, 24
Stereotyping, 290
Suggestion memos,
    140–42

T

Table manners,
    336–42
Talking. See also
    Small talk
  to yourself, 58–64
Tall people, 16
Teamwork (team-
    building), leader-
    ship and,
    215–17
Telephone messages.
    See Answering
    machines; Voice
    mail
Telephone tag, 123
Telephone (telephone
    calls), 109–28
  asking for recom-
    mendations, 367
  call screening eti-
    quette, 123–24

irate callers, 120–23
manners, 38
opening words,
    111–12
owning the call,
    115–18, 128
positive telephone
    attitude (PTA),
    111
preparation before
    making or answer-
    ing, 110
putting the caller on
    hold, 118–20
selling the call,
    117–18
to/from prospective
    employers, 365
voice for, 113–15
voice mail, 123–26
Temper, bosses with a,
    193–94
Territoriality, 40, 41
Thank-you letters,
    153–54
Thank-you notes
  to the host of a
    party, 324
  to job
    interviewer(s),
    371
Thomas, Roosevelt, Jr.,
    280
Thoreau, David, 27
Ties, 31
Time management, at
    meetings, 99
Tipping, at restau-
    rants, 342

Townshend, Robert, 90
Transactional Analysis (TA), 180
Travel, as topic of small talk, 80
T-shirts, 30, 31
Tyrannical bosses, 184–87

U
Undercutting yourself, 241

V
Verbal abuse, 271–73
Victimization, 237–38
  by bullies, 267
Victims, of sexual harassment, 302–3
Violence, 273–74
Vocabulary, 65
Voice
  small talk and, 84
  talking to your boss and, 179–80
  telephone, 113–15
Voice mail, 123–26
  after-hours message, 125
  buddy system for, 126

business-day and after-hours messages, 124
changing daytime messages daily, 125–26
effective messages, 124
getting your messages through, 126–28
information to leave on messages, 127

W
Walking, 17
Weather, as topic of small talk, 79
Whiners, 270–71. See also Complainers
  at meetings, 90
Who you know, importance of, 13–14
Wilde, Oscar, 256
Women, inclusion of, 284–87

Y
Yawning, 24

Z
Zanuck, Darryl F., 257

The *Unofficial Guide*™ Reader Questionnaire

If you would like to express your opinion about climbing the corporate ladder or this guide, please complete this questionnaire and mail it to:

The *Unofficial Guide*™ Reader Questionnaire
IDG
1633 Broadway, floor 7
New York, NY 10019-6785

Gender: ___ M   ___ F

Age: ___ Under 30   ___ 31–40   ___ 41–50
___ Over 50

Education: ___ High school   ___ College
___ Graduate/Professional

What is your occupation?

_____

How did you hear about this guide?
___ Friend or relative
___ Newspaper, magazine, or Internet
___ Radio or TV
___ Recommended at bookstore
___ Recommended by librarian
___ Picked it up on my own
___ Familiar with the *Unofficial Guide*™ travel series

Did you go to the bookstore specifically for a book on climbing the corporate ladder? Yes ___
No ___

Have you used any other *Unofficial Guides*™?
Yes ___   No ___

If Yes, which ones?

_____
_____
_____

What other book(s) on climbing the corporate ladder have you purchased? _____

_____

_____

Was this book:
___ more helpful than other(s)
___ less helpful than other(s)

Do you think this book was worth its price?
Yes ___   No ___

Did this book cover all topics related to climbing the corporate ladder adequately?
Yes ___   No ___

Please explain your answer:

_____

_____

_____

Were there any specific sections in this book that were of particular help to you?   Yes ___   No ___

Please explain your answer:

_____

_____

_____

On a scale of 1 to 10, with 10 being the best rating, how would you rate this guide? ___

What other titles would you like to see published in the *Unofficial Guide*™ series?

_____

_____

Are Unofficial Guides™ **readily available in your area?**   Yes ___   No ___

Other comments:

_____

_____

_____

_____

Get the inside scoop...with the *Unofficial Guides*™!

Health and Fitness

The Unofficial Guide to Alternative Medicine
ISBN: 0-02-862526-9 Price: $15.95

The Unofficial Guide to Conquering Impotence
ISBN: 0-02-862870-5 Price: $15.95

The Unofficial Guide to Coping with Menopause
ISBN: 0-02-862694-x Price: $15.95

The Unofficial Guide to Cosmetic Surgery
ISBN: 0-02-862522-6 Price: $15.95

The Unofficial Guide to Dieting Safely
ISBN: 0-02-862521-8 Price: $15.95

The Unofficial Guide to Having a Baby
ISBN: 0-02-862695-8 Price: $15.95

The Unofficial Guide to Living with Diabetes
ISBN: 0-02-862919-1 Price: $15.95

The Unofficial Guide to Overcoming Arthritis
ISBN: 0-02-862714-8 Price: $15.95

The Unofficial Guide to Overcoming Infertility
ISBN: 0-02-862916-7 Price: $15.95

Career Planning

The Unofficial Guide to Acing the Interview
ISBN: 0-02-862924-8 Price: $15.95

The Unofficial Guide to Earning What You Deserve
ISBN: 0-02-862523-4 Price: $15.95

The Unofficial Guide to Hiring and Firing People
ISBN: 0-02-862523-4 Price: $15.95

Business and Personal Finance

The Unofficial Guide to Investing
ISBN: 0-02-862458-0 Price: $15.95

The Unofficial Guide to Investing in Mutual Funds
ISBN: 0-02-862920-5 Price: $15.95

The Unofficial Guide to Managing Your Personal Finances
ISBN: 0-02-862921-3 Price: $15.95

The Unofficial Guide to Starting a Small Business
ISBN: 0-02-862525-0 Price: $15.95

Home and Automotive

The Unofficial Guide to Buying a Home
ISBN: 0-02-862461-0 Price: $15.95

The Unofficial Guide to Buying or Leasing a Car
ISBN: 0-02-862524-2 Price: $15.95

The Unofficial Guide to Hiring Contractors
ISBN: 0-02-862460-2 Price: $15.95

Family and Relationships

The Unofficial Guide to Childcare
ISBN: 0-02-862457-2 Price: $15.95

The Unofficial Guide to Dating Again
ISBN: 0-02-862454-8 Price: $15.95

The Unofficial Guide to Divorce
ISBN: 0-02-862455-6 Price: $15.95

The Unofficial Guide to Eldercare
ISBN: 0-02-862456-4 Price: $15.95

The Unofficial Guide to Planning Your Wedding
ISBN: 0-02-862459-9 Price: $15.95

Hobbies and Recreation

The Unofficial Guide to Finding Rare Antiques
ISBN: 0-02-862922-1 Price: $15.95

The Unofficial Guide to Casino Gambling
ISBN: 0-02-862917-5 Price: $15.95

All books in the *Unofficial Guide* series are available at your local bookseller, or by calling 1-800-428-5331.